THE WORLD SPINS BY

M000072844

THE WORLD SPINS BY

A Gift of Time, Love, and the Long Bike Ride Back to Myself

JERRY KOPACK

atmosphere press

© 2022 Jerry Kopack

Published by Atmosphere Press

Cover design by Ronaldo Alves

Map Designs by Allison Seymour, Gravity Girl Graphics.

No part of this book may be reproduced without permission from the author except in brief quotations and in reviews.

atmospherepress.com

"What's wrong with knowing what you know now and not knowing what you don't know until later?"

—Winnie the Pooh

My first bike, age 5
Marshall, Michigan 1979.

TABLE OF CONTENTS

INTRODUCTION – 3

PART 1: Africa

Chapter 1: We're Going on an Adventure 9
Chapter 2: Big Jer vs. Cool Hand Luke 23
Chapter 3: Cool Hand Luke Made Me Do It 27
Chapter 4: A Mad(a) Plan 33
Chapter 5: Stick to the Main Road 41
Chapter 6: Life, Itself 47
Chapter 7: Baby Steps, to *Being* 53
Chapter 8: Tsara Be 58

PART 2: Hospice

Chapter 1: What's a *Hospice?* 71
Chapter 2: The Sweet Potato
that Changed My Life 77
Chapter 3: Peaks and Valleys 83

PART 3: India

Chapter 1: Unplugging 93
Chapter 2: Christmas Came Early 98
Chapter 3: My Millennium Falcon 103
Chapter 4: I've Got Worms 123
Chapter 5: Mind if I Sleep Here? 126
Chapter 6: I'm Still Gonna Shine 133
Chapter 7: Let Me Go 143

PART 4: Nepal

Chapter 1: You're Going the Wrong Way! 153
Chapter 2: Unchecked Baggage 166
Chapter 3: The Illusion of Randomness 171

PART 5: India – Again!

Chapter 1: Counting Salt Rings 185
Chapter 2: Compromise, Shower Restrictions, and Resets 193
Chapter 3: Connecting the Dots with Selfies and Smiles 208
Chapter 4: Why Do You Come Here? 215
Chapter 5: Riding on Faith 227

PART 6:Thailand

Chapter 1: Barefoot, Beet Juice, and Cold Showers 243

PART 7: China

Chapter 1: Same but Different 255
Chapter 2: 3 Types of Fun 261
Chapter 3: The Chicken Soup of Buddhism 268
Chapter 4: Taking the Yak Track 275
Chapter 5: You'll Miss it When It's Gone 287
Chapter 6: It Was All a Dream 296

PART 8: Israel

Chapter 1: Don't Go to Israel! 313
Chapter 2: What Are You Entrepreneuring In? 324

EPILOGUE – 339

INTRODUCTION

The Tunnel of Doom
Himachal Pradesh, India

October 6, 2016

My luck ran out shortly after the peaceful secondary road rejoined the main artery at the town of Kullu. With a population of only 18,000 souls, it's not Delhi or Mumbai, however, when you're used to seeing three vehicles a day blasting by your bike, anything more can be a cardiac event. For two weeks, I had dragged my bike over countless 17,000-foot peaks that seemed to punch a hole in the Crayola-inspired, cloudless blue Himalayan sky. (I really think there should be a color named Himalayan Sky Blue.) Each subsequent soul-crushing climb was rewarded with the weightless euphoric feeling of flying down the backside of the pass—a permagrin plastered across my face.

The Leh Manali highway in northern India, just south of the Pakistan border, is roughly three hundred miles long and is open for only about four to five months each year due to snow. The bulk of the road, which is at best a dilapidated two-lane dirt track, and at worst a single-lane bombed-out cart path, sits at an average altitude of nearly 13,000 feet. The majority of the traffic seen here is Indian military vehicles due to the proximity to the Pakistan border, and also because they are pretty much the only vehicles durable enough to withstand the abuse. In this brown, barren moonscape, the slightest hint of rain can trigger a flood or landslide. Traveling this route from the north to south had been my life for the past two weeks as I worked my way further south toward the more densely populated tourist oasis of Manali.

But now, buses, trucks, cars, motorcycles, tractors—every imaginable motorized contraption—zoomed by me, blowing their horns, on busy streets too narrow to accommodate such speed. The horns in India are not intended to warn or even convey frustration, but rather they are a way to announce your presence and subsequently your place in the motorized hierarchy. With every approaching vehicle, a driver laid on the horn, simply to let others know they were coming. Up hills. Around corners. And in the current case of Kullu, even just blasting down the main street through town. In India, it seems everyone has someplace to get to, reducing my life expectancy by several years in the process. This seems all part of an understood etiquette of organized chaos that holds this country together.

Hold your line, I tell myself. *They see you and will go around you.*

White knuckles squeeze the bars of my bike in a vice-like, almost death grip. People step blindly off curbs, not expecting a white guy on a bike. I lock up my brakes. A man on a motorbike, his wife on the back and two kids sandwiched in between, each child carrying a live chicken, negotiates this mayhem while talking on his mobile phone, and careens around me almost as if I'm not there. Cars pull out in front of me, knowing that they are higher on the food chain and that I will stop. I lock up my brakes. Buses pass uphill, around blind corners, in town at speeds that would prevent them from stopping if something got in their path—like a guy on a bicycle—but that is of no consequence of course. They are the highest on the food chain, and everyone in this matrix knows it. Non-stop, everyone is blowing their horn, announcing their presence.

It is like a barking dog in the night, that initially may not be annoying, but it never seems to stop and gradually drives you insane. You hope that somehow the sound, although incessant, will fade away as you become numb to it—but you never do. Another horn, another vehicle comes barreling down the road at me, head-on. Again, I lock up my brakes. *Breathe*, I tell myself. *This is India. You signed up for this.*

Ninety minutes and twenty miles later (and two years removed from my life expectancy), I made the turnoff toward the sleepy mountainside town of Banjar where I hoped to find some quiet accommodations. Peace again, until up ahead, a tunnel.

In India, there are short tunnels and long tunnels. I had been through plenty. And then there is the *Tunnel of Doom*. It seemed like any other short, benign tunnel, carving through a mountain that sat innocently along a meandering river. As I rolled into the dark passageway, I expected it would simply and promptly flow around a bend and pop me out on the other side. As I ventured around the corner, the light from the entrance was immediately extinguished—and there was no *light at the end of the tunnel*. Absolute darkness, to the point that I was unsure if my eyes were even open. I squinted. I stretched. Whatever I could do in an attempt to find any semblance of vision or contrast. I slowed my pedaling but cautiously continued my progress, essentially pedaling blind. *Bikepacking Rule #1: When traveling solo, far from home, DO NOT GET INJURED.*

Without actually seeing, I felt the contour of the road trending subtly to the left. Around the curve, a single flickering bulb provided my first glimpse of the tunnel. The road was much narrower than I had imagined, but its condition was as I had expected, littered with countless watermelon-sized pockmarks—not big enough to swallow me, but enough to dislodge me from my bike. In the distance, a bus was approaching. The faint headlights were masked by the dust from the road and clouds of stagnant diesel exhaust. As it came racing toward me, the driver must have gotten a glimpse of this crazy cyclist and in traditional Indian form, blared his horn to announce his presence and make sure I knew who was higher on the food chain.

My heart was racing, my grip intensified as I held on for my life as the bus zoomed by, its wake threatening to blow me off my bike while choking me with that same toxic concoction of road dust and diesel fumes. My experience had been that Indian drivers are scary enough when I know they can see me. And if they can't? I reached into my pocket and pulled out my phone to use the flashlight. How long could this tunnel be, anyway? This will be good enough, I reasoned.

After five minutes of pedaling with one hand on my handlebars and the other on my phone, I realized that I was in for a much longer ride. With every pedal stroke, I was certain that I would see that elusive *light at the end of the tunnel*, and it felt far less dangerous to continue on rather than turn around.

However, I grew increasingly more terrified the deeper into the tunnel I ventured, as each subsequent potentially life-ending vehicle whizzed by me. Horns echoed off the tunnel walls, piercing my eardrums like icepicks. After the cloud of dust settled from the most recent bus fly by, I noticed an elevated sidewalk to my left. I quickly dragged my bike up on it while a person whom I did not even see walked past me. "*Namaste*," said the obscure figure as I pedaled by, only slightly faster than his walk. *Quit messing around, dumbass!* I told myself. *Smarten up and dig into your bag for those head and taillights you've been carrying!*

My heart was still racing from adrenaline. My lungs were wheezing from the lack of clean air, while my eyes burned from diesel fumes. I attached my front and rear blinky lights and confidently (sorta) pedaled along the sidewalk, which was barely wide enough for my handlebars. Horns continued to announce their presence, but they came from further away as now they could actually see me, so I guess that was reassuring. I tucked my chin, mustered whatever fortitude I had left. I had to be closer to the end than the beginning, I reasoned.

Fifteen minutes later, I finally saw that elusive light at the end of the tunnel. After being in near-total darkness for over twenty minutes, the late afternoon Indian sun was blinding. I exited to see the looks of sheer astonishment from several men on motorcycles who had evidently passed me in the tunnel. There are twenty minutes and another two years of my life that I'll never get back. *This is India. You signed up for this.*

PART 1

Africa

May 24 – July 10, 2016

"Everyone needs a friend who will call you up and say, 'Get dressed fucker, we're going on an adventure.'"

– Unknown

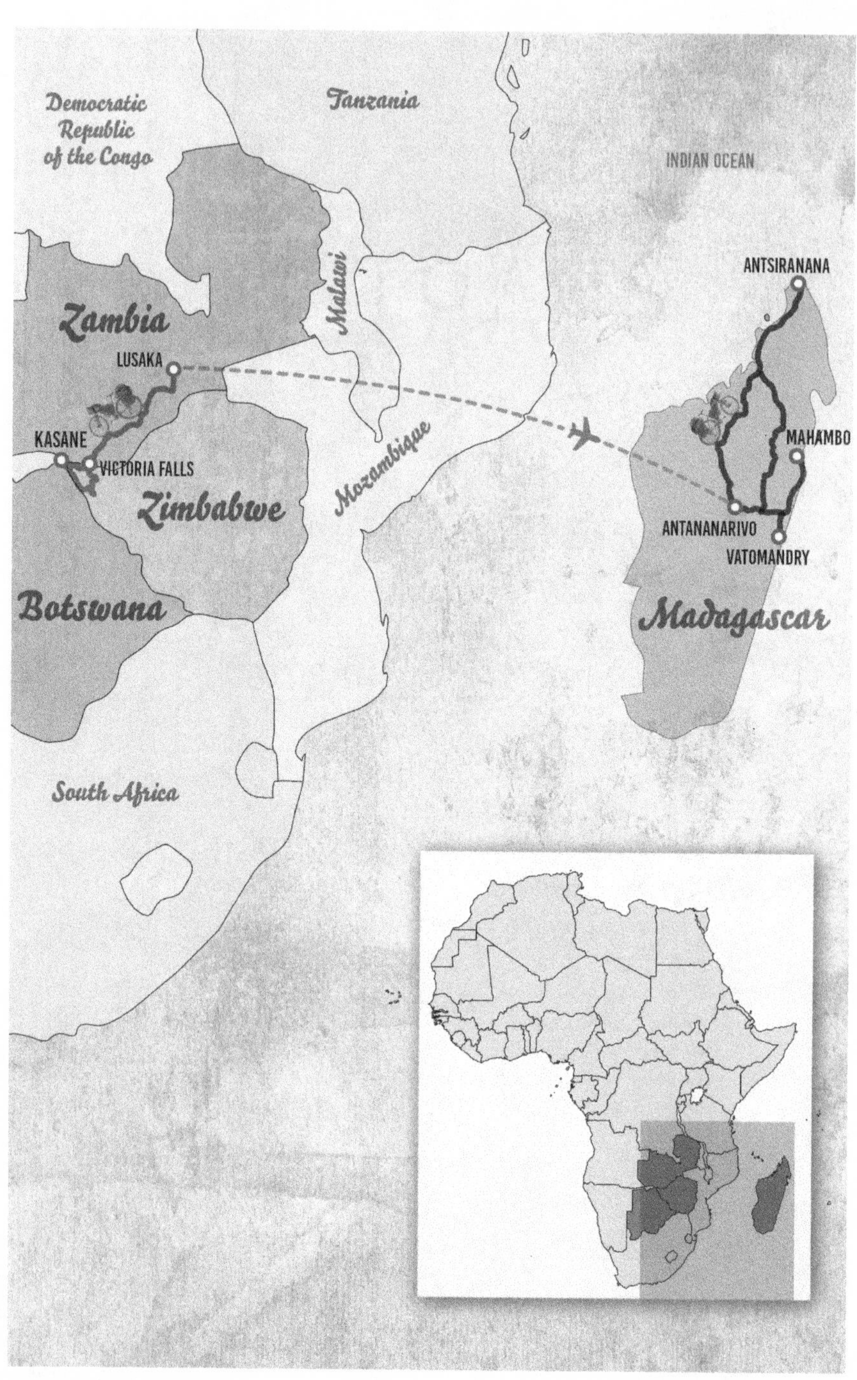

Democratic Republic of the Congo
Tanzania
INDIAN OCEAN
ANTSIRANANA
Zambia
Malawi
LUSAKA
MAHAMBO
KASANE
VICTORIA FALLS
Mozambique
Zimbabwe
ANTANANARIVO
VATOMANDRY
Botswana
Madagascar
South Africa

CHAPTER 1

We're Going on an Adventure

I grew up in Eaton Rapids, Michigan, a rural farm town south of Lansing with a population just shy of 5,000. It is a sleepy nook not otherwise known for adventure, and, on the surface looks like any other Midwestern town, with rolling hills, dense forests, and sprawling corn and potato fields as far you can see. If you did a search for "middle America" on the interweb, Eaton Rapids might just show up.

I am the middle child of five boys, splitting time between my dad in Michigan and my mom in Colorado. My parents had divorced when I was four, and honestly, I don't even remember them together. I lived with my dad in Michigan, while my other siblings were raised by my mom in Colorado.

Bobby is my only full biological brother, three years my junior. Dave and Bill are twins from my mom's first husband, eight years my senior. In 1989, we added our fifth brother, Joey, from my mom's current husband. We were and still are an unconventional sort of family, but somehow, we make it work.

How I ended up in Michigan with my dad and Bobby with my mom is still a somewhat grey area. The story I like best is simply that as my dad's firstborn, he fawned over me, and I wailed incessantly when he wasn't around. This led my mom, with two older boys and an infant, to simply throw up her hands and let me go with my dad. It wasn't that she didn't love me the way any mother would, but maybe more that she understood the connection my dad and I had.

I would see my brothers a couple of times a year on Christmas and over the summer and thought nothing of the oddity of that situation. Growing up essentially an only child meant I was an incredibly entitled and spoiled brat who was used to getting whatever I wanted. By the time I was eight, I was an accomplished traveler, flying solo back and forth from Michigan to Colorado several times each year, but otherwise, that was the extent of my awareness of the world.

About twenty years ago, I was bitten by the travel bug. It was the fall of 2003, my first trip outside of the United States. After graduating from the University of Colorado at Boulder, I decided to visit a college friend who was living in Berlin. Heidi was one of my closest friends from school. With her infectious smile, New York attitude, and love of all things hip-hop, we quickly became friends. I still like to tease her about how she routinely copied off of me in one of our classes, "Elements of Argumentation," and without me, she wouldn't have graduated (although she's now a hotshot in the advertising biz in New York).

Shortly after graduation, Heidi had moved to Berlin with her boyfriend, and over the course of many email exchanges, it was clear she needed some Colorado sunshine. She talked me into venturing out of Colorado, and more importantly, the US. Immediately upon landing in Berlin, it was like being in another world. "That grocery store is *weird.*" I was used to giant box stores with thirty-five kinds of cereal, twelve kinds of mayonnaise, and of course countless varieties of peanut butter (including crunchy, creamy, low salt, and then of course the all too clever peanut butter and jelly in the same jar). "Your apartment is *weird.*" Growing up in Michigan I was used to oversized houses, with large, sprawling yards that required a riding lawn mower because why would anyone walk when you can drive something? "The bathroom is *weird.*" What was this dual flush toilet, how do I use it, and why would I want to use less water to flush? To me, *everything was weird* and to say I had a *mild* case of ethnocentrism was putting it mildly. I was simply a product of my environment; a limited one for sure.

After several days of this, Heidi had had enough and finally quipped, "It isn't *weird*! It's just different than you're used to, *Culture Boy*. It's actually quite normal but you've never left the US." *Culture Boy* quickly became her newly-minted pet name for me since it seems I had none, based on my track record for travel. Up until this point in life, I had been naively fumbling through my tiny slice of the world with blinders on, completely content. It's like someone who had always been blind and never knew what color was but was suddenly given the gift of sight. It turned out there was a whole big world out there, and now, after two weeks in Germany, I had seen too much, and I wanted more.

In the summer of 2005, a high school friend invited me to visit her in Barcelona where she was working. It had been two full years since the initial foray into my limited glimpse of international travel, and thus I was immediately intrigued. While I was excited to explore Spain, I had a distinct and paralyzing fear of feeling stupid. Maybe it's a guy thing—but likely—it's just me. Fifteen years had passed since my last high school Spanish class, and having to figure out where I was going by asking someone for directions in a place where I did not speak the language was a guaranteed recipe for that. So instead, I bought a map and a used bike for $45 and hopped a flight to Spain. I had saved up enough cash and vacation days to allot for a ten-day trip—just enough time to further feed my intrigue. Heather was working during the week, so I was on my own in this new, and only slightly *weird* country with six days to explore Spain on my bike.

I grew up riding bikes as a kid and learned to ride on an old country road in rural Michigan when I was four, on a hand-me-down BMX-style bike. In my dad's basement are pictures of a gangly kid with a head befitting an eight-year-old, pedaling a bike made for an eight-year-old. I had to stand the entire time, shifting the bike side to side in order to reach the pedals. To stop, I would jump off the bike because I couldn't reach the ground while standing over the top tube. My friends and I would race up and down the dirt road between our two houses, a distance of maybe an eighth of a mile. As a kid, it felt like so much further. With the wind in our hair and grit from the road in our teeth (and occasionally our knees), the thrill was unquenchable. Bikes offered an immediate feeling of freedom. I knew then that bikes always win, and ever since they have been a part of my life.

This love seamlessly and effortlessly rolled into a passion during that one week in the summer of 2005. With all my love and enjoyment for bikes, however, I had never done a bike tour. How much do I take for a one-week venture? Are two pairs of socks enough? Do I need food? Where will I get water? Can I drink the water here? Where will I sleep? How will I carry everything? All these initial seemingly simple problems swirled around in my mind, overwhelming me with analysis paralysis.

Fortunately, my fear of feeling stupid is almost always immediately dwarfed by my inherent, unrelenting curiosity. As soon as I pushed my first pedal out of Heather's tiny flat in Barcelona heading for the mountains of the Pyrenees, everything fell into place. Instantly there was a symbiotic connection with the road, the bike, and my body that allowed me to relax, slow down, and experience the local culture in a way that I never knew was possible. Just like riding a bike as a kid, I could go where I wanted, when I wanted. It was the ultimate freedom.

Over the next six days, I climbed my vintage 1982 Peugeot road bike over countless mountain passes, stopping at small villages along the way for food, accommodations, and boundless smiles. My Spanish was still dreadful, but I made it work. The result was not only confidence but also inspiration. And I don't think anyone thought I was stupid.

A few years later, in 2007, this passion for the open road blossomed from a simple call from an old friend, Rex, inviting me to join him on a two-week bike tour in the mountains of northern Vietnam. This time, I didn't have two years of high school Vietnamese to fall back on. However, with the experience of the Pyrenees still fresh on my taste buds, I jumped. In anticipation of this new adventure, I upgraded to a used 1991 Specialized mountain bike purchased for $50, because I knew the roads would be considerably rougher. Rex and I worked together for several years back in Colorado until he was offered a job in Hong Kong. We had done plenty of one-day bike adventures together, but this would be different.

Upon landing in Hanoi, it was quite apparent that I was not in

Colorado anymore. As I exited the plane onto the tarmac, the area was flanked by armed soldiers with machine guns, which immediately got my attention. I'm not sure, however, which stood out more: armed military everywhere or the image of Rex and his 6′2″ frame and blonde hair, towering over hundreds of Vietnamese locals. At least he was easy to spot. We quickly boarded a van and were whisked out of the chaotic city to the beginning point of our tour.

Deep into the night, our dilapidated van lurched around single-lane dirt roads, high into the mountains along the Chinese border. In an effort to avoid falling asleep, the driver pulled over and stopped at a tea house around 9 p.m. The night was completely black, and the mountain jungle was alive. At best, the faint light cast an eerie silhouette of trees in the distant horizon, causing my mind to wander too much. I had never been in a place this remote.

The tea house was a tiny wooden structure with a thatched roof and, as it turned out, was really just someone's home. All the things I had seen growing up in movies paralyzed me with fear. In the black of the night, I was convinced that people were hiding in the jungle, ready to spring out at any moment. In my mind, I was definitely going to become a POW, even though the "American War," as it's called in Vietnam, had ended more than forty years earlier.

I refused to get out of the van, as if in some way that would have prevented me from being abducted. It's amazing what tricks your brain can play on you. Finally, after several minutes of coaxing (and a little teasing) from Rex, I got out of the van and sat on a short, handmade wicker stool and sipped some of the best green tea I have ever tasted. Rex and I spent the next twelve days exploring the northern mountains of Vietnam and experiencing the kindness and generosity of the Vietnamese people—further cementing my love for this form of travel.

By 2015, my desire to see the world this way had gotten more salient, the passion more intense. I was increasingly convinced that this mode of world and self-exploration was for me. I went all in and purchased a new, not used, Surly Karate Monkey mountain bike specifically for off-road bike touring. Although I wish it were, the name "Karate Monkey" is not mine. It's just the model of the bike from Surly, but it did seem appropriate. I had it custom-painted "Kermit

Green," because you know . . . it ain't easy being green.

This time, the plan was to connect with my friend Taylor from Boulder for three weeks in South America. He was attempting to ride his bike from Tierra del Fuego at the southernmost tip of South America all the way home—for as long as it took. Each day I was jealous of his freedom as I followed his progress from the desk in my office. I planned to meet him along the way from Bolivia to Peru to provide him with some company and also bring him a new tire and other supplies.

I had met Taylor a decade earlier through our mountain bike racing backgrounds, and since then, we had gotten ourselves into countless bike and ski shenanigans. Our mutual friend, Jason, appropriately gave him the nickname "Farm Truck," because like a broken down and beat-up farm truck with numerous dents and scratches that just looks rough, it still starts every day.

Taylor always has a freshly shaved head and a pearly white smile. That smile, however, was compliments of an orthodontist back in Wisconsin where Taylor grew up. The legend as I knew it was that he was pedaling his bike home from a late night out while in college in Madison, hit a pothole, flew over the bars, and knocked out the top six Chiclets in his grill. Knowing Taylor and his propensity for elaborate storytelling, it really could have been anything, though I do like that story best.

This trip to South America was not only the longest I had been away from work, but also the greatest distance I had bike toured. Unlike my prior two bike touring experiences where I rode from hotel to hotel, this time however Taylor and I spent the majority of our nights camping on high mountain passes or next to rushing rivers and cooking on a camp stove.

We pedaled deeper into the Andes and with the crossing of each mountain pass, I could feel myself letting go of more and more embedded fears—fears of being so far from anything familiar and *safe*. That is until I woke up one morning and couldn't get out of my sleeping bag. We had been cycling for about seven days along the Altiplano (*High Plains*), a region of the Andes between Bolivia and Peru with an average altitude of over 12,000 feet. Up until that morning, I had effortlessly churned the pedals over numerous high mountain passes like a machine. But on this morning, something was wrong, and I had no idea what it was. I felt physically paralyzed and mentally stupid. I couldn't move or even form coherent thoughts. I was convinced I had food poisoning, which is common when traveling and figured I would just ride it out.

"You have altitude sickness," Taylor quickly diagnosed. "It hit me out of nowhere when I arrived in La Paz."

I knew that the only remedy was to get down to a lower altitude, but this wasn't an easy task considering where we were—in the middle of the Andes, surrounded by total nothingness, having not seen another person other than each other for three days. All around were peaks that spiked up well above the 13,000-foot plateau we were on. And then that fear of "what if" seeped into my lethargic brain. Fortunately, my ailment was minor, and I spent the next four days slowly and methodically pushing pedals at a tortoise pace. At one point I stopped to rest on the side of a dusty mountain road while Taylor lagged behind to fix a flat tire. I woke up forty minutes later with Taylor hovering over me, flashing his perfect white teeth in a taunting smile. Eventually we made it down to the lower altitude in Cusco. The worst part was not the feeling of mental and physical paralysis but rather having Taylor carry all the food and prepare all my meals for four days—something he has never let me live down since.

Flash forward to 2016. This time it was Africa, and I was going alone. I was scared yet covertly exhilarated. There would be no one to tell me that my choices or decisions were crazy or dangerous. Perhaps of more importance, no one to bail me out if things went sideways. I would have to rely on my own internal judgment and experience. My previous trips had been to places I mentally deemed "safe." Africa, in my mind, was anything but.

I grew up watching National Geographic with images of a pride of lions devouring a wildebeest. It was exciting and fascinating to watch on television because it was another world that I would never see up close. It wasn't real, so it was safe, like any other movie or television show. But to actually go there, that was different. My friends and family propagated unfounded fears, which slowly crept into my thoughts and subconscious, much the way they had in Vietnam.

"You cannot just ride through Africa by yourself. There are wild animals everywhere," my dad cautioned me.

"Every disease in the world originates in Africa. They have diseases there that don't even have names yet. And don't forget about the big hitters like malaria, Ebola, and yellow fever," jokingly poked my friend, Bryan, who is a Physician Assistant in Colorado.

This wasn't helping. However, my old high school buddy, Ben, was working for the Centers for Disease Control and living in Lusaka, Zambia, with his wife and three kids and had invited me down. I rationalized if someone who works with infectious diseases every day was living there with his kids, that was all the assurance I needed. I booked my flight.

What do you bring with you on a two-month bike tour of Africa? The better question is, what *don't* you bring? This was so far beyond my comfort zone. I had gaping, voluminous panniers latched to the rear of my bike, eager to haul whatever I thought I *might* need, and in Africa, who knew what that might look like? I had the full spectrum of tools to fix any potential issues, even though I was a hack mechanic at best. Two pairs of bike shorts, rain pants and jacket, down jacket, warm upper and lower base layers, one "hanging out outfit" to wear when not biking, three pairs of underwear, three pairs of socks, sun hat, toiletries including an electric razor for my face and head (because there isn't any place to get a haircut in Africa?) laptop, Kindle, iPhone (for communication and navigation), and of course all the charging cables and necessary power converters since the power outlets are different in Africa. A tent, sleeping bag, air mattress, camp stove, pot, but only one pair of shoes—sandals, to ride in and for everything else. This—this was the only efficiency I had managed to achieve in my packing—my shoes. Fully loaded, it was pushing 80 pounds, without water. Right. I might need that.

Unlike my prior trips which had been driven by no more than whimsical responses to someone else's invitation, this one was different. I needed *something*. I needed a change. For the previous four months, I had been drowning in a turbulent sea of purposelessness, my soul desperately reaching for anything tangible to cling onto, to pour myself into. I have always been a driven, type-A guy who knew exactly what I wanted and would relentlessly stop at nothing to get it. I had the focus of a neurosurgeon, with the next twenty years of my life planned out by the time I was 20. My roadmap to success and happiness was carefully thought out, diagramed, and laminated.

I went to business school and graduated with honors in three years with a degree in finance and dreams of being a banker like Gordon Gekko from the 1980s movie *Wallstreet*. I fantasized about fancy cars, a big house, a beautiful wife, and hosting extravagant dinner parties.

For ten years, I worked in various soulless corporate roles from the Federal Reserve to telecommunications where I routinely slaved away sixty hours a week like a long haul trucker hopped up on caffeine, numb to his surroundings—just trying to make it to his next drop-off. The only motivation was to get to the weekend, though most of those were spent working as well. I chased a paycheck instead of my passion. Sure, I had a healthy income, but it didn't translate into a healthy lifestyle. I was only 31 but could already feel a part of me dying.

But in 2005, I co-founded a successful end-of-life hospice organization, with the added benefit of getting to work every day with my mother, one of three partners for the next ten years. We had a motto in our office: "Every day is an opportunity to improve someone's life." After years of unhappiness working in those other roles, with the hospice, I had found my purpose. In addition, I had a beautiful girlfriend named Emma. With her golden locks, British accent, quick wit, and love of all things adventure, I was off the market five minutes into our first date. A year later she moved in.

We lived in a terrific house that I had spent the better part of five years passionately remodeling into our "forever home." We had great friends with whom we did exciting things, including hosting those extravagant dinner parties. It was all coming together just like my laminated road map showed. However, it was all an illusion. While the foundation of the house I rebuilt was solid, my personal and professional life had been crumbling for some time even as I refused to acknowledge it. Emma and I were not as perfectly suited as I had tried to convince myself, and, nearly a decade into running the hospice, the conflicts in the office were tearing the family out of the family business. The dull murmur of discontent became unmistakably louder. These turbulent winds of my life were brewing into a near-perfect storm, whose initial vague trajectory was becoming ultimately more defined. The cacophonous rumblings seeping through the façade of my perfect life eventually became too loud to muffle. Something had to change. And actually—everything did.

I woke up one morning in December 2015, lost. Gone was my company, my partner, and with them, my identity. The clock had struck midnight, and the fairy tale ended. My perfect life was a mirage, seemingly within my reach but then faded, just past my desperate, outreached grasp as I got too close. For the first time in my adult life, I didn't have it all figured out. I was on the eve of my 42nd birthday and felt like a directionless 22-year-old who had just graduated from college, a far cry from my 22-year-old self with the laminated map. I had naively thought that I could will my way to fix anything, and it was humbling to realize that at least this time, I could not.

What would you do if you got everything you wanted? I had it. All of it. It's funny how we envision our perfect lives. Somehow along the way, I had lost something. Routine, I discovered, is paralyzing. When you learn how to get a job, pay bills, a mortgage, whatever society tells us is the norm, days fly by, and you lose touch with the important stuff. We no longer wake up excited about the possibility of a new day and what adventures lie ahead. We lose that childhood curiosity. I had lost mine, and so much more.

You know that old question: "What would you do if you knew you could not fail?" I think it's bullshit. It's a cop-out. It removes the anxiety, the tension, and the fear of a situation. It's that very uncertainty that provides clarity and brings out the greatness in people. Fear, when harnessed, can be a powerful engine. Instead, I prefer the question: "What would you do if time was not a factor?" This is a more poignant musing because most things in life, including life itself, are finite. Work, school, sports—they are all confined by time. When we are young, we want to get older. We work hard all week to get to the weekend. We dream of the day we turn 65, retire, and then can do all those things we've wanted to do our entire lives. We forget that there is beauty in the day-to-day struggles and living in *the now*. As I was bobbing in this turbulent sea, a good buddy paraphrased the late great author Alan Watts to me: "We don't go to a concert just for the encore . . ."

Through my hospice experience, I learned that we don't get to choose what happens to us, but we get to choose how we respond. This is where I found myself, with a choice. I was nearing my 42nd birthday and I had been given a gift of time.

Mine is not a story of a wide-eyed, naively optimistic 22-year-old recent college graduate who takes a year off to figure out what I want to do. Nor is it a story of a 51-year-old man suffocating inside the walled confines of a multi-decade career in middle management, who one day woke up to see an image in the mirror of the man he didn't recognize staring back at him; face wrinkled, hardened by time and stress. Instead, my story is somewhere in between. I was not a poor 22-year-old who had scraped together enough nickels to buy a bike for $50 and afford to take a two-month holiday. I had always been careful with money (my friends prefer the term "cheap") and with the sale of the hospice, I could afford to take some time off. Days prior, I had received a text from a close friend offering me support. It read: "Everyone needs a friend that will call them up and say 'Get dressed fucker. We're going on an adventure.'"

—

I landed in Lusaka, a modern city with a population of 1.8 million, and definitely not the Africa I was expecting from my National Geographic-fueled imagination. Pristine six-lane highways crisscrossed the bustling metropolitan city as skyscrapers peered overhead. Fortunately, Ben and his family lived just outside of Lusaka in a wooded area. We spent that first evening hiking with his kiddos in the woods behind his home, listening to the sounds of the Zambian night, sharing old memories, and creating some new ones. "I'm in AFRICA!" I giggled aloud, yet still in disbelief.

"Are you current on your rabies vaccination?" Ben asked casually the next morning.

"I'm not. Should I be?"

"It's probably a good idea but no worries," he replied. "It's just another one of those things you can die from down here. You can pick it up at the local pharmacy and inject yourself."

Right. Malaria, Ebola, yellow fever. How did I overlook rabies? I guess I would be able to check that off my bucket list: injecting myself with a rabies vaccination, in Africa.

The next day, I went down to the local pharmacy. It was not as I expected. I have no idea why, but for some reason I envisioned it to be somewhere out in the bush, the person behind the counter sweating profusely as he swatted away flies and malaria-harboring mosquitos. I realize that is a horribly misguided stereotype, and I really need to quit watching so much National Geographic. In reality, the pharmacy was an air-conditioned space in a local shopping center, not unlike anything I would have experienced in the US.

"I need a rabies vaccination," I said to the young female pharmacist behind the counter.

"To cure or prevent?" she replied in a very strong Zambian accent.

Caught off guard by that question, I stumbled, "Prevent!"

"Okay, no problem. It is $30 per dosage, and you will need three. Inject one today, another in one week, and the final three weeks later. You can pick these up in any pharmacy. It is very common. The vaccination will not actually prevent rabies but will give you a little bit longer to get to a hospital."

I guess that was somewhat comforting. The pharmacist gave me a bag complete with a needle, vile of serum, some alcohol swabs, all wrapped in ice. It looked exactly like what I would expect to see back in the States—except I would be administering it myself.

I like to think I have a pretty stout pain threshold, and needles have never scared me. However, I always had the option to turn my head if I chose. I wouldn't have that luxury this time. I'd never given myself a shot and I had no idea how to do it. People with diabetes do it every day. How hard could it be?

I went back to Ben's and FaceTimed my friend Sara, who is a nurse and has administered her share of shots. Sara and I worked together for five years at our hospice, and she had become one of my closest friends. She is a true gem, with a domineering yet kind heart, someone who no matter what would always tell it to me straight.

"Jeez, Jerry! What have you gotten yourself into already?" she inquired in a joking yet not-so-surprised tone. "It's easy. Inject your shoulder. It will likely be sore for a day or two so pick which shoulder you want to be sore. Now, relax your arm, swab the area with an alcohol pad, stick the needle in the vial, draw out the serum, then push it gently yet firmly into your shoulder—but relax! Oh, and yes, you will have to push firmly because you need to pierce the skin."

With a deep breath, I plunged the needle into my relaxed left shoulder, heard a pop as it pierced the skin, and deployed the serum. And this is how I gave myself my first of three rabies shots, in Africa.

I woke up the next day feeling very un-rabid, yet with a distinct ache like somebody had punched me in the shoulder twenty-seven times.

"Good morning!" Ben greeted me enthusiastically with a slap on my shoulder. "How ya feeling?"

I would have been better if he hadn't slapped me on that shoulder, I thought to myself as we ventured out to the backyard together.

"I know you're leaving to begin your tour tomorrow, but what are your plans today?" Ben inquired over a bowl of muesli. "If you want, the kids and I are going over to a friend's house this afternoon for a barbeque. You should come. She's American and her husband is from India. I think you'll like them a lot."

A few hours later, we pulled up to a house and were immediately greeted by a woman with short blonde hair, wearing a blue dress and donning a beaming ear-to-ear smile. Jessica immediately wrapped Ben in a full body hug and invited us inside. Not to be outdone, I went in for a hug as well. Since running a hospice, I had decided that this is how I'm going to meet new people from now on—whether they like it or not.

"This is my friend, Jerry," Ben introduced me as I was finishing my introductory hug. "We went to high school together. He's going to be bikepacking through Africa for a couple of months."

Jessica's eyes squinted, and her smile went crooked. "Where do you live?" Jessica prodded, with the tone of a detective trying to crack a case. "Do you live in Colorado? My friend Brian from Colorado mentioned he had a good buddy named Jerry who was going to be in Africa traveling by bike. Obviously, Zambia is a big country and Africa a bigger continent so I didn't think anything of it."

Then it was my turn as my smile when crooked. "Brian Taylor?" I inquired, relatively certain that it was just another Brian. The odds were simply far too long.

"Holy shit!" shrieked Jessica. "I went to college with Brian in Wisconsin!"

Shocked, I replied, "I was on a bike trip with Brian in Peru for three weeks. And to this day he has never let me forget how he *saved my ass* when I got altitude sickness in the Andes, and he carried all the food and made all my meals. Blah, blah, blah," I said with a joking disdain for my friend's 'heroics.'

"Oh, really?" inquired Jessica. "Let me tell you about all the times I *saved his ass* back in Madison!"

We laughed late into the afternoon, and the next morning I packed up my bags, eager to set off and see this magical land that I had been dreaming about. All the planning, the excitement, but mostly the fear would all finally come to a culmination.

"One last thing. Here. This will come in handy." Ben handed me a forest green Zambian national football jersey. "Wear this. I don't want you to stick out too bad," he said with a playful laugh.

CHAPTER 2

Big Jer vs. Cool Hand Luke

Nobody likes to feel dumb. Least of all, me. I'd like to believe that as I travel further down the road of life, ideally approaching *adulthood* (even though I'm in my 40s), these moments become less frequent—a demonstrated sign of growth. But every once in a while, I do something dumb that reminds me that I have yet to arrive, and maybe I can blame my dad?

Dad is a Korean War veteran and firmly believes in the military-style of child-rearing. Growing up with Big Jer was if nothing else, predictable. (My grandma would answer the phone, asking, "Jerry? Are you looking for Big Jerry or Little Jerry?") I appreciated this about my dad. I always knew his expectations and always knew where I stood. The line in the sand was drawn in my childhood sandbox even before I could walk. In his house, it wasn't quite a dictatorship, but certainly, it was a far cry from a democracy. There wasn't much room for discussion and even less for dissention. "It's my way or the highway," he would bark in his uncompromising, drill sergeant tone. "When you're 18, you can do what you want, but when you're under my roof, it's my rules." Okay, so maybe it was a dictatorship.

Big Jer grew up on the South Side of Chicago and used to tell me that he graduated from the "School of Hard Knocks." For sure, he has seen more than his share of them in his life. As an adult now, I relish any opportunity to hear him recount the shenanigans of growing up in a rough-and-tumble, racially-charged Chicago with the hooligans that he used to run with. He would tell me of fights he got into and how strict his single mother, raising three kids, was on him. After finishing high school, as a naïve 17-year-old, he followed his older brother and, against his mother's wishes, joined the Army as a paratrooper heading off to fight in Korea. I don't know if he looked at it as an adventure, or if it was just the simple impulsive, starry-eyed ambitions of a teenager. In any case, there was nobody who could tell him otherwise.

One time during jump training, his chute failed to deploy, but somehow, he landed on his brother's canopy and hit the ground without any major consequence. (Unbelievable, but true.) "Kopack, you're going back up," said his commanding officer. The thinking was that if you didn't immediately jump again after a traumatic experience, fear of the near-death event would set in, and you would never jump again. "Yessir," Private Kopack obediently replied, en route to another jump. It is clear to me that his experiences not only in Chicago but, absolutely in the military, *directly* made my dad the man he is today, which of course trickled down into making me who I am, although maybe *indirectly.*

To this day, Big Jer still has wavy brown hair, always dresses in a suit, and boasts a gregarious outgoing personality. Ironically, he has a tattoo on his right bicep of birds singing in a tree—probably another one of those impulsive decisions from his youthful military years. But just below this cheerful teddy bear surface, there is a layer that seems to goad, "Try me." He's my height but a solid 50 pounds heavier. Big Jer is in his 80s now and has what I call "old man strength," gained from years of hard work. He has a vice-like handshake and a bear hug that would make a chiropractor nervous. Growing up, I distinctly remember him doing pushups every morning followed by seemingly endless bicep curls with loaded water jugs. Big Jer is old school.

Like most kids in my town, I grew up watching cartoons. It began with shows like *Winnie the Pooh* but moved into *Bugs Bunny* and *Super Friends* as I got older. But on weekends, however, one of the things we loved doing together was watching movies, and we watched a lot. Sometimes we would go to the theater in Lansing and see three movies in one day; there really isn't much else to do in mid-Michigan in the winter. We would walk out of *Star Wars*, cross the hall to *Raiders of the Lost Ark*, and wrap up the day with *The Terminator*. We liked to think of it as the "buy one, get two free" package. With a trough of buttery popcorn and free refills on soda, our Saturdays were never dull.

Big Jer used to call me "Cool Hand Luke" after the movie of the same name starring Paul Newman. In the film, Luke was always pushing the boundaries of what he could get away with. The perpetual "why" was always asked because "that is the rule" never seemed to apply to him. Luke would use his smile and charismatic personality as currency to attempt to buy his way out of whatever bind he had inflicted on himself. Ultimately, however, it caught up to him, and he paid the price.

As a kid, I was just like Luke. Always questioning. Always pushing the limits. How far could I go? Sure, that is the rule, but is it *really?* I saw the line in the sand, but in my eyes it wasn't always so clear but rather more of a suggestion; an opportunity for negotiation. It seemed the stricter my dad was, the more I pushed and tested his boundaries. The worst thing I think was simply to question him, even on the most inconsequential things. "You need to go to sleep by 9 p.m." "If it's below 50°, you need to wear an undershirt." These were just some of the basics that we waged war over, much the same as most other kids did with their parents, I would assume.

Even if he was right (which he normally was), I still didn't back down and never accepted being wrong, either. "Why?" I would relentlessly prod. This burned my dad because, coming from the military, authority was never questioned. It was absolute and declarative. That was what he expected, and that was the approach he took to raising me. However, I could never take anything at face value. He would just smile at me, shaking his head, frustration building inside yet revealing a twinkle of pride in my inherent ambition and determination.

Thirty years later, I suppose that hasn't changed. I have always been driven by an unquenchable curiosity, especially when told *not* to do something. "What we have here, is . . . failure . . . to communicate" was the famous line from the warden to Luke, shortly after another act of defiance. My dad loved that line, and, every time I would push the limit too far, I would hear it just before the inevitable punishment came down.

Looking back, he was probably more right than not, but in those moments, I definitely felt the odds leaned dramatically in the other direction, and so I pushed. This tight lid on my freedom growing up fostered in me an unrelenting desire to rebel. It's no coincidence that, even today, I have genuine anxiety when I'm told what I can and cannot do, almost like I am being smothered under a pillow. This has led me down a lifelong road of perpetual curiosity and exploration, and again, not a coincidence why I now found myself in Africa, on a bike, about to do something—dumb.

CHAPTER 3

Cool Hand Luke Made Me Do It

In Botswana, elephants were everywhere, so I was told. Over the course of a week, I had made my way south, through Zambia, across a sliver of Zimbabwe, then finally into Botswana. From there, I had planned to pedal through Namibia before looping back to Zambia.

The ride from the Zimbabwe border to Botswana was about seventy miles on smooth tarmac, almost completely flat and straight, save for two hills (yes, I counted), and absent of any other remarkable topography. Little pockets of trees dotted the countryside, but it was otherwise a very forgettable stretch that blurred by without notice.

Occasionally I passed a cluster of small wooden homes. People would come out to wave and welcome me to their country with enormous smiles. Others would barely look up from what they were doing, sometimes glancing over at me with curious looks, perhaps wondering what I was doing. I was told that elephants frequented this region. With a perfectly flat road and zero traffic, I was constantly scanning for them, and considering the landscape, they should be pretty hard to miss.

I arrived in the small village Kasane, Botswana, and from there is a thirty-mile stretch of flawlessly paved road leading directly to Namibia, void of even a single curve. However, it cuts through Chobe

National Park, one of the wildest places in Africa. I had signed up for a safari through the roughly 4,500 square acre park the day before (picture National Geographic with an open-air Land Rover, a large, imposing guide, probably 6′4″ and 250 pounds, dressed in beige fatigues at the wheel, a Winchester rifle big enough to stop an elephant at his side). Giraffes, hippos, hyenas, and yes, dozens of elephants all came out to say hello. But to be fair, this paved route through to Namibia was not the same dusty road through the bush that we had followed on our safari, so it was probably safe, I reasoned. Why would wild animals hang out along a paved road with all the available surrounding woods and bush that we traveled through yesterday?

I loaded up my gear, ready to get back on my bike and cross into Namibia. I asked no fewer than seventeen people around Kasane whether I could pedal through Chobe National Park, and I got no fewer than seventeen variations of the same thing, "Are you crazy? There are elephants and lions in the park!" I did however ask one final person who said, "Go up to the gate and find out." So that is what I did.

The guard was an overbearing, intimidating man, a pistol on his hip and that same familiar elephant stopping rifle in his guard shack. He appeared to lack any real interest in my presence or have any patience for me given his abrupt manner.

"Can I pedal through the park on this road?" I naively asked.

With an emotionless face, and barely acknowledging me at all, he said dismissively, "No, there are elephants and lions in the park. See there, elephants crossing the road," as he casually pointed off into the direction where I would start my ride, before he turned and walked back into the guard shack to enjoy his coffee.

Yup, sure enough, fifty yards down the road, a dozen adult elephants were crossing. Right. I was told by my guide the day before that elephants are even more dangerous than lions. Their population density in this region means you can't avoid them, and their sheer size makes any encounter potentially deadly. These were African Savanna or bush elephants, which weigh up to nine tons and stand ten to thirteen feet at the shoulder. If one of them turns aggressive, there's really not much you can do. I read later that some reports had shown that human deaths from elephants range from one hundred up to five hundred per year, a statistic more than enough to convince me of my flawed ambition. Instead, I made the turn back—back to Zambia.

—

After a long day of cycling through dusty, brown, forgettable landscape, essentially on autopilot (thus bypassing Namibia), I was once again approaching the Zambian border and began to see dirt roads spurring off to the south toward the Zambezi River. It was the first time in four hours that I had actually ventured to lift my gaze from the perfectly straight, yellow lines on the road that had methodically lured me into a trance. I could see on my map that these roads wrapped around and ran parallel to the river and would take me back to Livingstone, where I had begun. Needing some distraction from the monotony, I took the first spur, which led me shortly to a game lodge about a mile in—the gateway to Mosi-oa-Tunya National Park. I stopped at the guard shack and inquired what animals were in the area. The guard stepped out, and with a large welcoming smile, "Elephants, giraffe, zebra, buffalo!" he replied emphatically.

"No cats?" I asked, almost prodding.

"No cats." He retorted with confidence.

"Can I cycle down this road and follow along the river into Livingstone?" I asked hopefully.

"Too dangerous. Also, you're in the park and need a permit. No bikes."

Disappointed, and still a bit upset about being turned around in Botswana only to have it happen a second time, I headed back toward the predictable monotony of the tarmac, relegated to just get back and hang out in Livingstone before making my way north to Ben's house. As I plodded back along the same dirt road I came in on, I saw another dirt road just before the tarmac that I had overlooked when I first approached. I paused, knowing this was likely that dumb idea that apparently I had yet to grow out of, but the thought of riding another hour on tarmac with trucks zooming by as I entered the city felt like brain damage (and potentially body damage). *Hmm . . . it's just a dirt road that parallels the main road. What's the difference?* My dad's words crept back into my brain. "What we have here is . . . failure . . . to communicate." *Shut up, Dad,* I defiantly mumbled back as I made the turn.

The sun was high in the sky, and in the distance a cluster of billowy, white cotton balls etched a contrast into the otherwise clear blue sky. A warm breeze was making the leaves in the thirty-foot forest canopy dance playfully overhead. I had envisioned a peaceful trek through the woods, but almost immediately I was overcome by a suffocating anxiety. The woods were denser than I expected. The track was narrow and dusty and quickly degraded into a footpath. Unbeknownst to me, I had entered into the park. (*Unbeknownst? Was it? Really?*)

My pulse quickened. My breath became shallow. I felt like I was in *Jurassic Park*, and at any moment I would roll up on some animal, patiently waiting for me to do—just that. Even with as much as I had learned about the number of elephants in the area and reported stories of the deaths they caused, the child inside me still feared lions—a paralyzing fear of being stalked. For whatever reason, being stalked by an elegant killing machine seemed more terrifying (and likely) than being stampeded by a group of lumbering, clumsy elephants—so I told myself. These thoughts dominated my mind, and no matter what I did, I could not banish them. *But he said there were definitely "no cats." Breathe.*

The deeper into the woods I went, the more my heart raced. For some reason, I couldn't bring myself to simply turn around, the lament that boredom was somehow worse than this. I feared that the sound of my knobby tires lumbering along the dirt track would prevent me from hearing an animal lurking in the bush waiting to pounce—which was foolish thinking anyway since this was their home, and they would know about me way before I knew about them. It's amazing how adrenaline affects your mindset.

After about a mile, the road abruptly stopped. To my left, there were railroad tracks, which I was pretty sure continued all the way into Livingstone. Just like the old TV show, *Let's Make a Deal* with Monty Hall, where contestants were given the option to choose from a safe, but boring known quantity (like a sectional couch), or give it back with the hope that behind door #1 would be something amazing (like a new sports car), I was presented with a pressing decision: I could play it safe, take my couch, and retrace my tracks through the woods before once again being deposited back onto the tarmac and rolling unadventurously back into Livingstone. Or, with the hope of that sexy new sports car, I could see what was behind door #1, and plod along the train tracks further into the park, all while continuing to scan left, right, and especially, definitely—behind me. *He said there were no cats, right?*

I could see my dad's face, his eyes squinting, shaking his head. However, I knew that so many of the opportunities I was presented with in my life were the result of being Luke, so instead, I chose door #1 and stubbornly lugged my bike up the short embankment and began thumping along the wooden train tracks.

There's nothing peaceful or relaxing about riding on train tracks, the front wheel thumping over one wooden tie a split second before the back tire hits one. *Ka thunk, ka thunk, ka thunk.* But, I was sure that I had made the right decision. It was a warm day but far from hot, and I was in the shade of a dense forest. However, my head was seeping sweat like a faucet that I could not shut off, down my forehead and stinging my eyes. The green Zambian football jersey clung to my back, splotchy and saturated. I was pedaling slowly, but my pulse continued to race. Forty minutes rolled by, but given my anxiety, it really could have been two hours. I came to a fence line. (*Unbeknownst? Oh, c'mon. Yes. I'm IN the park. Shut up, Dad.*)

The tracks I was riding along continued through a break in the fence. There was, however, a road leading left, presumably out of the park and past a shack housing a guard—who would definitely have a pistol on his hip and that ubiquitous rifle just an arms reach away, and definitely not expect a cyclist to come strolling out of the national park, a place where bikes are explicitly not allowed. Bad idea.

Just as I was about to play it safe and continue pedaling along the tracks, at the last instant, I looked down and saw that there were some wires on the tracks directly at the fence line; likely a powerful electric fence meant to keep very large animals in. Of course. Worse idea. This was that moment, emphatically confirming the fact that I had done something dumb, and Cool Hand Luke wasn't going to be able to talk himself out of this one. I was trapped, without any good options. I had long since ruled out retracing my route along the tracks and dirt road all that way back through *Jurassic Park*. Monty Hall and my dad were both grinning at me because it was clear that this left me with the option of trying to cross the electric fence line, with its promise of a potent zing since it is there to keep animals much larger than myself in the park. Or, I could head up the dirt road (door #2?) and inevitably past a very soon-to-be surprised and angry guard. I have no idea what the punishment is for foreigners who do this sort of thing and was not eager to find out. So, like Maverick in *Top Gun*, I decided to buzz the tower.

The guard shack was facing me, and I knew the guard would have me in his sights, so to speak, for the seventy-five yards of approach before the gate. I set off pedaling slowly to conserve energy before ramping up my speed at the very end—I didn't plan to stop. As I got closer, the guard was understandably surprised to see a bright green bicycle coming toward him at Mach speed, and came out to inquire (read: intercept, detain, and reprimand). Expecting this, I tucked my head and charged forward, flying past by him as he chased me on foot. He yelled something, but it was all a blur with the wind in my ears and adrenaline throttling through my veins. It was about a hundred yards on the dirt road past the shack to the tarmac, where I turned right and continued pedaling feverishly, never looking back for what felt like several miles. I heard more yelling, but it probably wasn't because he wanted to talk to me about my Zambia football jersey.

CHAPTER 4

A Mad(a) Plan

"Hey! Welcome back!" Ben beamed. His scraggly beard seemed to have filled in a bit since I last saw him two weeks prior. "What are your plans? Wanna go for a ride?"

After touring around bits of Zambia, Zimbabwe, and Botswana, the boil of my initial African fears were slowly being reduced to a simmer, allowing my inherent curiosity to percolate. But along the way, I had gotten comfortable knowing that there was always a safety net back in Lusaka if I needed it, leaving me feeling like I was never really "out there." I needed to be on my own, detached from the comfort of the familiar. With six weeks left before my return flight to Colorado, I packed up my bike, after hardly ever getting it dirty, and concocted a plan to go to Madagascar.

I had read about travelers who toured through Africa from north to south, connecting all the countries along the way while never skipping around because it would compromise the authenticity of the tour. I had no such ambitions. Once the idea of Madagascar got lodged in my brain, so too did the romantic idea of once again hitting the open road and riding my bike through Zambia, around the war-torn country of Malawi, through Mozambique to the coast where I would find a boat patiently waiting to port me across the Indian Ocean. It seemed so perfect and idealistic, but after about two days of rudimentary internet searches for boat transport options, I came up empty. Instead, like a spoiled child reeking of privilege, I begrudgingly and very unromantically hopped a plane.

I was met at the airport in Antananarivo (Tana) by my new Malagasy friend. Her name is Njara (pronounced En Zarrah), and she was 27. I connected with her through a mutual friend in Boulder who had spent three years in Madagascar in the Peace Corps. Njara stands barely five feet tall, is slender in stature but with a smile that is twice her size. She was wearing crisp red jeans, a black leather jacket, and had a colorful silk scarf wrapped around her neck. Her father who stepped out of the car as we approached stood at most two inches taller than her, was in his early 50s, also sharply dressed, with a thinning hairline and a smile showing exactly where Njara got hers from. For some reason, Njara, this person whom I had never met, living on the other side of the world, offered to pick me up and take me into her family home.

The Tana airport is a pressure cooker of culture, mayhem, and overall disorganization. Because the country is so poor, locals come at weary travelers from every angle, offering to give them a ride, carry a bag, or simply give directions—all with the hope to make a little bit of money. Although endearing and heartbreaking, in this melee, I was relieved to see a pseudo familiar face in the dizzying madness.

Njara and her father picked me up in his compact, 1970s Renault four-door hatchback. It was faded white with a few dings and blemishes, but given the vintage, it was in remarkable condition and showed a true pride of ownership. France had stopped exporting them to the US in the early 1980s but because Madagascar is a former French colony, if you're looking for one, come to Tana, where I estimate that no less than 50 percent of the cars here are like this one. It's like opening a time capsule.

They quickly loaded me and my bike into their car and whisked me out of the buzzing capital city, but not before stopping for gas. We pulled up at the full-service petrol station, and a smiling man in his 30s with splotches of grease on his face and shirt walked across the dusty lot and approached our car. Njara's father reached down and pulled out a plastic container from between his legs. It was about the size of two two-liter bottles of soda and had a hose in it snaking out from somewhere under the dashboard, which her father removed before handing the thing to the attendant. Somehow, this was the gas tank? I suppose it's possible I was still reeling from the frenzy of the Tana airport, so what I thought I was seeing wasn't registering. However, five minutes later the attendant handed back the container, now full, and Njara's father placed it on the floor between his legs, put the hose back in it, and fired up the engine. With a puff of grey smoke, we were on our way.

We chugged and rattled along a broken dirt road that would make the Land Rover in Botswana cringe. It was lined with clusters of trees, and periodically chickens would dart out and around our lumbering Renault. My head was still spinning from the fact that two days prior I was in Zambia hanging out with an old high school friend enjoying yogurt and fresh fruit on the patio in his backyard. With zero planning, I had no idea what to expect in Madagascar, but it already felt like the right call.

Njara's family's home, which was located a half-hour from the chaotic city center, was a simple yet immaculate brick structure with whitewashed walls and polished tile floors. We were greeted at the front door by the outstretched arms of Njara's smiling mother and the smell of dinner. She had short wavy hair, and like her husband and daughter, was also very sharply dressed with the same radiant and welcoming smile. She was even smaller in size than Njara and nearly disappeared inside my hug. I already felt at home.

Njara's mother and father spoke no English, so Njara translated our entire interaction. Even absent words—it is amazing how a smile can convey so much kindness. After a traditional Malagasy dinner of rice, beans, and greens, her father shared some of his home-brewed cinnamon-flavored alcohol made from sugar cane called Toaka Gasy. The name simply means "Malagasy Rum." It is one step removed from gasoline and most probably causes blindness. I politely indulged in a thimble-sized sip of this potent elixir and felt my nose hairs curl and eyes water, much to the amusement of Njara's father.

The following day Njara and her father drove me into town, but before sending me off, she told me a disturbing yet appropriate joke.

What do you call a person who speaks multiple languages? Multi-

lingual.

What do you call a person who speaks three languages? Trilingual.

What do you call a person who speaks two languages? Bilingual.

What do you call a person who speaks one language? American.

Sigh . . .

After a day's reprieve, the chaotic frenzy of the city was now exhilarating. Tana is the capital of Madagascar with a population of about 1.3 million people and sits at an elevation of 4,200 feet. It is a beautiful and densely populated city, nestled in rolling hills, in the center of the island. A web of cobblestone streets and bridges meander throughout the city. The architecture is distinctly French, dating back to their occupation from 1897 to 1958.

Madagascar, called "Mada" by the locals, is about 226,000 square miles, roughly the size of California, although with only about two-thirds the population. It is the fourth largest island in the world, and it is estimated that 90 percent of the country's plant and animal species exist nowhere else on Earth. The island has only a handful of roads outside of the city, and the mountainous Ankaratra region runs through the middle, creating a natural weather shield whereby the east side is tropical, and the west arid, with a picturesque coastline all the way around.

Sadly, the old French charm cannot hide the dark fact that Tana is a poor, impoverished city. Children as young as three are taught to beg for money and even pickpocket. On more than one occasion, I saw a child likely not older than six carrying a baby and asking for money, while the mother likely in her teens or early 20s slept in a stairwell, too tired and weak to do anything else.

Njara dropped me off at a local backpacker's hostel, called the Madagascar Underground (the *Underground* to those who know). It is located on a side street in a quiet part of town and is a nice melting pot of travelers of varying ages on very like-minded journeys. I walked into the Underground and dropped my gear, already slowly being worn down by the mayhem of Tana. There was reggae playing over the speakers, and several guests were sitting around on the brilliantly colored couches, passively conversing while tapping away on their Apple laptops and smartphones. It seemed like a standard backpacker hostel and an easy place to stay for a few days, to meet other travelers, and to get a feel for the local scene before heading out on my bike.

"This place is cool, but if you want someplace a little more chill, I know a place."

This is how I met Jenna, as she put down her guitar and paused the song she was singing. Immediately, we hit it off like two childhood friends, one of whom had moved away from the small town where they lived only to reconnect years later as if no time had ever passed. Jenna was 25, from San Francisco, with long wavy brown hair draped over her shoulder, subtly caressing her peeling, sunburned face. She was wearing an oversized white and brown crocheted sweater that she told me she had picked up for $3 at the local market.

Jenna has a booming yet fluttering singing voice that is a combination of Adele and Bonnie Rait, and she was slowly teaching herself to play the guitar. On this occasion, I had unintentionally interrupted her rendition of a Beyoncé cover she was working on. In only a few minutes, I learned that she was in year two of her three-year Peace Corps stint and, as a result, was fluent in Malagasy. When not in Tana for some "socialization," she lived in a small village on the east coast of Madagascar named Tsarasambo. Most Peace Corps volunteers work in very remote and isolated villages, and it is common for them to all congregate in Tana periodically so they don't lose their minds—so I was told.

After nearly an hour of chatting, we walked down the side street, approximately two hundred yards away, to the Chalet de Rose, an upper-scale hotel with a private room for $20 per night. In a whirling sea of blaring horns and continual accosting, I had an oasis.

I checked into my room and opted for a shower to help me relax. Clearing the soap from my squinting eyes, I glanced at the tile on the shower wall and noticed the "circle of life." It is a squiggly spiral line that wraps around into a circle and was also the logo for the hospice that I founded. I took a deep breath, choked back a stray tear, then smiled proudly. Perhaps a not-so-subtle sign that being in Mada was right.

The next day, my new friend and I hopped a ride on a *taxi breusse* and headed across town to the stadium to watch the international rugby match between Madagascar and Senegal. A *taxi breusse* is the main form of budget mass transit around Madagascar but is really nothing more than a dilapidated Toyota Previa from the 80s. As a *breusse* approached, Jenna waved her arm to hail it. The driver slowed down just enough for the driver's handler to open up the sliding side door, drag us inside, take a few ariary (the local currency), and quickly sputter away down the road.

Once inside, it was clear that Toyota's eight-person seating was a mere suggestion. I counted nineteen people, not including myself or Jenna, as people were stacked on top of one another, everyone just happy to have a ride. Immediately I noticed that the handler wasn't only opening the sliding door and taking the rider's fare, but he was actually holding the door shut since the latch didn't work. We stopped every few minutes to cycle people in and out, the handler somehow maintaining the correct fare for each rider. A few minutes later, we signaled to the driver to let us out and then climbed over four people and arrived at the stadium.

On match days the local markets outside the stadium are especially electric. Colorful fruits and vegetables filled the stalls while slabs of meat swarming with flies hung from hooks in another alley. All of the people working in the area put on their best hard sell as we passed. Without any preference, I quickly grabbed three bananas and then walked across the street to the clothing side as the sellers continued to push their fruit on me, even as I was walking away. Since I was still wearing my Zambia football jersey, I felt like I needed to look more *local*, so for $3.00 I picked up a white Madagascar rugby jersey, and like that, I was a local. Well, sorta.

As we approached the raucous stadium, the fans were queuing up, many already drunk on *Toaka Gasy*. There were two ticket options, with the stadium divided this way—sections for Locals and VIPs. The locals were of course the local Malagasy people, and the VIPs appeared to be a small collection of white travelers looking for a true Madagascar experience. The price for a local's ticket was $3 or $9 for VIP. Having a tour guide who spoke the language fluently almost felt like cheating when negotiating a ticket price from the guy hocking them out front. No doubt Jenna saved me some money if I had otherwise tried to purchase the tickets myself, but probably only a dollar or two. The ticket line for the locals went around the corner, so because of this, we ended up splurging for the VIP tickets.

Entering the thundering 22,000-seat stadium, segregated and buffered by police, felt like a scene out of a movie. There were at most 150 of us on the sprawling and spacious VIP side with the remaining fans crammed into the other side, somehow into an equal amount of real estate. Immediately, I felt like "one of them," a rich, white, entitled person, sitting under a canopy of privilege in a reclining padded, red velvet seat, watching a sporting match in a predominantly black country. I didn't want to be on this side of history, or the stadium. I felt ashamed and longed to feel the energy and inclusion of the local Malagasy people.

"Let's move," I said to Jenna.

"You sure?" She replied while waving her Madagascar flag. "I thought you would like it over here."

"I hate it. We might as well be watching on television. So what do you think?"

"Hell yes," she replied excitedly.

We made our way down three rows, around the track, and over to the gate separating *us* from *them*. The guard who opened the gate to the other side looked at us like we were crazy and told us there were no *vazaha* over there. (Vazaha was the first Malagasy word I learned. It simply meant "white people," not so much in a derogatory way, but rather just matter-of-factly.) Evidently, he thought this was a deterrent but really it had the opposite effect. With my Madagascar rugby jersey and my local tour guide, we plowed our way through a sea of crazed fans while stepping over countless others, likely passed out on *Toaka Gasy*.

It was shoulder to shoulder as we surfed our way through the flowing sea of screaming fans trying to get to midfield, optimistically looking for a place to sit. If there were 22,000 seats, there were 25,000 fans squeezed into every crevice of available real estate. We were already saturated in sweat and *Toaka Gasy* from the frenzied crowd when I faintly heard a woman call down to us and offer space next to her. We climbed over six rows, past and over more hysterical fans, into what felt like the eye of a hurricane of emotion. There really wasn't any space, but she did her best to carve out a slice. Every time Madagascar would score, the tidal wave of the crowd's energy would toss us around like a cork on the sea. It was intoxicating, like *Toaka*

Gasy, but without the side effect of blindness and amnesia. The crowd was singing and swaying in unison throughout the match, and, even though I didn't know the words to any of the songs, it was impossible not to sway along. The people around us were surprised to see us there, but nonetheless thanked us for supporting them.

Just as there was no order to the seating, the flow of people exiting the stadium two hours later was even more chaotic. I immediately got the sense of what a stampede would feel like. Just like a powerful undertow in the ocean, we were held at the whim of the crowd—utterly powerless—and it was terrifying. Pinned without any sense of choice, we were continually driven forward, sweat and alcohol coating us. Thousands of people pushed from behind as only several people at a time could be squeezed and forced through the few exit portals. I felt a flutter on my leg and when I glanced down, I saw a child, no more than seven years old, fidgeting with the zipper on my pants pocket, trying to get at my mobile phone. I politely tapped him on the top of his head and waved my finger at him. Undeterred at being caught, he simply slipped away to case out his next mark.

We finally reached the exit and were granted some much-needed space to move and breathe. When I finally caught my breath, I looked down and saw urine cascading down the concrete stairs like a river as countless Malagasy men were standing to the side and relieving themselves following the day's excitement. An hour later, I arrived back at Chalet de Rose and promptly rinsed off the day's *culture*.

I woke up the next morning, restless. Anxiety was again building inside me, becoming pervasive inside my head. Memories stirring from the life I left in the US, barely two weeks ago—emotions yet to be dealt with. The only thing that has historically quelled this in the past is movement. I needed to leave. I needed to start pedaling again.

After a discussion with Jenna, I made a plan to travel to the east coast and continue up to the northern tip before returning to Tana five weeks later for my flight home. It would be nearly a thousand miles of remote roads, plenty of time for me to release all the things that were still going on inside my mind. In addition, there was another thing going through my mind on a continual loop all day, something that Jenna had told me. "There are no secondary roads in Mada. Stick to the main national road." Oh, hello again, Cool Hand Luke.

CHAPTER 5

Stick to the Main Road

I set off on a sunny, warm, and especially chaotic traffic day in Tana. Renaults seemed to be packed in as far as I could see. Fortunately, I was on a bike. On my map, there were two routes: the main road, and a faint, distinctively smaller secondary road. I had time to mull it over since the slog to get through morning rush hour in Tana took nearly two hours of exhaust asphyxiating brain damage. I weaved my way through a tangled web of cars jammed into the narrow and winding cobbled streets and at my decision point stood two options: more congestion and exhaust, literally choking the passion out of me—or—clean and pure freedom. I again heard Jenna's voice in my head, "there are no secondary roads in Mada. Stick to the main national road." Anxiety was coursing through my veins, and I felt trapped by the city. I was being choked by the fumes but more so by my own inner turmoil. In my mind I saw Big Jer, shaking his head decisively, a line drawn in the sand, daring me—and I took the bait and chose door #1.

The cobbles quickly gave way to broken pavement, and I began clawing and winding my way up 2,000 vertical feet before rolling through the heavily forested green countryside, leaving all the *Madness* behind. *This wasn't so bad*? I mused.

Two hours passed by and the whirl of Tana was a distant memory.

My smile returned, and I had a renewed optimism as I let out a gigantic decision-affirming exhale. But the road I was following began to narrow, and then narrowed some more, becoming a mere broken and overgrown footpath that was barely visible, before reaching a dead end at a creek crossing. "Shit!" I cursed audibly. I pulled out my phone and looked at the map. Yup. I was still on course, even though the road that I was following was gone. It was Day 1 and I had already managed to get lost.

I could hear Jenna, "There are no secondary roads in Mada. Stick to the main national road." As I lamented the dreaded "tuck tail and backtrack" (something I did NOT do while in Zambia in *Jurassic Park*), I could see Big Jer, again shaking his head with an "I told you so" half-cocked grin on his face. If I turned around, I could be back in the city at the junction to the national highway in less than two hours, or I could forge ahead like my dad would expect Cool Hand Luke to do, not knowing where I would end up but letting my curiosity play out. I couldn't bear the thought of going back to the traffic of the city, but worse would be letting Big Jer win and accept the fact that I made a mistake.

Yvon Chouinard, mountaineer and founder of Patagonia once said, *"The word adventure has gotten overused. For me, when everything goes wrong—that's when adventure starts."*

With this in mind, and without really knowing where I was going, I pushed my bike across the creek, up the other side, and began dragging it up the footpath that was much too steep to pedal. This went on for about ninety grueling minutes as sweat flowed down my forehead like the stream I just crossed. For some reason, I chose to wear sandals on this trip, which work well for pedaling and stream crossings, but were ill-equipped for clawing my way up a scree field. I checked the GPS every ten minutes. Yup, still on course, but how was this *path* on the map? Finally, I crested the hill and joined a larger dirt road as the lactic acid of muscle fatigue was bubbling inside my legs. I had gone only about a mile, but I was euphoric yet dumbfounded because somehow, I was still on the route.

I continued pedaling along this seldom-used dirt road for another hour. I checked the map again just to make sure I didn't miss a turn, even though there were not any other junctions for me to miss.

"DAMMIT!" I cursed. I had missed a turn nearly a half-mile back. I backtracked and saw yet another footpath heading up a ridiculously steep hill where a man was walking his cow. I made the turn and began heaving my fully loaded bike up the incline once again, cursing the hair clippers, laptop, and three pairs of socks tucked inside the panniers, while never gaining on the man with his cow. He looked back periodically to see if I was still pursuing this foolish endeavor. Sadly, I was.

Another forty-five-minute war ensued with me slogging my bike up this hill, loose rocks careening down behind me. At one point it got so steep that I slid down the hill backwards with my bike on top of me. In the face of absurdity, I was somehow defiant. Even if I wanted to turn around, it would have been harder to prevent my bike from catapulting down this hill and shattering into a dozen pieces—and I with it. I pressed on and again was rewarded with an overgrown, never used dirt road. Oddly, this time there were white arrows (but for sure no actual street signs) painted into the dirt informing me that this was indeed a *used road*. I was still "on course."

Throughout the day, I was greeted by the kind smiles of people in the small remote villages that I passed through, who I'm certain were perplexed by what they were witnessing. Finally, after about six hours of this absurdity, a single-track trail dropped down and joined the paved national highway before rolling into the village of Manjakandira.

—

It was getting dark and about to rain. Manjakandira is a small, dusty village with a single road running through it, a few homes scattered to either side. I had traveled fewer than thirty miles from Tana, but it may as well have been three thousand. I was in rural Madagascar, a seemingly completely different world, and I was shattered. Dirt was caked thickly on my face as if I had just finished working a double shift at the coal mine. I needed to find a place to sleep and eat, ideally, before the rain came down and totally dissolved me. I cruised back and forth through town three times, looking intently on both sides of the road for a hotel. Nothing. I resigned myself to camp but was not looking forward to it.

The ominous grey sky slowly opened up, faint thunder growled, and a light rain began to fall. I felt myself becoming more anxious. With one last-ditch effort, I began trying to communicate with people, even though I spoke no Malagasy and they spoke no English. I gave the international sign of sleep with my ear laying on my hands. Nothing. Even my tried and true charades seemingly were in a foreign language. Where this had once gotten at least a laugh, now I was instead looked upon with bewilderment. A small crowd was slowly forming around me. Apparently, they didn't experience many people looking like me rolling through town, making all kinds of strange gestures. Finally, a woman who knew a couple of words in English, who was now standing in front of me with her two small children, offered to let me stay in her home if I didn't mind an empty room with no furniture or electricity.

"Yes!" I exalted, just as the rain began to lash down.

The woman was in her 30s and her two children were probably 8 and 10. They were all well dressed, despite the pervasive dusty town that is Manjakandira. In my current state, I could only imagine what they thought of me. As we walked up the hill to her home, I was glowing from the pure kindness and generosity that this woman was showing me, while her children were walking next to me flicking the bell on my handlebars. Yet, I was dumbfounded because somehow this woman was okay with allowing a filthy stranger into her home. I wondered if I would do the same if the roles were reversed and a grubby stranger from another country showed up in town, making wild gyrations. Although she spoke only a few words of English, she smiled brightly, and made continual hand gestures indicating that it was only a little further.

Fifteen minutes later, we arrived at her home. It was again a two-story, whitewashed home, evidently a common style in Madagascar. The first floor was unfinished, just as I was told, and her family lived on the second floor. It was new construction, and the smell of drying concrete emanated from the walls, creating a cold and damp atmosphere. There was no electricity, bathroom, or running water, but it was shelter and I was happy. I began to roll out my air mattress as the cracking thunder boomed outside shortly before the lightning illuminated the space. I pulled out my headlamp and moved further away from the window to avoid the cold rain that was coming inside due to the lack of glass. I peered through the open window to see rivers of mud flowing down the hillside. Cold and wet is a truly dreadful combination. Cold, wet, tired, and hungry are far worse.

A slender, well-dressed man in his 30s with a kind smile entered the room behind me as I was blowing up my air mattress. He was her husband and had just arrived home from work, donning pressed black pants, a crisp white shirt, and shiny black shoes. He motioned for me to follow him upstairs. Curiously, I did. Upstairs, the home was warmly furnished with handmade wooden furniture and ornate rugs covering the tile floors. A patio overlooked the village, and fresh flowers garnished the room. There was no running water but there was a gas range for cooking and the smell of simmering rice permeated the air. He showed me a bedroom. It was a small space, barely large enough for the single bed, which was adorned with fresh "Hello Kitty" sheets. Posters of Katie Perry were plastered on the wall. Evidently, one of the children had given up their bed to me for the night.

I was still in my battle fatigues from the day's cycling war, and a damp chill was beginning to seep into my body as my blood sugar continued to plummet. I desperately wanted to clean up and put on dry clothes, but people kept coming into my room. It wasn't just the wife and her young children. Apparently, the word was out in town. No less than a dozen people squeezed into this tiny room and oozed out into the hallway, all wanting to communicate and practice their English but mostly just to connect with this strange, dirty-faced *vazaha* on a bike who had somehow arrived in their small village.

For over an hour, we traded laughs and smiles, no one really understanding the other, while the warmth of their kindness gradually thawed out my encroaching shiver. Finally, the husband asked if I would like to clean up. The shower room was a basic, dark, unfinished concrete room without a light, but with a bucket and a drain. It was maybe four feet by four feet, slightly larger than a traditional shower stall and with just enough space to get undressed and bathe. I hung my headlamp from a hook on the wall so I could see. As the first shocking dose of cold water flushed down my back, taking with it the day's adventure, I could feel myself coming back to life.

Once clean, my hunger began to take over and after my shower, I made a move for the door, so I could head into town to find some food. Immediately the mother grabbed my arm with one hand while waving her other and pointed to the table with a smile. They heaped a mound of rice on my plate half the size of a basketball. Tonight there was only a small portion of greens and I felt guilty for taking any, so instead, I did my best to make a dent in the mound of plain white rice on my plate. Somehow, everyone, even the children, had an amazing intrinsic rice-consuming ability. I was the only one who did not join the clean plate club that night, even as hungry as I was. After dinner, everyone seemed to passively drift off to bed. I tucked myself into the Hello Kitty sheets with the sound of rain thumping on the metal roof above me—happy to be dry.

Even though they expected nothing of me, I wanted to show my immense gratitude the next morning. I gave the father 10,000 ariary. He looked at me like I handed him the winning Lotto ticket. It was about $3.00. He refused to take it and after going back and forth, I finally put it in his hand and closed his fingers around it. Somehow, his look of gratitude was as big as mine. As I pedaled away, a smile, nearly as big as the Malagasy sun cresting the hillside, lit up my soul. Not even the mud splashing into my face from the overnight rain could cover it up.

CHAPTER 6

Life, Itself

"Are you Jerry?" a young woman, about 25, asked as I came downstairs from the hotel room where I was staying in Vatomandry a week later. She was the first *vazaha* that I had seen since leaving Tana, and happened to be standing in the lobby of my hotel at 8 a.m.

"Uhhhhh . . . yes?" I replied curiously, clearly caught off guard.

"I thought so," she replied. "Jenna told me about you." Dee was in the Peace Corps and lived in a neighboring village, and of course, was a close friend of Jenna. Apparently, the word was out that an American was cycling around Madagascar. This is a big deal because, as I was told, no one does it.

"I met Jenna back in Tana a few weeks ago, and I'm meeting her this morning. She's going to take me to her village," I explained with enthusiasm.

Moments later, Jenna and another woman entered the hotel lobby, both smeared with beaming smiles.

"Hey, stranger!" Jenna called across to me before wrapping me in a hug. "This is Vanessa. She's the Country Director for Mada Peace Corps."

Dee was also in Vatomandry to connect with them and do site visits to their villages, which amounted to assessing the progress of their projects, communicating any vital national directives, but mostly checking on everyone's mental state. The mental trauma of extended isolation in remote villages has been known to wreak havoc on Peace Corps volunteers' psyche, causing many to melt down and quit.

"So Jerry, what are you doing in Mada?" Vanessa asked me as we all sat down for breakfast.

"An old high school friend invited me down to visit him in Zambia. From there, I just found my way over here I suppose."

"And how has your experience been?"

"Well, it seems like it's been pretty easy to meet people, once I met Jenna, the mayor of Mada," I joked.

"What does your friend do in Zambia?" Vanessa inquired

"He used to work for the CDC but now is working on a startup in Lusaka."

"I used to work for the CDC as well. What's his name?" Vanessa prodded with a squint in her eyes.

"Ben Bellows."

"Ha! I went to school with him at Berkeley!" Vanessa exalted after her mouth dropped.

At this point, maybe Ben was the mayor. First with Jessica in Zambia, now Vanessa in Mada. Africa is big, but thus far it felt like anything but.

—

The Madagascar Independence Day, *Vingt-Six*, was today, and Vanessa made it clear that none of the Peace Corps volunteers should be anywhere near Tana. There was simply too much potential for danger and mayhem. Apparently, the Malagasy people look for any reason to get a little rowdy and break up the monotony of their daily lives. Fortunately, Tana was already in my rearview mirror. Instead, Jenna and I were on our way to her rural village, Tsarasambo, ten miles to the south. It was a quick one-hour pedal down a sloppy dirt road, dodging lingering mud puddles along the way while keeping a close eye on the impending storm, unfortunately lurking over the area where we were headed.

Tsarasambo is a tiny village of at most a few hundred inhabitants, all living in thatch-roofed huts, without running water or electricity. Jenna had been at this site for just over a year, and upon our arrival, it was clear that she was well known and adored. Her simple, very primitive hut was maybe twelve by fifteen feet and was by far the nicest in town, which was not a grandiose claim. The main "upgrade" was a concrete floor, which made it easier to keep the inside clean when the likes of the current storm blasted through and created rivers of flowing mud through the dirt floors of the other huts. Besides the concrete floor, it was not unlike any of the other huts, with stick walls, thatch roof (lined with plastic), two doors, and one window. She was also fortunate to have a cooktop stove fueled by a small propane tank. Outside was her *ladosy* (place for bucket showers), and her *kabone* (essentially a shed with a hole for other needs). Jenna tried to introduce me to the rat that lived in her roof, whom she ironically named "Ratsy" (which means "bad" in Malagasy) and shared graphic tales of being woken up on countless nights by Ratsy scurrying across her chest.

Food in the village consists of rice, every day, every meal. As a result, many local villagers are malnourished. There was a small market in town that sold the minimal amount of rice and a sparse display of seasonal vegetables. The people of Tsarasambo are representative of so many other villages. They exist on very little means but have been some of the kindest people that I had met in the country. As we walked through the village, everyone was happy to greet us and share whatever food they had, and of course to meet another *vazaha*.

After listening to Vanessa's cautions, I was relieved to be in a quiet remote village, away from the mayhem of Tana. To my surprise, but more my concern, even the small village of Tsarasambo was gearing up for the celebration. The village center is perched on a small hill with makeshift dirt steps essentially kicked into the hillside. Through Jenna's window, I could make out about ten local villagers battling the now deluge of rain, surfing through the tidal wave of mud, and dragging speakers as large as themselves up to the town center. I was terrified not solely by the size of the speakers, but also by the proximity to Jenna's hut, which was at most a hundred yards away. Fortunately, it was pretty much monsooning outside, with a river of mud cascading down the makeshift stairs, effectively preventing the villagers from ascending up to the hillside to dance and celebrate. Initially, the diesel generators kicked on and music started, but then stopped again after an hour. "All right then, I guess there won't be any celebration tonight," I conceded.

I learned that the people of Mada are nothing if not willful, and by 6 p.m. it was on. Twelve hours of nonstop bone-rattling, brain cell-killing Malagasy celebration ensued. Through the buckets of rain lashing down on the village, I could see an expectedly vacant town center, yet unexpectedly, the music went on uninterrupted through the rain and the night. Why was the music still throbbing when nobody was out? The thundering five-foot-tall speakers reverberated off of the walls in Jenna's hut, and I could see the plastic liner on the inside of the roof vibrating while the exhaust from diesel generators permeated the hut. This was hell; something even Ratsy couldn't tolerate. I hoped that the rain would eventually drown their spirits (and maybe the actual DJ), but I suppose when you go through all that effort to set up a venue, you just wanna use it.

Back in 1993, I lived in a three-bedroom townhouse in East Lansing, Michigan, with five roommates, just off of the Michigan State University campus. Because it was technically off-campus, it meant that mostly normal, non-students lived there, people who had day jobs, possibly families, and thus didn't want to be kept up all night long by a "fundraiser."

We were all 19 years old, and this was our first time living on our own. Rent was $615 per month, so we each paid $102.50, which even back then seemed insanely cheap. If we could have found another roommate to make the rent cheaper, we would have. Although we all had jobs and could cover our share, each month we had a "Make the Rent" party. A friend who was 21 would buy a half dozen kegs of beer, and we would charge $5 for a cup, which simply meant for a $5 cover charge you could come to our party and drink your face off.

At any given time, we would have 75–100 people crammed into our apartment or congregating out front in the yard. I had a six-disc CD player with four-foot-tall speakers whose thunderous sound would shake the neighbors out of bed with the first track of Dr. Dre's *The Chronic*. After the first party, the decimation to the interior of our townhouse was so catastrophic that it took us two full days to make it feel like we might actually get a sliver of our security deposit back. The next month, we smartened up and bought old carpet remnants to put down over the existing, already nuked-out carpet to soak up the bulk of the spilled beer and subsequent vomit deluge.

I remember during the third or fourth fundraiser, my neighbor, a man probably in his late 20s, maybe with a wife and kids, was sitting on his front porch. His head was buried in his hands as I walked outside to work the door. It was *only* midnight, maybe, but the look of despair was unmistakable.

"Hey man! Do you wanna come over? I won't even charge you," I said, genuinely believing this would mediate his misery.

"Can you please stop? Please?" he pleaded.

I wasn't even fazed as I began taking money from the line of people snaking up the walkway out front, most of whom I didn't even know. It wasn't until about 1 a.m. at every party that the police would show up and break it up, but not before we had easily made the rent.

I was now that decimated guy on the porch with his head buried in his hands. In Jenna's hut, we tried closing the single window, but all that did was turn the hut into a sauna. Instead, we opened the window and the door on the other side to create a cross breeze. Within minutes, mud began to flow onto the concrete floor of the hut through the open door. We scrambled to put a towel barrier down to divert the mud, but not before the entire floor was glazed with a two-inch coating of slop. We toweled off our feet, finished our dinner of rice and veggies, then laid down on the bed and hoped for a miracle. For the next eleven hours, until 6 a.m., the music pulsed while my head rattled. I could feel my internal organs vibrating as the thumping bass of the island dance music roared throughout the village. I'm not religious, but I tried appealing to a higher power to bring down enough rain to demolish the speaker system. Through my delirium and the buckets of rain emptying from the sky, for a moment, I thought I saw Noah building a boat. By 3 a.m. I somehow managed to pass out from sheer exhaustion.

"Mana un!" We were awakened the next morning by a cheery voice. With a welcoming smile, Jenna's neighbor stopped over to offer some food. My head was still thumping, but the music had stopped. The sun was out, and birds were singing. Most local villagers were cleaning their huts from the storm, theirs having not fared nearly as well as Jenna's. Others were conversing in the street, some making their way to the market through the ankle-deep field of mud that had once been the road.

"Holy shit!" shrieked Jenna as she was poring over an email from Vanessa on her phone. "There was a free concert at the stadium in Tana on *Vingt-Six,* and apparently someone brought in a hand grenade and threw it into the stands, killing two and injuring eighty others."

While truly terrible news, it was even more startling because we had been in that stadium, in that section, just a week earlier watching the rugby match. The news, combined with my failed attempt for a peaceful night in a rural village, left me fractured—both physically and mentally.

Inside Jenna's hut was a disaster. There were towels on the floor, fully saturated with rainwater and mud, yet even so, puddles still remained. Our clothes were soaked, bodies battered, and brains scrambled. I was filthy, exhausted, and grumpy. It looked like I was wearing mud socks up to my ankles. I wanted out of Jenna's flooded-out, rat-infested hut. As I was fantasizing simply about being dry and clean, Jenna began singing and proceeded to scrub out her hut and go about the day.

Here Jenna was, smiling. She was the DJ of the morning shift. Every other person in this remote village was also smiling, cheerfully going about their day. But weren't they left *Sleepless in Madagascar* with me too? Why did my mud socks come with a scowl while theirs came with a smile?

And then reality hit me: Although I had tried to blend in with my Mada rugby jersey, I was a tourist, the person I had tried to avoid being—that entitled foreigner I dodged at all costs. If I chose, I could simply pick up and leave in situations like this. Jenna and the rest of the villagers could not. This was their life, itself, every day and for Jenna, what life had been for the previous thirteen months. I had a one-day dose of their world—and it shook me. It was a week later before I realized that I had gotten this gift, another rare glimpse into the *real* Madagascar, the reason that I had come here—to see the spirit, the kindness, and the resilience of the people.

CHAPTER 7

Baby Steps, to Being

Growing up in Michigan, there was always water around, and our parents made sure we could swim almost before we could walk. Lake Michigan was about a ninety-minute drive from our rural town, and when I was six, it seemed like forever to get there. In the summer, my three brothers and I loaded into my dad's wood-paneled station wagon, each of us vying for the coveted flip-up seat in the *way back* that faced backwards. My older brothers were eight years older than me, so they typically sat there, leaving my younger brother Bobby, who was three years younger than me, to wrestle in the back seat. This was the 80s, child seats and even seat belts weren't a thing.

With its powdery sand beaches and endless blue water, Lake Michigan was the closest that I would get to an ocean until many years later. When we pulled up, Bobby and I, in our matching Stars and Stripes Speedo bikini suits, would spring from the woody wagon and run haphazardly into Lake Michigan without fear or a care in the world. We would jump as many waves as we could as we entered the water before diving over the next wave only a split second before it took our legs out from under us anyway. My parents divorced shortly after, and my mom and brothers moved to Colorado, but those summers spent along Lake Michigan instilled a sense of freedom and calm that still resonates with me today whenever I am around open water.

After leaving Tsarasambo, I made my way up the coast for three days before arriving in Mahambo just before 3 p.m., knowing that my pedaling was done for the next five. It's a largish town of about 26,000 people, situated on the coast with regular ferry crossings over to the tiny and serene island of Île Saint Marie, where I would once again meet up with Jenna. Île Saint Marie, about thirty-five miles long by less than six miles wide, is located off the east coast of Madagascar. It became a popular base for pirates in the 17th and 18th centuries due to its close proximity to the maritime routes of the East Indies. I can't help my brain from conjuring up images from the 1980s movie, *The Goonies,* remembering the lovable character "Sloth" as he yells out, "Hey you guuuuys!" while swinging in from the ship's mast to save the day. And now, I'm sure you can't help it either. You're welcome.

I had been cycling next to the ocean for the past couple of days, smelling its salty allure, so as soon as I found the first deserted beach, I stripped down and went for it. I had been fantasizing about being in the Indian Ocean from the moment I landed in Madagascar. The seemingly gentle waves beckoned to me like the songs of the sirens and reminded me of those summer trips to Lake Michigan. Like that young boy, I ran cackling down the powdery sand beach, jumping waves, and dove headfirst into the tide. The water was nourishing and bathed me in a cool salty lather that oozed life back into my fatigued body.

There was something so peaceful about swimming naked in the Indian Ocean—that is, of course, until the deceptively diabolical undertow dragged me across the rocks. Without warning, my feet were yanked out from underneath me, and I was churned like a pair of old socks in a washing machine. As I consumed a liter or so of water, I did my best to get onto my back with my feet out in front of me because, well, I had less sensitive skin on my backside than the front. I was never in fear of drowning, but rather just of being filleted by the rocks and serrated coral. Remarkably, I managed to escape with only one layer of skin removed from my butt, which I immediately counted as a win.

"You're great at *doing*, but *harrible* at *being*," was the voice message I received from my friend Sara, trying to disguise her closeted New Jersey accent. "Just be." For the first time in my life, I felt the truth of that statement fully. I was so accustomed to always being on the go, but now, in Madagascar, I truly had no place to be. It was a feeling that I didn't know how to process. Having worked with Sara over the years, she had seen me at my best, and also at my worst. She knew what drove me professionally and also emotionally. Sara was one of my closest friends and knew what buttons to push. And most of the time, her insight was spot on. In my world of running the hospice over the past ten years, I was much better with a daily routine, being on the go, and generally oversubscribed. Although having too much going on in my life gave me a mandated focus on the day-to-day deliverables, it prevented me from ever fully delving into deeper emotional queries. Being in Madagascar, where nothing ever happens on time or schedule, I was slowly learning to dial back my drive and *roll with it*. Each mile that I ticked off on the bike, I could feel the weight of those ten years slowly cracking and flaking off like the dead skin on my sunburnt neck, revealing a vibrant new layer.

Slowing down even more on my bike and in my brain, I realized I was still very much reeling from the events in my life back home that had shaken me so deeply. On many occasions, I felt lonely, in spite of the fact that *alone* is exactly what I initially wanted. The isolation of traveling solo can be therapeutic in many ways, and it had so far given me valuable time to process many of the conflicts simultaneously raging in my brain. Other times, however, the solitude can allow demons to creep in and set up camp. I desperately needed to meet them head-on and eventually dispatch them, but in small doses, and right now, I wasn't ready. I just wanted to laugh and resign myself to live to fight another day.

While waiting at the beach with Jenna for the ferry to Île Saint Marie the next morning, I struck up a conversation with a Malagasy man who noticed my still shiny Kermit Green bike. Tahiry was about my age, of slight build, with thinning hair and smart, wire-rimmed glasses. He was a teacher and, as a result, spoke remarkable English, which was something I was thus far unaccustomed to hearing in Mada. He glanced down and noticed Jenna's guitar.

"Will you play something?" Tahiry asked Jenna.

Initially, she was shy and reluctant. Jenna is a perfectionist, and her vocals reflect that, but she still lacked the confidence to play the guitar publicly. Feeling this hesitation, Tahiry flipped through the songbook Jenna was carrying, grabbed her guitar, and started to strum. Thankfully, he landed on "Don't Stop Believing" by Journey, a song that everyone I grew up with in Michigan knows by heart and, when they hear it, will immediately drop everything they're doing and belt out the lyrics. As Tahiry began playing, other locals took notice and gathered around. He played. She sang. We all sang. *"Just a small town boy . . . born and raised in SOUTH DETROIT!"* It's pretty amazing that a song about Detroit from the 80s made it around the globe, and I'm sure somewhere Steve Perry (the lead singer of Journey) was proud.

Moments later, we had picked up another guitar player and an ensemble of singers. There we were, two Americans and five Malagasy, singing, laughing, and belting out American classics on a beach in Madagascar, waiting for our boat to leave and wondering who was going to choose the next song. Five hours later our boat finally shoved off—because, of course, Malagasy time. There is no rush here. In fact, there isn't even a word for it. Instead, just *be.*

Well, that blissful feeling ended—quickly. Ten minutes into the two-hour boat passage to Île Saint Marie, I felt a gurgle in my stomach, then pinballed my way through the crowded cabin, out the back door and projected my breakfast over the edge. Not surprisingly, I wasn't the only one, but rather just the first. The boat churned and lurched on the turbulent Indian Ocean as more people without their sea legs joined me with their heads hanging limply over the edge. I spent the remaining time on the boat sprawled out on the deck, in the rain, drifting between violent seasickness and complete lack of consciousness, as my head routinely bounced off the rail each time the thirty-foot ferry would heave over another wave. Fortunately, or not, I had plenty of company from dozens of others who were anxiously anticipating the end of the passage.

I awoke to discover that Jenna had put my rain jacket on me just as we were pulling into the dock. The ship's crew were anxiously rounding up the people on the deck and guiding them back inside the cabin. On all the seats, there were vomit bags, most of them used by people who couldn't make it outside. The stench nearly induced another round of vomiting, but I simply had nothing left inside me.

I stepped off the boat onto solid land, although my knees buckled beneath me as if I was still adrift. Similar to getting off the plane in Tana, locals congregated around us like vultures to roadkill, smelling the vomit and offering to sweep us away to their cush beach resort.

Eventually, I sobered up from the malicious ocean crossing, and we found a basic, rustic bungalow on the beach. It was about ten feet by ten feet, with clean(ish) sheets and a (mostly) non-leaky roof. Fortunately, Jenna and I were both well-accustomed to this, and we probably wouldn't have known what to do with anything nicer. Sometimes we had electricity. Sometimes we didn't. One thing we did not have was a toilet seat which really wasn't that odd at all in Mada.

For five days, the gentle breeze and blissful lapping of waves were meditative, and gradually I could feel the knots in my neck loosen in the calming blissful waves that I swam in each morning. It was a complete shutdown and something that was so far removed from my normal mindset. Being continually on the go in a foreign country, with each day an undertaking just to find food and shelter, while exciting, was at the same time debilitating. Île Sainte Marie provided a necessary pause, a reset for my body. But it was even more so for my mind.

However, after five days my brain was once again churning. I was antsy and ready to get back to the mainland and start the wheels rolling again. Sorry, Sara. Baby steps, I suppose.

CHAPTER 8

Tsara Be

In tenth grade, I learned about the laws of physics, specifically Newton's First Law of Motion, which simply states that *an object at rest will stay at rest unless acted on by an outside force.* After five days of *being at rest,* it was time to get moving. Motion creates emotion. A week later, I had made my way to the northernmost tip of the country, an island named Nosy Be.

Nosy Be simply means "big island" in Malagasy. It is the largest island in the archipelago, located about five miles off the coast of Madagascar. I spent my first night in Hell Ville (yes, that is the name of the main city on Nosy Be, and actually rather appropriate). It is a historic, dusty, dilapidated town with decaying French colonial architecture. There is however a delightful market, with a gorgeous coastline, and the scents from the ylang-ylang trees (its yellow, star-shaped flowers are used for making essential oils and perfume), coffee, cacao, vanilla and sugarcane plantations permeate the air.

The topography of Nosy Be was formed by volcanic activity and is thus one of many hills punctuated by two distinct peaks—Mount Lokone (1,476 feet) and Mount Passot (1,148 feet). After grinding my way to the top of Passot, true to their origin, both peaks seem to explode out of the center of the island and are surrounded by eleven volcanic lakes that appear as puddles on a saturated lawn, left over from the rain.

While the landscape was captivating, after two days on an island dominated by mostly tolerable French tourists, I once again felt my tension begin to climb. I was trying to recapture the feeling of *being*, but I felt trapped, craving something less—*easy*.

I arrived at the boat dock the next morning to make my way back to the main island. It was crowded with affluent French tourists on one dock and local Malagasy families and workers on the other. The toll for the express boat was $15 for the half-hour trip. As I prepared to board the express boat, I was informed of a new safety rule passed by the government two years earlier prohibiting bicycles and motorbikes on these small speedboats. I could understand motorbikes, but bicycles? The irony of Madagascar passing "safety" rules was almost comical, but the crew actually showed me the law, and for the first time in Madagascar, something wasn't negotiable. By default, I was thus relegated to the $3.00, *it will take as long as it takes*, ferry ride, complete with chickens, motorbikes, of course, and anything else that needed to slowly chug its way across to the mainland.

Standing at the dock, I enviously looked on with conscious entitlement as the tourists boarded the speedboats and zipped off, skipping across the water and quickly disappearing over the horizon. As I was about to board the thirty-five-foot cargo barge, a young man blew by me in a flurry, up the stairs, vomited over the edge, then feebly made his way below deck, back to his fetal position next to the humming warmth of the diesel engine. I could feel a déjà vu beginning to tie knots in my stomach, and I hadn't even stepped foot on the boat yet.

I watched as two men delicately hoisted my 80 pound bike off the dock, passed it to two other men on the boat, flipped it sideways, and gently finessed it through the barely three-foot opening, down six stairs leading to the lower deck where all other items were stowed for the trip. I felt reasonably confident that the guy in the fetal position likely would not be sifting through my bags. Up top, I found a seat on the sunbaked deck, with my feet dangling freely over the edge of the bow. After an hour of patiently cooking under the early morning sun, I learned that there was no real schedule for departure: the boat leaves when it's full. Of course, Malagasy time. I knew this. Another hour later, after a parade of chickens and countless more families crammed their way on board, we shoved off.

The sound of the ramped-up diesel engine was deafening, and the fumes suffocating. The boat was jammed, and the only shade from the blistering sun was below deck, where the diesel engine roared and spewed its toxic airborne excrement while dozens of caged chickens loudly expressed their discontent as well. Somehow the man who vomited over the edge hours ago still had not moved. I assumed he was alive.

Around me, mothers sat quietly while their children played, and the men congregated and smoked cigarettes. Dozens of speedboats went buzzing by. "I should be on one," I sighed, once again the despair of stolen privilege invading my mind. "I would be there by now." Instead, I was a captive on this broken-down jalopy, with no idea when we would actually arrive.

Soon enough, we were out of sight of the shore. I looked up and noticed the captain who had come out onto the shaded upper deck to sit comfortably while his first mate steered the boat as it slowly chugged through the translucent, turquoise sea. He was about my age, dark-skinned, wearing a blue, short-sleeved polo-style shirt. A white captain's hat completed the uniform. I glanced up to him and gave him the "Can I come up?" look. Surprisingly, with a beaming white smile, he waved me up. I eagerly climbed the pole like a ring-tailed lemur and perched myself next to the captain, away from the chickens and diesel fumes.

I pulled out my iPod, cued up Bob Marley's *Legend* album—and resumed *being*. The anxiety that had been building inside me drifted away, and I somehow forgot that I was supposed to be seasick and passed out by now, my head thunking off the floor of the deck, vomit crusted on my face. The captain, who spoke fewer words in English than I did in Malagasy, looked over at my iPod curiously. I placed an earbud in his ear. "Three Little Birds" was playing. His eyes lit up, and he began singing aloud at the top of his lungs. "*. . . cuz every little thing's . . . gonna be all right . . .*" I took the other earbud and put it in my ear as we sang along to the entire album together. Although he spoke almost zero English, he knew all the words, likely without knowing what any of them meant. Just like on the beach waiting to transport over to Île Saint Marie, music was once again the bridge between our divides.

The road the next morning quickly turned into a battlefield, revealing the scars of decades of erosion and disrepair. For the most part, it was dirt, sprinkled with occasional bits of pavement chunks, reminders of a time when this had been a French colony with more resources. The countryside, while hilly, was brown and destitute, a near barren landscape. After six weeks, I was now used to these *roads and* nonchalantly weaved and zipped by the over-loaded rusted and dented *taxi bruesses* as they screeched to a near stop to navigate around the *taxi bruesse*-sized craters in the road, then zoomed off again, expelling a cloud of blue diesel fog in their wake. After being in one in Tana, I had a pretty good idea what the twenty-six people stacked on top of one another inside the van must be feeling.

The day's ride would turn out to be seventy-five miles of this undulating, punishing, yet gratifying track, marking the end of my bicycle tour in Madagascar. It was a date that always seemed "out there," but the finality never quite sunk in until today. Although the road was filled with literal ups and downs, my spirit was soaring as I was riding a euphoric emotion of the "now"—knowing that this was my last day and I was intent on savoring every inch of these relentless, bombed-out rolling hills.

At one point, I came across a broken-down *taxi bruesse* leaning on the side of the road. Throughout the prior six weeks, it was far from an uncommon sight. The man who had his head buried inside the engine looked up as I was rolling by, dropped his tools, and ran across the road, just to give me a high five. It had been these tiny human experiences that made Madagascar so amazing. Whenever I had been frustrated, confused, humbled, and knocked down (which was a lot), small things like this just reset the score.

After about four hours, the road smoothed out, displaying noticeably less carnage, tilted slightly downhill, and a tailwind whipped up. Madagascar was once again giving me a final high five as I cruised into the city of Diego Suarez and quickly found a hotel.

I awoke the next morning, sluggish and disenchanted, no doubt a byproduct of the mental angst of knowing that I was going to the airport. A one-hour flight, and I would be back in Tana, with one day more to pack up my bike before heading home.

Normally, flying with a bike in any other part of the world that I've been to typically involves at least $200 in excess baggage fees, with most airlines having a bicycle-specific surcharge, if for no other reason than that it is simply a bicycle. You are also required to pack it in a box or other special case for transport. You can't simply roll it on the plane. If it is over a certain size or weight, you'll enjoy an additional tax as well. It's maddening. However, in Madagascar I've learned nothing is at it seems, and aside from bikes on boats, everything is open to negotiation. I walked up to the only gate at the small airport, and immediately the two men behind the counter looked at my bike, waved their hands and tried to send me away.

"Not possible to fly with cycle," I was told in not-so-vague terms.

After a few minutes of back and forth of them telling me that my bicycle would "not fit" on the plane and me trying to choke back the laughter at the absurdity of that statement, the men recessed for a meeting. They returned a few moments later with a solution. One man pulled me aside and held out his hand behind his back, below the counter. I looked over and casually made eye contact with the military officer at the gate. In a panic, my eyes darted down to the floor as I tried to look cool. No doubt he had seen me and seen what was about to transpire, but apparently, this was nothing new. Calmly, I reached into my pocket and pulled out the equivalent of $5 and slipped it to the man. He smiled, grabbed my bike, and wheeled it away. Turns out it would fit on the plane.

As I was waiting for takeoff, I met an American couple from India. The wife was a professor in Maryland, and they were visiting a former student in Mada, who of course is in the Peace Corps and was definitely friends with Jenna, of course. I realize that this is probably just a *random* coincidence, but Madagascar is big, really big. Though it is the fourth largest island in the world, ever since I arrived, it had felt just like the small town I grew up in in Michigan, where I couldn't even go out for ice cream at the Quality Dairy without inevitably running into someone I knew.

I confessed to her that I was sad to be leaving after six weeks of traveling through Madagascar by bicycle, at which she immediately shrieked in her barely evident Indian accent, "By bicycle?" giving me that shocked and terrified look that I had come to expect throughout Madagascar.

"I get that a lot," I replied with a smile.

She could see the passion and excitement in my face. "Oh, if you like traveling by bicycle in Madagascar, and you were not scared, then you *must* go to India!"

When I pushed a bit further about India, her dark brown eyes lit up with unbridled passion, while her Indian accent became noticeably more distinct. She gushed when recounting tales of growing up in the shadow of the mighty Himalayas. I could feel the excitement dripping out of her, and I tucked away this emotion as we boarded the plane.

Mostly on schedule, an hour later I stepped off the plane to the familiar buzz of Tana. It was a strange feeling, being back in the place where my journey began nearly six weeks earlier. The noise, the crowds, the traffic, the feeling of chaos—they were all still here—just as I left them. After being in the rural parts of the country for several weeks, the intensity of Tana was suffocating. Like being followed by a stranger in a dark alley, anxiety began to creep over and asphyxiate me. My heart began to race as people from every direction saw the tall white guy wheeling out the bright Kermit green bicycle from the terminal into the parking lot, and they began to converge. Everyone just wanted to help, but all I wanted was to get as far away from the airport as possible where I would be a little less conspicuous—if that was even possible. Though it felt like a whole year had passed, I recalled this sensation from only six weeks ago when Njara and her father picked me up and rescued me from this madness the first time, whisking me out of the city before I was engulfed by it. But now I was on my own, and I just wanted to get moving.

I still needed to make some minor adjustments to the bike, things that happen as a result of simply wheeling a bike onto a plane and pitching it haphazardly into the cargo bin. I suppose that is what a $5 bribe gets you. I threw a leg over my bike and quickly began to pedal away as the hordes of people anxious to help me continued to swarm.

"ARGH! FUCK!" I screamed in pain, but mostly in fear.

I had reached down to adjust something near my front wheel while I was pedaling, and someone in the mob inadvertently bumped me, sending my entire hand hurling into the spinning front wheel.

With my arm entwined in the spokes, my bike screeched to an abrupt stop and thrashed me down to the potholed street. Other people across the way heard the commotion of my shriek and the sound of metal crashing onto the broken concrete and quickly rushed over to join the swarm of people already chasing me from the airport. I quickly dislodged my arm from the wheel, kicked my bike off me, and climbed out of the muddy, trash-filled pothole I had landed in. I took a quick stock to make sure everything that was supposed to be attached to the bike (but mostly to my body), still was, then scurried away before the adrenaline wore off and the realization had set in that I had just broken travel rule #1: Don't get hurt. Fortunately, I suppose, this happened on my last day, so I hadn't *technically* broken the rule, but still . . .

I tucked my chin and pedaled as fast as I could for about a mile until I was sure that nobody who had witnessed the trauma was near. I pulled off onto a quiet side street and assessed the severity of the situation. Blood was seeping down my forearm, wrist, and all along my hand, which had begun to swell like a cartoon, resembling what it would look like if you blew up a rubber glove. The only antiseptic I had was a bottle of hand sanitizer, so I emptied the contents on any area that had blood seeping from it—the feeling of a dozen knives stabbing me all along my arm.

Ninety minutes later, I walked into the Chalet de Rose looking like I had been run over by an errant *taxi breusse,* which I'm sure is what the hotel staff thought when they saw me, likely not an uncommon occurrence. The blood on my arm had dried into a crusty paste. My shirt was ripped above the shoulder, and the entire right side of my body was brown from the murky pothole I had landed in.

"What the . . .?" Jenna gasped upon seeing my war-torn condition. After leaving Île Saint Marie, we had made plans to get together in Tana before I left, and she was waiting for me at the hotel. "What did you do?" she inquired.

"Well, I did something pretty idiotic," I replied with a playful, embarrassed laugh, not knowing how else to behave in light of the situation.

Jenna went across the street and grabbed a bag of ice and an Ace wrap to hopefully mitigate some of the swelling that had already taken over my hand. Although purple and swollen, I could wiggle all my fingers, and nothing was overly crooked, so it seemed like a win. I jumped in the shower and scrubbed out the rest of the road grime, took six Advil, rewrapped my wrist, and went out to dinner with Jenna, intent to not let this bit of idiocy spoil my last night in Madagascar.

—

"Tsara Be" (pronounced tsarra BAY) is an expression that I used a lot in Madagascar, and for good reason. Simply, it means "very good." I used it to describe the food, the landscape, but overwhelmingly, the people. The physical act of saying those words makes your mouth turn upwards into a smile. Six weeks here was more than enough to make me feel at home. I underestimated how comfortable I would get in a place that was anything but, and thus how difficult it would be for me to leave. Every day was an exercise to just *figure it out.*

After Jenna and I parted ways for the last time, she sent me a text that I read on the flight back to Zambia that made my heart swell, further confirmation of this new path I was on.

> *"You give Madagascar the benefit of the doubt. A lot of people judge when they are visiting and don't look beneath the surface for why things are, how they are, or why people do what they do. A lot of people think "different" is wrong. You look at Malagasy people as equals. Even some of the most self-proclaimed "worldly" people still look at foreigners as exhibits at a zoo."*

As I sat on the plane, a quiet calm came over me, the entire time reflecting on the fact that the adventure that I was on, was over. The finality up until that point had not fully sunk in. I had been operating on this distant timeline whose endpoint would seemingly never arrive. But in a few short days, I would be back in Boulder, back to my normal life.

It's amazing how time slows down when you're not on any schedule or part of a routine, because the routine I've learned, makes time fly by. We get so caught up in the hamster wheel of life that life itself stops being amazing. When we're able to separate ourselves from that routine, the little nuances of each day become more magnified. Simple things like finding a place to sleep, or even just food and water, take on an entirely new significance. I had gotten so used to being on the go and figuring out the new hiccup or quirk that occurs every day in this strange and unique land. In an unexpected way, this lack of predictability had been comforting because it had been the complete antithesis of my former life, a life where everything was calculated, measured, and predictable.

I wondered how I would adjust, how I would deal with *re-entry*. Would I quickly return to work, falling back into the same ruts and monotony, or would I see things through a different lens? Life back home would be easy for sure, where anything and everything is available. Dogs won't bark all night. Any kind of food is possible. I can turn on a faucet and drink what comes out, and my toilet seat will not be broken. I had no idea what my plans were, but I had a few ideas that were not so subtly placed into my imagination from some people I met along the way. *Tsara be!*

First ride in Africa—with Ben

Decisions...

Njara and her family

Stick to the main road!

Arriving in Jenna's village

Every little thing's...gonna be alright

PART 2

Hospice

April 5, 2005 – November 30, 2015

*"Life all comes down to a few moments.
This is one of them."*

– Bud Fox, played by Charlie Sheen
in the 1987 film, *Wallstreet*

CHAPTER 1

What's a Hospice?

November 30, 2015. My head was throbbing, I was nauseous, and my entire body ached. I couldn't get out of bed. It felt like someone had spent the last four months punching me in the gut because that's ultimately when this unstoppable hurricane had begun to form. Today was closing day for my hospice, the company I had co-founded with my mom and her husband a decade earlier. It was being sold to a national healthcare conglomerate at noon, and I needed to show up and begrudgingly sign it away. I didn't want to. I had never wanted to. Nobody on our staff and community wanted us to. Only my two business partners wanted us to, and I would venture a guess that only one of them actually did.

A family business can either be a dream or a nightmare—and over the course of ten years, somehow it was both. I had always liked my step-father. Luther had helped me with dozens of house projects over the years and had always been there for me in a pinch if I needed anything. He was a good guy who took care of my mom, and I was glad that she had married him. However, it was no secret that he and I did not see eye to eye on most things financial and were thus driven by different motivations.

In his younger years, he looked like Richard Gere, a suave fella with wavy brown hair and squinty eyes. But he grew up poor in Louisiana, and as a result always appeared to be image-conscious, eager to show the world that he had *made it*. Luther had done well for himself as a stockbroker for over twenty years and had developed a taste for nice things, especially fancy German cars. I remember a time early on when we had just recently opened our doors of the hospice and were working on a financial project together. He turned to me beaming and said, "Jerry, we're gonna make so much money at this!"

My mom, on the other hand, is about 5′5″, a petite woman with hair so long and blond that she could have been one of Charlie's Angels. Her favorite pastime was driving her beloved Subaru to all the local thrift stores in Boulder, intent on finding the best deal. "Jerry, Wednesdays are 50 percent off everything in the store at the Salvy (my mom's slang for Salvation Army thrift store). "I got this Ralph Lauren sweater for $5 and this North Face jacket for $9. It looks like they weren't even worn!" My mom wasn't cheap or ever poor, but she just loved a deal and didn't see the point in overspending on anything, and thus she never focused on the dollar signs of running the hospice. She just wanted to do something important.

Maybe because I had gone to business school and started my career in banking, Luther saw a little of himself in me. I was young and motivated, with my eyes set on a bright future, so perhaps there was a little bit of truth to that at the time. But his comment struck me. I squinted my eyes and tried to process what I had just heard, hoping I had misunderstood the intent. Sure, going into business for yourself, one of the goals is to make money, a desire that does not inherently make someone a bad person. But at that moment, I felt alone, a foreshadowing so dark of the imminent battles to come for the three of us over the next 10 years. For my mom, the hospice was her dream, to do something consequential for a community that she loved and to which she felt so connected, and I was slowly becoming engulfed by her vision and passion.

In February 2005, I received a phone call from my mom to tell me about her dream. While it wasn't odd for her to call, it was odd that she called me from Mexico. She and Luther were on holiday, and while there, they'd met a couple who lived in New Orleans and immediately hit it off—my mom's new best friends.

"Jerry! I have an idea!" I could feel the excitement exploding from my mom's voice through the phone.

"Why are you calling me from a beach in Mexico?" I inquired in a confused tone.

"Jerry! Listen to me! I met this amazing couple down here. They're from New Orleans, and they own a hospice. I want to start a hospice in Boulder!"

"Ummmm . . . a hospice? There's already one on campus, and I don't really want to start a company for a bunch of twenty-something transients," I replied in an even more confused, yet snarky tone.

"No! A HOSPICE. Not a HOSTEL," she belted back.

"What's a hospice?" I asked.

I was 31 with a business degree, still intent on climbing the corporate ladder and becoming the next Gordon Gekko. If you're unfamiliar with the 1987 movie *Wall Street* with Charlie Sheen and Michael Douglas, Gordon Gekko (played by Douglas) was an investment tycoon who made an untold fortune in not-so-ethical ways. Bud Fox (Sheen) was the up-and-coming broker, willing to compromise his soul and make his own fortune by bagging the elephant of a big-ticket investor: Gordon Gekko (aka "Gekko the Great"). After getting lured into the depths of deception, greed, and betrayal, at the end of the film, Fox has a moment of moral clarity and turns on Gekko.

This film was pretty much Business School 101, and it just seemed that every kid I went to B-School with owned a copy and could recite any scene on request. For whatever reason, we all romanticized the vision of a lavish salary and cushy lifestyle in the banking industry. Sure, we would sell our souls and forfeit the first twenty years of our youth, but who cares? We would be players. Looking back now as my 40-plus-year-old self, I shake my head at that dream as those ambitions seem so absurd and shallow. It turned out that I didn't actually want to be Gordon Gekko. I just wanted to be Bud Fox.

When my mom called, I had zero knowledge, experience, or especially any interest in working with people who were dying. Where clearly I lacked any vision outside of my own short-sighted goals, my mom had this angle figured out, though she wasn't as well versed in the business of business. But together, we made the perfect team. When she arrived back in Boulder later in the week, we got together for dinner to talk about her trip, but mostly to talk about this dream of hers. It was hard to not be at least a little bit intrigued simply based on her contagious excitement. She definitely had enough to go around. The more we talked over the following weeks, the more I began to see this as potentially my dream as well.

At the time, I had a high-profile role working for a small insurance company that provided coverage for hurricanes. Overall, it was still a soulless corporate job. But, hey, I had gone to business school, and I thought that is what my career was supposed to be about. I played the usual corporate games in order to climb the ladder, get a little bit more money, and with it more responsibility and, of course, more work. I came in early. I stayed late. I went to company-*recommended* events, just for the face time. I even developed this ploy to demonstrate just how dedicated I was to the company (although I doubt I was the first one to use this tactic). I would concoct a very well-thought-out and detailed email to my boss with elaborate analysis rolled in and then save it to "my drafts." I went to sleep but would set an alarm to wake me up at 1:37 a.m. or some other random absurd time when nobody should be working, let alone be awake—and click "send." The intention was, of course, that when my boss showed up the next morning for work, he would see that incredible email from me with a timestamp of 1:37 a.m. and think, "Wow, this guy is really dedicated! We need to promote him and give him more money with a more important-sounding title!" I would pull this ruse about once per week, on various days, sometimes even over a weekend, but never more because otherwise it just wouldn't seem believable—as if it even was? To this day, I have no idea if it worked.

Even with my mom's unwavering commitment, I still needed to know more before I signed up to this idea of working with dying people. It was just the linear thinking business brain in me because everything I did came down to the opportunity cost—keeping with my corporate map of success or pouring myself into this new vision. The next step was a trip to New Orleans to meet this dynamic duo who had sparked such a fervent passion in my mom.

"Hey, baby!" Opal yelled out as I stepped off the plane. "Welcome to NOLA!" Without ever meeting or even speaking to me, she met me at the airport and wrapped me up in a spine adjusting bear hug. Part of it was just good old-fashioned southern hospitality, but really, it was just Opal.

She was a physically imposing black woman in her early 50s, with a take-no-bullshit persona. If I had to guess, she was about 5′11″ and 190 pounds and could put the fear of God into you with just a look if you crossed her. But as a lifelong nurse with a heart of gold, she could just as easily wrap you up in one of her giant southern hospitality hugs and invite you to her house for a bowl of gumbo. Opal had a laugh and personality more boisterous than all of New Orleans, and when she opened her mouth either to talk or simply to laugh, everyone took notice. Her partner, Jackie, was a smaller, more reserved white woman in her 40s. She stood about 5′6″ and 140 pounds with short brown hair and a quick-witted yet soft-spoken demeanor.

"Hey, y'all. This is my friend Jerry from Colorado. He and his momma are opening a hospice up there, and we're gonna give them whatever help they need," commanded Opal the next day as she and Jackie paraded me around their office. With that support, I built a business case, and after several weeks of analysis paralysis, something apparently I'm hardwired for, in April 2005, Family Hospice was born, just two months after my mom's crazy call.

We quickly set up contracts with hospitals, nursing homes, and assisted living facilities with the plan to provide care in a patient's home, wherever that may be. Next, we rented a small space in a dilapidated 1970s office building that was occupied by a half dozen struggling attorneys. The owner was an older attorney nearing retirement who was touched by the work that we did, so he offered us the basement office for $100 per month. It was only about a hundred square feet, and my mom's desk was next to the bathroom, which also conveniently had a steam shower. At any given time of the day, people would come downstairs to use the toilet and sometimes take a shower. It was odd, but it was ours, and we were on our way.

For the first two years, my mom was the only partner who was a regular full-time employee and thus collected a paycheck. I continued my job with the insurance company, and Luther worked as a stockbroker. He and I moonlighted for the hospice on nights and weekends working on contracts, billing, payroll, and really anything else that needed to get done outside of the day-to-day operations that my mom oversaw. Early on, the three of us did whatever we needed to do, and whatever we didn't know we figured out—many times with the support of Opal and Jackie.

If I'm being honest, although I was fed by my mom's passion, I thought the hospice made sense purely from a business perspective, and I planned to only get involved as an outside supporter in helping my mom achieve her dream. Although I was smitten by the vision, I was still only 32 and was clinging to my own playbook. I never knew the hospice was going to change my life.

CHAPTER 2

The Sweet Potato that Changed My Life

Wielding her father's ax at age 95, Francis would still drag her oxygen tank outside in the middle of winter to chop wood for her stove. She was one of our first patients, a frail yet resilient woman who lived in the mountains above Boulder in the cabin her father built and she grew up in. It was a simple wooden structure, maybe eight hundred square feet, dimly lit but cozy, with decades of black smoke emblazoned on the walls and ceiling from the woodstove. Francis had COPD (Congestive Obstructive Pulmonary Disorder) and as a result, was continuously on oxygen. I'm sure it didn't help that she was living at 9,000 feet, but at 95, it was her home, and she wasn't moving. Francis stood at most five feet tall and including her oxygen tank weighed maybe 98 pounds. She had a well-honed talent for woodworking and would carve the most intricate figures into the handles of walking sticks, which she also whittled. Francis was fiercely independent, even after she came on service with us.

When Luther and I found out about Francis' wood chopping heroics from her hospice nurse, he and I drove the twenty-five minutes up to her house the next day, through the mostly snowed-in driveway, and spent the evening splitting and stacking wood for her. This type of "working late" was a far cry from what I was used to and was quickly weaning me away from my corporate job. I went up to her homestead several more times just to spend time with her. It was so much more rewarding than concocting senseless emails for an insurance company to be sent out in the middle of the night. I relished in her stories about what Boulder was like in the 1940s and how much it had changed. Over the first couple of years, there were countless other "Francis's" that I spent time with that began to tug at my heart—causing it to open and deepening my connection to the hospice beyond that of any financial goals.

Shortly after hurricane Katrina had decimated the southeastern US, one of the territories that I oversaw, I got called in for a meeting with my boss at the insurance company. Our company had to write some pretty hefty checks as a result of the damage, and they were "revisiting some of their direction." Translation: they were letting me go.

I had never been fired from a job before, well, except for that time when I was a nineteen-year-old busboy in a four-star restaurant in Lansing, Michigan and got fired for snatching little pinches of food off plates before they went out to the customer. I probably earned that one. This was different, and even though it felt personal, it wasn't. It was just math, something I knew well but it didn't lessen the feeling of being blindsided; my master plan disrupted. I had just purchased a house earlier in the year and was already "house poor," just trying to survive while also co-funding the hospice. I had been spending more and more time with the hospice, falling in love with it and helping it mature. It still wasn't large enough to support another salary but if it was ever going to be more than a side project, now was the time. I felt that I had to commit and jump in with both feet.

Going without a paycheck for twelve months was terrifying, but I remembered what a former colleague said to me before he left to start his own gig: "If I work as hard as I do for as many hours at a job that I don't like, what will happen if I did that for something I'm passionate about?" Up until this point, I had been playing it safe and sticking to the playbook. I had gotten good jobs and climbed the ladder, slowly and steadily. My life had been going exactly where I wanted until this, and I thought to myself, *if I could fail at doing something I didn't love, why not take a chance at something that I did?*

I called up my mom and told her what happened and that I wanted to join the company full time, but would defer any salary until we could actually afford it. She was excited to have me in the office with her, and for another $100 per month, we expanded our space to include a tiny sixty square foot shoe box on the third floor, barely big enough for my desk, but fortunately without the distraction of people walking by my office after a trip through the steam shower. It was a leap of faith, but I was definitely more passionate about Family Hospice than I was about an insurance company. Even though I wouldn't have to send silly emails at 1:37 a.m., there would be plenty of late nights to come, but with the hospice, I was okay with that.

By 2007 we had grown to seven mostly part-time staff (including myself), and things were beginning to happen. There were already a couple of well-established hospices in the area for thirty years, but we saw how their service was fading, becoming less passionate and more bottom-line driven, at the expense of not only their patients but also their staff. My mom had a vision to restore the practice of hospice to its grassroots, one that focused not on death and dying but on living well. When these other larger hospices began to take notice of us, we knew we had something special.

In this second year, many of our competitor's staff who had become just cogs in their bureaucratic machine began to submit applications to us and before long, we had more interest than positions. Business quickly accelerated as physicians and local residents soon learned of us and were eager to give us a chance. We began hiring as fast as we could to keep up with our growing demand and quickly outgrew our first tiny office space.

By 2009, Family Hospice was four years old and a successful company. I was making a modest salary, and everything was back on track. I turned 35 and was proud and passionate about what I was doing. I would regularly meet people on the street and would tell them what I did for a living. More often than not, their first words were: "Wow, that is really hard work. It sounds so depressing to be around death all the time." This was of course after they asked how someone so young was in the *business of dying*.

It was true, it was hard work both mentally and physically, but I quickly learned from our staff that the people who work in hospice are a special breed—they have the "hospice heart," as my mom called it. We had an incredible *family* that taught me so much about life, perspective, and the value of the ultimate commodity: time. We saw our work as rewarding and not depressing because we were helping patients and their families to enjoy their remaining time as peacefully and comfortably as possible. Our internal slogan was "Every day is an opportunity to improve someone's life." How many other jobs can make that claim?

Even with these valuable lessons being taught to me each day, I was still a naïve, know-it-all 36-year-old kid who needed a slap in the face from time to time. In the fall of 2010, I had just gotten home from a bike race and was making dinner. It was about 6:30 p.m. on a soggy, drizzly Saturday evening in Boulder. Muddy and shivering from a late October storm, I pulled out a sweet potato and was about to put it in the microwave to cook before quickly jumping in the shower to rinse off and thaw out. In my haste, instead of using a fork to poke holes in the skin and aerate it, for whatever reason, I chose a butter knife. As I began stabbing at the potato with this very blunt utensil, my hand inadvertently slipped and slid down the handle, across the edge of the *blade*, and nicked my pinky finger just above the first crease. Without any real pain, I calmly put down the knife and saw blood beginning to seep from my finger and dripping down my palm. I had had enough medical training to know that I likely needed a stitch, so I wrapped my finger in a towel with some tape and drove myself to the emergency room.

"Hi, so I cut my finger. Nothing bad. I probably need a stitch," I calmly explained to the ER doc an hour later.

"Actually, you cut a tendon, and it will need surgery. See, you can't close your finger," she explained after a quick assessment.

"Surgery? Nah. It's just a small cut. It will heal," I fired back, trying to convince her.

"You're a young man, and if you ever want to use this finger again, we'll see you back here in two days," the doctor retorted, unconvinced by my pitch.

The surgery was simple, but the recovery was eight weeks, with my right arm completely immobilized in a plastic splint—the concern that any use or movement would disrupt the healing and undo the surgery. This meant of course no biking, but also that I would have to use my left arm to type, write, eat, dress, brush my teeth; essentially everything. At first, it was just an annoying new challenge, but I underestimated how difficult it was to not be able to use my arm at all, especially since it was my dominant one. Physical activity was such a vital component of my life that the realization of not being able to bike, ski, run or do anything sent me into a dark hole of depression.

After four weeks, the muscle in my right arm had atrophied such that it looked like that of a nine-year-old boy. I came to work one day, fresh from the gutter of depression that I had been living in, a permafunk from having (in my mind) my entire world upended by this stupid avoidable *trauma*. As I sat in our conference room about to lead a staff meeting, my arm withering away in its familiar blue plastic splint, my mom walked in and noticed the glum look on my face. I'm sure it was a look that she and others had noticed over the past three weeks and had grown increasingly annoyed with but somehow tolerated.

"What's wrong?" she asked in a modest attempt at concern.

I could read her underlying tone but didn't care because I was wallowing so deep in my own depression that I figured she and everyone else would understand. "Because of the stupid sweet potato, I haven't ridden my bike in a month. I can't exercise. I can't do anything!" I said with solemn conviction.

In a calm yet direct tone, she replied matter-of-factly and only subtly disguising her annoyance, "What is wrong with you? Do you know where you work? We are taking care of people who are *dying*. Sara (our volunteer coordinator), just got diagnosed with breast cancer, *again*, and you're depressed because you can't ride your bike? Your *bike*! Are you serious? Knock it off!" she scolded, the flip side of that nurturing, protective momma bird.

Smack! There was my mom, not my business partner, squarely and sternly planting that metaphorical slap across my cheek, just like I was a little boy again, and she needed to snap me out of whatever melodramatic tantrum I was having—booting me out of the self-pity doldrums. It was a valuable lesson in perspective that I have never forgotten.

Shortly after this exchange, I found myself in a clinical meeting.

The first words I heard as I entered the meeting already in progress were *fecal transplants.* I did my best to not be that adolescent child who burst out into laughter when the discussion of poop arose (and had just gotten slapped in the face by his mother twenty minutes earlier). Fecal transplants are exactly what they sound like. It entails taking feces from someone who has a healthy gut biome and transferring it to someone else with a compromised one, a proposed treatment for a patient who recently finished a strong course of antibiotics which consequently robbed his gut of healthy bacteria, allowing the bad guys to propagate. It was still an experimental procedure at the time but did prove successful in a number of cases. I cannot confirm or deny that the words *turkey baster* and *blender* were or were not discussed but will confirm that I was not the only one to laugh at a poop joke. Fortunately, I've learned that, while hospice clinicians have an incredible heart, they also have a colorful and dark sense of humor. It's a job requirement, necessary to maintain sanity. So I guess they choose door #2?

CHAPTER 3

Peaks and Valleys

At our peak, we had sixty-one employees and seventy-three volunteers. We were a family, one that spent time together outside of work and took an interest in our staff's lives, even their kids and pets. As the years passed and the company grew, I took on a more active role in leading the organization—gradually surpassing my mother and Luther in leadership roles. Looking back, I can see how this may have felt to them, like I had usurped those roles and marginalized their value to the organization, but it was never my intent. That informal coup early in the growth phase of the company would lay the foundation for resentment and mistrust in the years to come. At that time, however, it just seemed like a natural evolution for me on the way to achieving my own professional goals. I possessed a strong business acumen stemming from my education and prior professional career. They were both in their late 60s, and I felt like maybe they were slowing down, which was fine and something they were entitled to do. Conversely, I was more than willing to pick up the slack. I was intoxicated by this passion of building something exactly as I wanted, almost like a LEGO set but one whose pieces were made from bits of real life. I had a strong conviction of how the hospice should be run and was intent on making it happen, as if the current status still somehow was not up to my high expectations.

The more we grew, the more the community learned about us, and the more motivated I got. The necessary numbers portion of my job, spreadsheets and budgets and such, were the least of my passion. I still came in early and stayed late. I worked weekends and rarely took a day off. I sat in nurse meetings, enthralled by their stories of real passion and dedication. I sat vigil with patients nearing the end and held their hands when they didn't have family or friends to do it. I was driven to push harder and make us better. I worked more hours but was less burned out than roles in my former corporate life; a testament to the rightness of this new path I was on. It was addictive.

Business was thriving, but as a result of my drive and time commitment, Luther's role in operations continued to become more and more diluted. Not surprisingly, our personal and professional relationship soured as well, essentially guaranteeing a reckoning date in the not-so-distant future. Simple discussions among the three of us exploded into shouting matches whose rancor inevitably seeped out into the business. As much as we tried to hide it, the staff knew that storms were brewing. In addition, new hospices began to spring up all over the area, catching us off guard. Slowly, Family Hospice was feeling less like a family.

The point of no return occurred one spring day in 2013. Luther had taken his Jaguar in for some repairs and was going to pay for them with the company account, something the three of us did since all of our cars were company vehicles. Instead of spending the $700 or $800 for the repairs, he rolled into the parking lot with a new BMW 5 Series emphatically making his position known: he refused to be marginalized. "What the hell is that?" I exploded at Luther as he walked in with the look of a child who had just gotten a new toy, my mom, clearly embarrassed, looking on in the background trying to avoid another conflict.

"Leave it alone," she finally chimed in, breaking up our shouting match just as Luther stormed out of the room. "I can't deal with the daily battles. You have no idea what it's like living with him right now. This will make it better. Just let him have it."

Looking back now, it's clear to me that this was the day that sealed the fate of Family Hospice.

I needed a break, and in 2014, I took my first vacation away from hospice since we had started in 2005. Emma and I had decided to celebrate our 40th birthdays with a bikepacking trip to Vietnam for two and a half weeks. We had been living together for over two years, and I had been so invested in the hospice that we seldom had time together outside of the after-work bike ride.

I returned from the trip, once again invigorated. I revamped the entire marketing plan from our website all the way down to our logo. Our business doubled in only a few short months. My heart was racing with enthusiasm again, like someone had shocked me with a defibrillator, even though my relationship with my partners was still on life support. While on the surface they appeared rejuvenated, I soon learned they were only motivated to grow the business to make it more appealing to potential buyers.

In July 2015, with the hospice once again on track and growing, I took the opportunity to meet my friend Taylor in South America to bikepack through the Andes from Bolivia to Peru over a three-week period. One week into the trip, I received an email from Sara, our new Clinical Director.

> *"Hey, do you know some guys named James and Ed? Your mom said they were consultants doing some QA for the hospice. However, it seemed odd. And with you out of the country, I did a quick Google search and discovered that they own a large hospice in Texas that has been acquiring a lot of smaller hospices."*

I lied and said I didn't know who they were, but in actuality, I did. They had been soliciting me for well over a year to sell to them, but I had always blown them off, never giving them even a cordial consideration. Family Hospice was thriving, and I was passionate about what I was doing. I felt confident that I could somehow suppress the underlying tensions amongst the partners and that our overall success would further coat that result. The arrogance of my overbearing Type A personality falsely led me to believe that I could fix this. Sadly, I was wrong. The two men were in our office doing a site visit, an assessment of our operations, and thus our overall viability and value.

In my egocentric view, it was the ultimate betrayal. Over the years, where my mom had trouble separating business from family, I was always laser-focused. It was black and white. What happened between those walls was business, not personal, and surely not family. She and I were partners, not mother and son, and our job was to fulfill this vision that she had intoxicated me with. But this—this somehow felt personal. This was my mom, seemingly betraying me, siding with her husband. How could my own mother do this? The impact felt wasn't the disorienting, blunt force concussion felt by being clubbed in the head. Instead, it was a knife to the heart that drove a wedge between us. It wasn't until years later that I could remove myself and my emotions from the situation enough to realize that whatever I felt in that moment must have paled in comparison to my mom's feeling of betrayal to *herself*. She had to choose between keeping her home life happy or ultimately betraying *herself* by closing the doors on her dream.

Still reeling from this sucker punch, two days later I received a devastating message from Emma that took the air from my lungs. *"Hey, I hope you're enjoying your trip, but I have something to tell you. Cynthia is in hospice."*

I knew she had been silently battling breast cancer for several years, but this floored me. Cynthia was one of my favorite people in the world. We had just gone for a hike a few weeks before I left for Bolivia, and her progress seemed encouraging. She of course knew of my trip and how stressed I had been at work. I can only imagine that she had not wanted to burden me with her story. That's just the way she was. Cynthia was 45, a southern girl living in Boulder who had an unquenchable thirst for life. Over those two days, I felt like I had been dealt a colossal one-two punch.

Though shocked with the news from Sara, I didn't really feel any strong current of impending doom. After all, I owned a third of the hospice, and even though a couple of investors were walking around the office, nothing seemed imminent. Instead, I switched to the news from Emma and my focus on Cynthia. I made a few calls and determined who her power of attorney was, and called her.

"Susan. Hey, this is Jerry. I just heard. I'm in a pretty remote part of the Andes, but I can catch a bus and be on a plane in two days," my voice trembling with anxiety.

"Jerry. Stay in Peru. Continue your adventure. It's what Cynthia would want. She'll be here when you get back."

The confidence in Susan's voice tamed my anxiety, and a few moments later I received a text photo from Cynthia of the two of us at a Halloween party a few years back. It was, and still is, one of my all-time favorite pictures, both of us decked out in giant afros and disco attire, and both of us displaying a similar arrogant "We're too cool for you" smirk. I choked back a waterfall of tears because I knew what it meant to be admitted to hospice, but I felt confident that I would see her again.

Three weeks later, I arrived back in Boulder and rushed to Cynthia's house, excited to see my old friend. She perked up when I walked in the door, but I was devastated by what I saw. She had shaved her head and was confined to the couch with only brief, fleeting moments of lucidity. Cynthia was now a shell of the girl who I knew and loved, and it was apparent that she was already gone. We spent about an hour together as I held her hand and told her about my adventures in the Andes while she drifted in and out of coherence. When she finally fell asleep, I swallowed a mouthful of emotion and walked out the door, knowing that would be the last time I would see her. I had held countless patients' hands over the years, but this was different. While tragic for anyone to die, it's easier to accept the passing of Francis, a 95-year-old woman living in the mountains, believing *she had a good run.* This was personal and no amount of training or experience could prepare me. Cynthia was 45, the finiteness of her life and proximity of her age to mine, leveled me.

I returned to work to face my other emotional battle, the feeling of rage and utter betrayal that I felt from my mom and her husband. Even before the final betrayal, the last year of our coexistence had become so toxic that Luther and I could not be in the same room with one another without an explosion happening. My mom was understandably torn between her son and the company that she dreamed up, and her husband of twenty-five years. I can only imagine the emotional burden she carried with her, even after she left the office each day.

At home one night, I cried in Emma's arms, my partner who I had lived with and who had been by my side for four years. My rock. She had seen the ups and downs with the hospice and my relationship with my parents. I had lost Cynthia and could feel myself losing the company that gave me so much life. These storms, however, were clouding the other very real fact that Emma and I were also falling apart and had been for nearly a year. Death by 1,000 paper cuts.

It's easy to understand how you can be lonely when you're alone, but being lonely in a relationship to me feels far worse. Since our Vietnam trip, each day Emma and I drifted a little further apart. I could feel her slowly pulling away, and it seemed the harder I tried to pull her back, the more fiercely she recoiled. First, she was just sleeping in the basement if one of us was sick. Then it was because she was studying. Finally, one indiscernible day, she was just living down there as my roommate, not the person I used to know intimately, deeply—but now just someone living in my basement.

There are always at least two sides to every story, and I'll never fully know hers. But there weren't any hardline instances like infidelity, abuse, neglect, or distrust. I could say that we simply fell out of love, and that wouldn't be inaccurate. Honestly, to this day, I have no idea what went wrong. We just lost our way, I suppose.

The South America trip was not only an opportunity to see Taylor, my mountain bike racing friend from Boulder and get a much-needed vacation from work, but also from my relationship with Emma. I had hoped that a three-week breather would provide some clarity and allow us the space to gain some perspective to work things out. I was wrong about that as well.

The culmination of these three emotional storms was palpable, and something had to give. On November 30, 2015, everything did. Even though I controlled a third of the hospice, that was still less than the two-thirds of the partners who wanted out. The dream was over.

Family Hospice was about family, not just my mom and me, but our staff. This was their family and their hospice as well, with many of them having been with us since we began in that tiny basement office. They had bought into our vision, ridden the waves of our growing pains, and stuck around to see us flourish, becoming the community beacon that everyone envisioned. My mom's ultimate goal was always for Family Hospice to leave a lasting legacy in the community. With the sale, the vision that we created and the legacy that we had sought to establish, was gone. Under the new corporate management, most of our staff quit, the patients either died or transferred, and the doors closed forever. Family Hospice, too, had died.

I woke up on December 1, 2015, to an empty house and an empty heart. Cynthia was gone. Family Hospice was gone. Emma was gone. My relationship with my mom, was gone. Forty-one, and adrift. On May 31, 2016, after six months lamenting the loss of the hospice, I boarded a plane for a two-month trip to Africa.

Mom and I at the Family Hospice holiday party

Too cool for you—With Cynthia

December 2015. Final picture of Family Hospice. (not present: Luther and Mom)

PART 3

India

September 14 – October 23, 2016

"This is your last chance. After this, there is no turning back. You take the blue pill—the story ends, you wake up in your bed and believe whatever you want to believe. You take the red pill—you stay in Wonderland, and I show you how deep the rabbit hole goes."

- Morpheus, played by Laurence Fishburne in the 1999 film, *The Matrix*

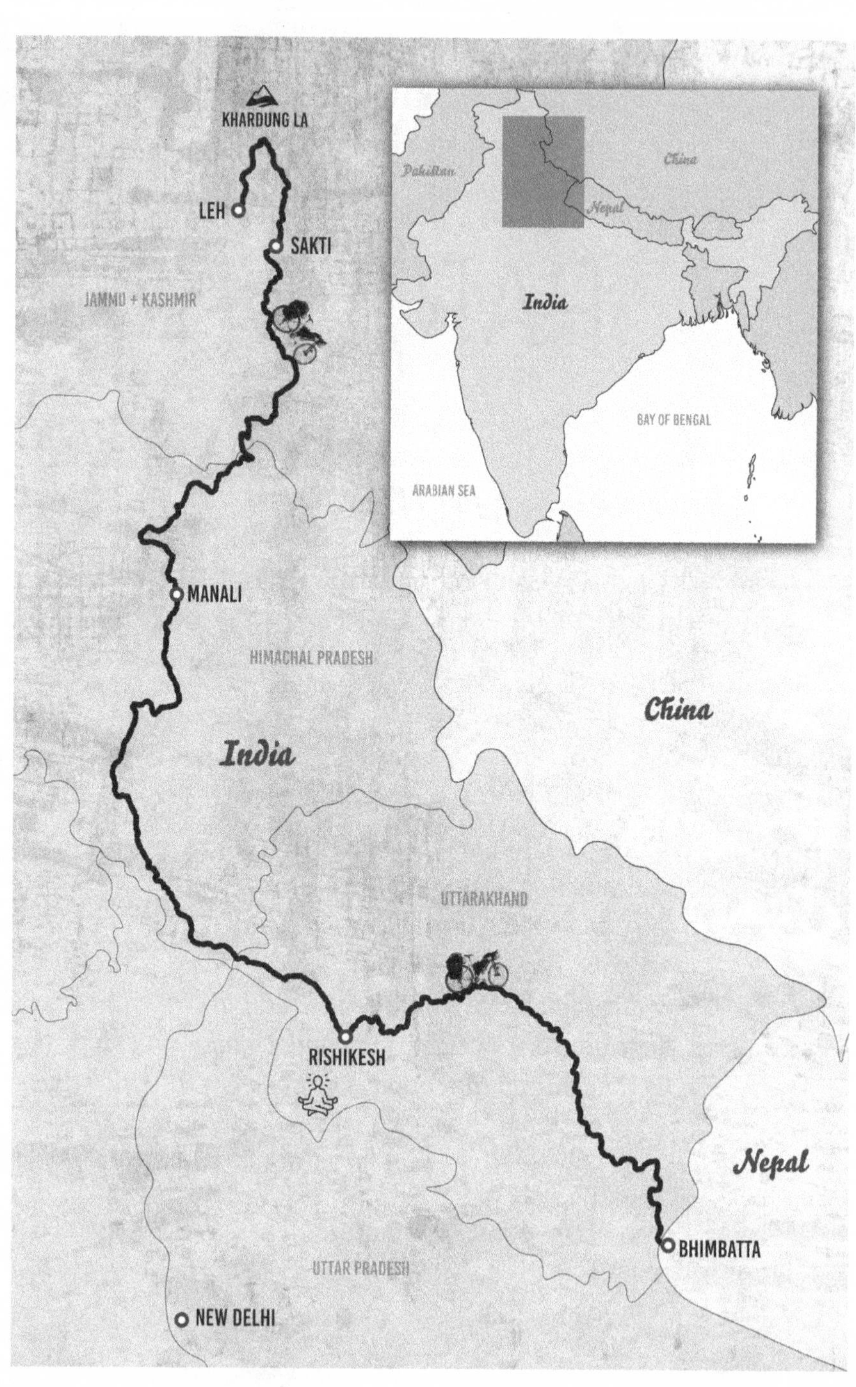

KHARDUNG LA
LEH
SAKTI
JAMMU + KASHMIR
MANALI
HIMACHAL PRADESH
India
China
UTTARAKHAND
RISHIKESH
Nepal
BHIMBATTA
UTTAR PRADESH
NEW DELHI
Pakistan
China
Nepal
India
BAY OF BENGAL
ARABIAN SEA

CHAPTER 1

Unplugging

I arrived home from Africa after two months, and it was just as I remembered: predictable, calculated, and measured. People were going out for their 6 a.m. run or rushing to yoga before scurrying off in traffic on their way to work. This was normal. This was the life that I had left behind two months earlier. It was still a great life, and Boulder was still an amazing community that most of the country dreamed of living in. *The New York Times* had recently run a story rating Boulder as the best city in America to live in for quality of life, and as a result, people were migrating here in droves. However, I felt like so much had changed within me, but nothing had changed in Boulder. I have no idea why that surprised me or what I expected, but for whatever reason, we no longer clicked.

These unsettled feelings had not come out of nowhere. Two weeks before my departure from Africa, the nightmares began again. It was the same recurring nightmare I had ten years prior when we were just starting Family Hospice, and for five years prior to that when I had been running the hamster wheel of corporate life—before Family Hospice was even a glimmer in my mom's eye. Many people, I'm sure, have had the nightmare of coming to school either naked or unprepared for an exam, or worse, naked *and* unprepared for an exam. My dream was similar but with a more professional and topical spin. I was coming to work, back in my *Matrix*-like corporate life. As in the movie, there were no distinct colors, only varying shades of grey that made up the diluted, hazy visuals in my periphery. I step off the elevator to an endless sea of equally non-distinct cubicles, stretching as far as I can see. Each one has a nameplate, and inside is a drone of a person attempting to look busy, but really just counting the hours until lunch, and then until 5 p.m. when they can go home and do something they actually enjoy. I wade through the maze of cubicles, past caffeinated, faceless employees and arrive at my cubicle only to realize that I didn't get the report done for my boss, so he can't present it to his boss, and his boss's boss. He calls me into his office. For some reason I haven't shaved, my pants are wrinkled, and my shirt is untucked. I look like I slept in my car, and I feel completely disheveled. For sure, I'm getting fired. With each step I take inching me closer to his office, my pulse ratchets up. The anxiety is so real in my dream that I wake up in a sudden, violent spasm, my chest dripping with sweat.

I was coming home to Boulder, back to my life, and it was a great life. It had been a two-month discovery, but my journey was ending. I needed to have all the answers because I knew the first question would be: "What are you going to do now?" But I didn't have the answers. What I did know was that I wasn't right for this structured world anymore and, like in the *Matrix*, I just wanted to unplug.

In the first few weeks of being back in Boulder, I talked to a few companies about jobs. I didn't know what I wanted to do, but it was clear what I didn't want to do. Friends asked me about my trip. "Wow, you were gone for so long!" they would say, marveling at my two-month experience, but to me, it sailed by in an instant. In my former life, I never took vacations or really any time away from the office. I had a playbook that I was following, but after being away from it for only two months, it was evident that the rules of the game had changed for me.

Although only home for less than a week, a malcontented restlessness was already creeping over me. Over the next two months, I slowly began to settle back into the familiarity of my world back home, but my mind was racing, still fixated on the encounter I had in

Madagascar with the woman I met from India. No matter what I did, I couldn't shake it. I was supposed to return home with all the answers, but all I had were more questions. As soon as my visa for India was processed, I was on a plane, this time with a one-way ticket—to the Himalayas.

—

I arrived in Kathmandu on a Friday after over thirty hours of travel. I completely lost Thursday. Kathmandu hosts a major international airport catering to spiritual and adventure tourists from around the world, but you couldn't tell by looking at it. Signs were vague, cows roamed freely, and organization was merely a suggestion. If I hadn't experienced the chaos of Madagascar, this might have been shocking, but instead, I felt once again alive and more at home than in Boulder.

I cleared customs and hopped a taxi into the heart of the city, the Thamel district. It is a melee of narrow, busy streets lined with small shops, vendors, and stupas (dome-shaped buildings erected as Buddhist shrines). Prayer flags traverse the alleys, while throughout the town a spider web of twisted and convoluted cables provides electricity to the ancient stone and wooden buildings. There are shops like North Face and Mammut for all of your last-minute active endeavor needs, while down narrow corridors, countless other shops sell those same items at a remarkably reduced price. But judging by the stitching and the logo, maybe they aren't the *same*.

The traffic was paralyzing, and it had taken over an hour to travel the nine miles from the airport to my hotel. A two-lane road was filled with four lanes of busses and rusted-out cars belching blue clouds of diesel. The taxi creeping along next to us was close enough that the driver had to roll down his window to tuck in his side mirror before angling in and inching in front of us.

Immediately I could see evidence of the scars from the 7.8 magnitude earthquake that rocked the city in April 2015, killing more than 8,000 people and injuring some 21,000 more. Many structures were destroyed but were in the process of being rebuilt. Some of them are more than 6,000 years old. Many buildings had a series of ten-foot-tall boards nailed together in a line, attempting to provide support for the structures whose foundation had been compromised—which was most of them. One end of the board was anchored to the ground while the other was pitched at a forty-five-degree angle and tethered to the side of the building, effectively supporting it until it could be repaired. It looked like they would immediately collapse into a pile of rubble if someone kicked loose one of the boards.

My taxi brought me down one of these narrow alleyways, a passage that in any other place I've been would have been far too narrow, yet drivers here are adept at negotiating these ancient nooks. The driver blew his horn to clear the walkers and motorbikes as we zoomed down the broken, cobbled corridor, only to be stopped for a few minutes by a cow, casually standing in the middle, oblivious to us or anyone else.

In Kathmandu, cows patrol the streets and have the ultimate right of way. The taxi driver again laid on his horn while the cow glanced away with an overwhelming ambivalence as traffic began to back up. We sat patiently in the claustrophobic alley as diesel fumes began to asphyxiate me while a symphony of horns blared. Finally, a shop owner came out to shoo the cow out of the way, thus freeing up traffic, albeit momentarily. I glanced back, and once we had passed, the cow returned to his place, once again completely content and oblivious.

I arrived at my hotel and quickly felt the warm Nepali culture. “Hello, Mr. Jerry, welcome to Nepal!” beamed Renu from the front desk. She was 24, with a petite frame, dark flowing straight hair, and a gushing smile. She was wearing a traditional pink Nepali skirt and a white blouse. Renu was shy and humble about her English, but nonetheless anxious to practice with me. Her husband, Bikash, was 31, about 5′7″ with a lean build and wore pressed black slacks, shiny black shoes, and a crisp white button-up shirt. Bikash, with a similar smile, quickly grabbed my luggage and showed me to my room. The hotel was a four-story oasis, set back down a long corridor, isolated from the mayhem of Kathmandu.

After only two days, Bikash and Renu made me feel like family, as we shared many laughs and stories. I had quickly become accustomed to the discussion and the looks of stupefied bewilderment at my cycling plans and routes, even in an area as accustomed to adventuring as Nepal. Ironically, I always find amusement at their thoughts of my impending peril. "Oh no!" Renu would continually warn me. "This too far to go by cycle. Maybe you take bus instead? Will be very cold too!"

Like Africa, I had a *rough* plan. I would touch down in Kathmandu just long enough to catch my breath before another flight north to the mountainous area of Ladakh in Northern India, near the Pakistan border. From there, I would begin my journey along the Leh Manali highway (the term "highway" is a bit generous, as I would find out), before finally making my way back to Kathmandu—and like my buddy Taylor—for as long as it took.

Unlike Africa, I had a one-way ticket, fully prepared to cash in this "gift of time" that was given to me. The route is about eighteen hundred miles, crossing some of the highest mountain passes in the world, including Taglang La and Khardung La, both at over 17,000 feet. I was short of breath and light-headed just thinking about it. The weather window is narrow to be cycling (let alone traveling) at that altitude as the area becomes even more susceptible to storms and heavy snow this time of year. The monsoon season there is real and had just ended, so this was the time before winter blanketed the high passes in snow.

The Ladakh region in India sits at an average altitude of more than 13,000 feet and is so barren and remote that in many areas there is no permanent human habitation, only *dhabas*, temporary roadside tent communities where tourists, military, and road crew can find shelter. This rough outline made Africa seem mundane. What should have struck me as a more mentally daunting endeavor, but instead, I couldn't leave soon enough.

CHAPTER 2

Christmas Came Early

When I was a kid, one year I found my dad's secret hiding spot for Christmas presents. It was 1981, and I was 7. Young enough to be innocent, yet old enough to be crafty and resourceful. *The Empire Strikes Back* had just blown up the box office and taken America by storm (or by *force?*). My parents had divorced when I was four, and I quickly learned to leverage the concept of two Christmases, a fortuitous byproduct of divorced parents. I had been openly campaigning for the Millennium Falcon. It was all I wanted, and it was all I talked about.

"How was school?" my dad would ask over a dinner of frozen fish sticks and a can of creamed corn.

"Great. Did you know that the Millennium Falcon has retractable landing gears and a cockpit that opens so Han Solo and Chewbacca can fly it around? It's great because I already have Han and Chewy!"

I knew that Santa (the stocky, jolly guy with a white beard, draped in red velvet cruising around in a wooden sleigh) likely wasn't going to bring it, so I started pushing my dad (the stocky, jolly guy with a brown beard, draped in puffy Gore-Tex and cruising around in a wood-paneled station wagon). I'm sure he was utterly annoyed by my incessant pitches for weeks leading up to Christmas about how good

I had been that year, but I didn't care. I wanted the Millennium Falcon.

I had covertly been looking around the house, and a week before Christmas, I found the spot. There it was, the Millenium Falcon, tucked up on the shelf in my dad's closet behind a bunch of boxes and wool sweaters. I could hardly contain myself upon the discovery. I already had the X-Wing Fighter and Tie Fighter, and the Falcon would complete the collection. I heard years later that dads had camped out at Toys "R" Us before the store opened just to get their hands on this gem.

Now, could I hold it together and not blow it? All I had to do was act cool for a week and it was mine, all mine! (Yes, I realize I sound like a typical spoiled kid, and I was.) The galaxy was ripe for the taking. I couldn't sleep. That week was like being on a perpetual Mountain Dew buzz. The anticipation was coursing through my veins, and combining that with the fact that in the 80s I regularly drank Mountain Dew like water–imagine what I was like that week for my dad.

The week had agonizingly crept by, and somehow, I had kept it together. No one knew that I knew. Christmas morning came, and there was no letdown. I launched out of my room, down the stairs, and dove under the five-foot artificial Christmas tree, knowing exactly what I was looking for. I politely dug through the smaller boxes that likely contained more Star Wars action figures, flippantly dismissing the softer packages that clearly concealed the sweater from my grandma, and locked my tractor beam on the large box tucked in the corner under the tinsel-draped tree. I tore through the wrapping paper and box, turning them into material resembling Death Star shrapnel, revealing what I already knew was there. Even today, more than thirty years later, it is still stored in a box in my dad's basement in Michigan. And no, Dad, I'm not coming to pick it up yet.

The Himalayas. This was my adult Millennium Falcon. I had been reading about this magical place for years. Flying over them in the plane from Kathmandu was like finding that hiding spot. I couldn't touch them yet, but I now had confirmation of their existence. I had talked to people. I had read blogs and seen pictures, but nothing could fully prepare me. I was overcome with a feeling of exuberance and uncontrollable anticipation. My diet had changed considerably since the 80s, so for the first time since I could remember, I had that jittery Mountain Dew buzz again. The seatbelt sign was merely a suggestion as I scrambled from one side of the plane to the other to get another and perhaps different view.

I landed in Leh, the capital of the Ladakh state of the Jammu and Kashmir region. It is perched at 11,482 feet, deep in the Himalayas in Northern India, at the base of the "highest motorable road in the world," Khardung La, at over 18,300 feet. Of course, I had already tagged that as my starting point. Ladakh is a stone's throw from the Pakistan and China borders, and in the periphery lies a host of other daunting peaks over 22,000 feet.

I stepped off the plane at 7 a.m. to a crisp, cloudless 38° morning, the sting in the air instantly vanquishing any residual sweat that I brought with me from the muggy, swamp-like climate of Kathmandu. Instead, I was surrounded by a dry, barren, moonscape that almost immediately sucked the moisture from my mouth and chapped my lips. All around were brown, desolate peaks with the occasional Bob Ross-esque "happy trees" sparsely dotting some of the neighboring valleys.

Glancing around, I immediately became aware that I was near the border in a contentious region. There were military everywhere, all carrying automatic weapons. Nobody smiled. The airport is surrounded by ten-foot-tall stone walls topped with razor wire. A long and turbulent history of violence and unrest exists between India and Pakistan in the Kashmir region, the roots of the conflict lying in the countries' shared colonial past. From the 17th to the 20th century, Britain ruled most of the Indian subcontinent. Over time, however, Britain's power over its colony weakened, and a growing nationalist movement threatened the crown's already weakening grip. Fearing a civil war between India's Hindu majority and Muslim minority, Britain faced increasing pressure to grant independence to its colony, and following World War II, Parliament decided British rule in India should end by 1948. Unfortunately, where Britain drew the lines between India and the new country of Pakistan, it created a territorial dispute between the two countries—specifically claims to religious sites, something that to this day has yet to be resolved.

The city of Leh felt far smaller and more intimate than its 30,000 population would suggest. Whitewashed stone buildings made the monochrome brown hills seem slightly less bland. There is a quaint main street that serves as a market, adorned with an intricate mosaic tile walkway. All along the three hundred-yard long stretch, dogs sun themselves on the warm tiles. The nine-story Leh Palace, which was built in the 16th century in traditional, whitewashed stone Buddhist architecture, looks down over the main bazaar, buzzing with commerce.

After a few days of acclimatizing to the altitude, I decided to do a final tune-up ride to test out my bike, but mostly to test out my lungs. While riding some of the high roads around Leh, I decided to stop at Shanti Stupa. It is a picturesque place of worship, inhabited by Buddhist monks, set high on a mountaintop overlooking Leh, some 1,500 feet below. As I was admiring the timeless, simplistic beauty, one of the monks approached me, enamored by my bicycle. His name was Lobzang, and his flowing burgundy robe, eyes filled with the wisdom of his 60-plus years, and compassionate smile made me feel immediately grateful for this chance meeting. I shared my story with him, and he invited me inside to have tea and hear more of my travels.

His home was an intimate yet welcoming room, approximately ten feet by ten feet. The smell of incense permeated the space, and the view from the cracked, single-pane window overlooked the Leh valley. Ornate rugs draped across the floor, while pads for sleeping flanked the perimeter of the room. The walls were jubilant with color and had photos of a smiling Dali Lama. There was a small table where we sat and enjoyed our masala (chai) tea. In this peaceful stillness, I was compelled to just be present, sitting quietly and observing the space, feeling grateful for this experience. Until his iPhone rang and broke the silence. Lobzang looked at me, embarrassed, and apologized for the interruption. I chuckled, mostly at the fact that he has an iPhone—actually an iPhone 6, which was newer than my iPhone 5.

After his call, Lobzang offered me some *tsampa*. Made from barley, sugar, water, cheese, and congealed together with yak butter, it is a brown, doughy paste that you squish with your hand to form into a ball. It's an acquired taste... that I quickly acquired.

We took some photos and shared several laughs and a heartfelt hug before parting. It turns out he is on Facebook, and we're now officially *friends*. Before departing, Lobzang gave me a small bag of his barley for my travels. “It’s good for health. Will keep you strong on your journey,” he told me.

CHAPTER 3

My Millenium Falcon

Every time my dad visits me in Colorado from his home in our old rural farm town in Michigan, he looks at the mountains and skyline with seemingly new eyes—and he has been to Colorado a dozen times over the years. Maybe I had taken "my mountains" for granted having lived in Colorado for twenty-five years, but now in India, I understood what my dad experienced each time he visited me.

On my adult Christmas morning, I awoke mesmerized by the grandeur of the Himalayas. Thinking of my dad, I was left pondering . . . how do you describe a blue that is bluer than any blue sky you have ever seen? My dad always asks rhetorically while gazing off at the mountains in Colorado, "How do you describe something that is indescribable? It would be like describing color to someone who has always been blind."

The sun was just barely peeking over the mountains, with seemingly one eye open, wondering if I, too, were awake. This warming glance began to melt off the thin layer of ice on the ground from the prior day's storm, and by 8 a.m., instead of running to the base of the Christmas tree to tear open the Millennium Falcon, I set out on my journey into the Himalayas and up Khardung La, the highest motorable road in the world.

Just before pushing those first pedals, I received a message from Jenna back in Madagascar.

As you begin another cycling journey, I hope . . .

That the road is curvy but kind

That the hills lift you to new heights within yourself and the world

That the cold nights are cradled by the warmth of fulfillment

That the people you meet leave a print on your heart, and that you leave prints on theirs, next to the tire prints left on the road

That you forge your own path, and the unknown embraces you as you embrace it yourself

That the fierce winds in every direction remind you of all of the people who love you and are sending that love your way

That the world spins by, but not too quickly, because every sight and every moment is precious.

With that additional push of inspiration, I began pedaling my fully loaded, rotund bike up the mountain pass, each pedal stroke lurching forward like I was spring-loaded. *Dial it back*, I told myself. *Control your youthful enthusiasm, at least a little.* The Leh Manali highway is just under three hundred miles, but I would tack on a few more with the detour over Khardung La. How long would it take? Based on the condition of the road and altitude, it was anyone's guess.

I had a daunting task for day 1 of over 7,000 feet of climbing spread harshly over the next twenty-five miles, but it was no matter. The sky was blue; that indescribable blue. The cool breeze gently kissed my cheeks, and the single-lane paved road was all mine.

The first fifteen miles were a meditative, gradual, winding ascent cut into the side of this behemoth of a mountain. In some places, it was easily a five hundred-foot sheer drop off to the chalky brown valley below. The distant mountain peaks rocketed out of the valley and clawed their way further into that indescribable cloudless blue sky, continually coaxing me forward. The air was only about 45°, but the intensity of the sun at 15,000 feet made it feel like 70°. The sun climbed higher in the eastern Himalayan sky, luring me and my childlike curiosity. My mind was at ease, and the pedal strokes flowed freely. I reminded myself that only a few weeks earlier, I had been in Boulder, uncomfortably interviewing for a job. But now, I was in my place, and everything was as it should be.

A few hours up the road, I came upon an Indian couple whom I had met a few days prior in the main plaza in Leh. They were in their early 30s, wrapped snuggly in puffy down jackets, and riding custom bikes made from bamboo. Their heads cocked sideways when they saw me pass them while riding in shorts and sandals. I remembered that they were from the southern part of India, so I guess it's whatever you're used to?

We pedaled for an hour together up to the first permit checkpoint and, while there, chatted over an egg sandwich and several cups of chai. Today was their final day, and my first. I listened enthusiastically as they told me tales of their journey throughout India by bicycle, churning even more inspiration within me. They were only going to the top of the pass and then back down, but I planned to go over the backside to the Nubra Valley. We wished each other safe travels, exchanged several warm hugs and went our separate, but same ways.

Five miles up the road, the pavement turned to dirt. My new Indian friends had described it to me as a "bad road." I suppose that was all perspective. In that instant, the road climbed steeper and more ruthlessly. It was the kind of road that showed the weathering effects of being at 17,000 feet through cycles of warm and cold, wet and dry, freeze and thaw, expansion and contraction. Lingering chunks of rubble were littered casually about.

A few minutes later, uninvited clouds rolled in, bringing with them—snow. The temperature dipped, and the water created from the melting residual ice began to once again glaze over the road. Gone were all the memories of the heat of Madagascar and the sauna of Kathmandu. I was back in the mountains and relished every biting slush flake that stung my cheeks as I battled the last six miles to the summit. Around each corner, through my frozen eyelashes, I could see the road clawing higher. Each time I thought I was nearing the summit, I was sternly scolded by another broken, loose switchback that dove deeper into the canyon.

The altitude ticked higher, taking with it any fleeting hints of oxygen. The muscles in my legs whined while my brain felt stupid as I struggled to form coherent thoughts. Maybe in the moment, this was a good thing as my brain became numb to the conflict that I was inflicting upon my body.

Finally, after a couple of hours of unrelenting war, I saw tattered prayer flags, signaling that the summit was near. For some reason, Mother Nature winked at me and opened up the sky to a glistening, indescribable blue that reflected off the mirror of ice and slush that carpeted the broken road. And for a moment, the howling wind was calm, and the prayer flags were still. I basked in the shimmering light for only a few minutes before the weather window began to close. I needed to get rolling before the next lashing.

Then, the road worsened, as if that was possible. The droves of tourists taking selfies at the summit had turned down the way they came up—happy after just seeing the summit. I once again felt like I was "out there," in a foreign and exciting world that few, if any, got to experience.

The hillsides were dusted in what looked like confectioner sugar from the recent storm. Landslides, evidence of the effect of the constantly changing weather patterns, were everywhere. Entire sections of the dirt road simply fell away and tumbled down to the valley below. A recent slide had closed the road and backed up the few cars that had ventured over to this side of the pass. Another advantage of being on a bicycle is that roads are rarely ever closed to you. I simply pedaled my bike around and over the debris and continued on because *bikes always win.*

Oddly, as I lumbered down the beaten mineshaft mistaken for a road, in a moment, it turned to tarmac and began paralleling the Shyok river, which eventually led me to the tiny village of Tangyar a few hours later. It was the first place I'd seen that even remotely resembled civilization. Several dilapidated, yet now familiar stone, whitewashed buildings were cut dauntingly into the mountainside, displaying the only proof that people lived here. The only way up to them was via a scree field of loose rocks with a suggestion of a footpath. My body was approaching total failure from the day's effort, so I laid my bike down, crossed a makeshift bridge over the river, and scrambled up the path to a building with "Homestay" hand-painted on it. Up close, the building was even more debilitated than it had appeared from across the river. Decades of Himalayan weather had battered it to the bone. I yelled around, peeked in windows (which were simply holes with no glass), but there was nobody there, and it looked like there hadn't been in years. The buildings all had dirt floors and thatched roofs, while the only inhabitants I could see were the cows that roamed freely.

I wandered around for an hour while my *check engine* lights were blaring. The village was only a few structures built into a hillside overlooking a river, so I'm sure I must have looked like a crazy person wandering in circles. Just when I thought nobody actually lived in Tangyar, I came across a gentleman in his late 50s, wearing a black North Face fleece jacket, exactly like the one I had in college.

"Homestay?" I asked as I had learned that most people at least knew that expression if nothing else in English.

"Four o'clock," he replied with a subtle smile as he pointed at the seemingly abandoned building with "Homestay" painted on it.

Right. It was barely 1 p.m., and I was shattered. I did my best to convey that I just wanted to lay down and hopefully have some food. He pointed off in the direction across the river on the other side of the valley to another structure.

"Four o'clock."

"Okay," I said in a confused and dejected way while trying to smile and show my appreciation, unsure why he pointed across the valley.

I drank some more water that I had taken from the melting snow feeding the river, ate a pinch of *tsampa* from my bag, then scrambled back down the loose rock path and crossed the river over to the other side of the valley. The few buildings over there seemed to be of slightly newer construction, some with actual windows. It was clearly a more residential part. I had never looked on this side of the river because I was immediately drawn to the only building with "Homestay" painted on it.

I began walking around the cluster of five homes, attempting to find anyone who knew about a potential homestay in Tangyar. After an hour of unsuccessfully knocking on doors and peeking in windows (with actual glass), I saw the same man still wearing his North Face jacket and heading my way.

"You need homestay? Food?" he asked, holding his hands up to his mouth in an eating motion. By this time it was still only 2 p.m.

"Yes!" I replied enthusiastically, as my spirits began to rise, anticipating that something might have changed.

"Three o'clock." He pointed at the home he was walking toward.

I felt once again like Monte Hall was playing a game of "Let's Make a Deal" with me, but three o'clock was better than four o'clock, so I resigned myself to optimistically sitting on a rock and waiting out the next hour—still unsure what that "homestay" option was or where.

I had a ton of food, and I was following a river, so water wasn't an issue. There was plenty of daylight so I could have kept going. However, the past couple of days, which were really only my first two cycling days in India, had crushed me, and I just didn't have the motivation to push another pedal. I could have camped along the river, but I was told that there wasn't much, if any civilization in this area, so I wanted to take advantage of it when I did find it.

Seeing me slump down on the rock, defeated, the man motioned for me to follow him up the path to his home.

"You stay with me," he said in a welcoming yet non-negotiable way.

I leaped from the rock that I was perched on, dragged my bike up the loose gravel path to his home and joined him inside. It was a simple home built of solid concrete, and, like others in town, it had a whitewashed exterior and a thatched roof. He led me to a colorful room with bright red velvet carpet, wood paneling on the walls, and ornate rugs sitting atop cushions for seating and sleeping.

"This your room. Sit and rest." After a pause, he smiled and asked in quite passable English, "Where you begin today?"

"Leh!" I replied enthusiastically.

"Very long journey. You are very strong! You alone?"

I nodded yes with a smile but definitely felt something far south of strong at the moment and very content to not pedal any more that day. He seemed surprised that I was out here by myself, but I wasn't. I'm not sure I would have had it any other way.

I collapsed onto the cushions and after a few moments, the man returned with traditional Ladakhi tea made with butter and salt. I don't think there was actual tea in it, but rather hot water, yak butter, and salt. To this *tea*, he added barley, more butter, yak cheese (which is quite salty), and sugar to form a soup, which was the same potion my friend Lobzang had made for me back in Leh—though in a soup form. It tasted a little like rich, chalky dirt (think: butter and barley), however, sugar helped, and I was starving.

"Do you like *maggi*?" he asked.

"Yes!" This was something I could get into. *Maggi* is essentially instant ramen noodles, the kind we all lived on in college.

He disappeared again and returned a few minutes later with a steaming bowl of *maggi* and a large thermos of chai. I graciously inhaled his entire offering as I felt the calories circulate through my bloodstream.

"You need wash?" he offered a few minutes later, seeing the dried salt plastered on my face. "Warm or cold water?"

"Cold. It's no problem," I replied with a smile, not wanting to be any further burden. I was already so grateful for his kindness and generosity.

"After long journey, warm water is better."

I finished my snack, and he led me to the backyard where he had a solar hot water system. He filled a five-gallon container with hot water and showed me the washroom.

"Oh, one more thing," I asked, "where can I get water to drink?"

He pointed to a hose in the backyard, the same place he'd gotten my bathing water.

"It's okay to drink?" I inquired cautiously.

"From glacier. Very good water. No sick." He pointed up the mountain to the snowcapped peak and the stream flowing directly down from it.

"I must work now. You stay and rest. Be back 4 o'clock and make you dinner."

He informed me that he was a teacher and was going back to the school. Shortly after he left, his wife, daughter, and son came home and warmly greeted the clean, well-fed, and once again energetic stranger seated in their home. By 7 p.m., we were all sitting around a table on the floor, sharing a family dinner of rice, dhal (lentils), potatoes, and curd (yogurt). He apologized for making me go without a proper lunch and waiting this long for real food. All I could do was smile.

I awoke the next morning, well-rested, and asked my host how far it was to Karu.

"Too far," he replied nonchalantly as he brought me some morning tea. "By cycle? Two days. Maybe 90–100 km. Very remote. Steep road. No homestay invitation."

That was apparent when I looked at the map and saw what looked like a squiggly, perfectly cooked spaghetti noodle. Had I looked closer, I would have seen that the spaghetti on my map was another high pass, this one at over 17,000 feet.

From Tangyar, the road immediately deteriorated, with loose rock, dirt, sand, and some broken pavement greeting me resoundingly within my first hour of the ride. Even when the road became modestly paved for a few miles, it was still so steep that it was a constant battle with physics just to keep the bike moving forward and not tip over.

By early afternoon, ominous clouds began to settle in and cast shadows on the brown sugar-coated ground. The higher I climbed, the more I slogged, and the colder it got. The seasonal stream coming down from the top now had ice on it, and in preparation for the final battle, I punched a hole in the stream and topped off all my bottles. Glancing around, it was clear that this mountain range was so high, so cold, and so barren that nothing could live here. It was a canvas of chalky dirt everywhere I turned, with remnants of landslides careening down from the peaks.

This was my second day in a row riding at over 15,000 feet, and it was starting to show. With continual road stretches so steeply sinister, the best I could do was get off and push. I didn't have any altitude issues unless you count extreme fatigue, trouble constructing clear thoughts, and a mild headache, but I just figured those were more a function of the prior day's onslaught. Higher, steeper, colder, and less oxygen—that was the continual punch line in what was becoming a comical undertaking. I could see the top, and it wasn't close. I looked at the map and confirmed it. I had yet to approach the spaghetti part of the road. Sometimes it's more depressing to be able to see how far the end actually is rather than toil in ignorance.

Finally, I simply sat down and started laughing at the absurdity. There was no one around to hear me. There were no people driving by with thumbs up or words of encouragement as when I was ascending Khardung La. Just me, in my head. I saw only two cars the entire time, both momentarily before my laughter outburst. One zoomed by with hardly a hesitation. The other slowed down and asked if I was okay. I guess with the speed I was traveling, the cold in the air, and the look of utter defeat on my face, it was a fair question. I very nearly said, "No." Nearly—but instead smiled and gave a thumbs up. I was fading. Clouds were rolling in. The temperature was below 30°. It was still only 2 p.m. so I had plenty of daylight, but I just didn't have any more legs or, more importantly, any lower gears.

I started thinking of options. Camping at this altitude would seriously test the 20° rating of my sleeping bag, but I wouldn't freeze to death, assuming I could find a flat space in the frozen, pitched scree field. I had been climbing for six hours, and to go back down would just mean a complete do-over of the day, so that was out. During the peak of my laughter, a subtle calm seeped into my oxygen-deprived brain. Maybe it was delirium. I had everything I needed, and I was in a place of unquenchable inspiration—more remote than any place I had ever been. The only option—was up.

I pushed on, dragging my bike around countless loose, steep, and broken switchbacks, too steep to pedal. After an hour, hunched over to catch my breath, I came around another crushing switchback and noticed prayer flags a little way up the road. With renewed enthusiasm, I chugged along at a slightly less annihilated pace and arrived at the summit a half-hour later, immediately realizing that the spaghetti was on the backside! By this time, the temperature was officially biting, and the wind was howling. I quickly dug into my "oh shit" bag, layered up, and pointed downhill. (My "oh shit" bag is just a place at the top of my panniers where I have quick access to emergency clothes like a down jacket, Gore-Tex jacket and pants, beanie, and warm gloves, because, at this altitude, storms come crashing in without notice or invite.)

The road going down from the summit looked as if a backhoe had just come through and torn everything up, leaving piles of loose rocks where a road once had been. I did a quick bolt check to make sure everything on my bike and racks were secure, then smashed through the quarry with renewed vigor. Somehow, the past six hours were immediately vanquished from my brain, possibly the effects of oxygen deprivation caused by crossing another 17,000-foot mountain pass, but mostly the realization that I wouldn't need to camp up there in the fast-approaching storm.

Ten minutes into my off-road descent, the sun came out, and the road (at a line) immediately turned to a newly paved, single-lane tarmac that extended the next twenty-five miles down a spaghetti noodle through the valley and into the small village of Debring, rejoining the Leh Manali highway.

—

A *dhaba* is quite simply a temporary shelter of either tents or other basic construction. There is usually a hard-packed dirt floor and a stove used for cooking, but it is shelter. If you're staying in one, hopefully you know enough to have brought warm clothes. Because the route from Leh to Manali is so long, these offerings are necessary for people to sleep and eat. There simply is nothing else in between. In the particular *dhaba* I found myself in, there was one shared tent that slept a dozen people in the back of the restaurant (if you could call it that), which was also a tent. That's it.

I walked into the main tent (restaurant) and saw a woman who looked to be in her 30s, and her mother, likely in her 50s, both dressed in dirty, yet colorful puffy coats and wrapped in makeshift skirts of heavy, brown yak blankets. They had inviting smiles, but the wrinkles in their faces and the bent posture of their backs told the story of a hard existence. There was a stove in the tent's center, kicking off heat that immediately drew me in. All around the circular, white canvas tent were cots set up for seating, but ultimately for overflow sleeping later in the night. The woman and her mother who ran this *dhaba*, seeing the chill and fatigue in my face, quickly presented me with a bottomless plate of dhal, rice, and roti, and of course, endless cups of chai tea. They spoke no English, and I wonder if they had ever seen a foreigner on a bicycle walk through the door. Moments later and true to form, the winds began to howl, whipping the canvas walls into a thundering chorus. I huddled around the stove and enjoyed my meal while the heat slowly poured back into my bones.

I was the only person in the *dhaba*, so as soon as the ladies saw me scraping the last of my food, they quickly came by and plopped another heaping portion of rice, beans, and roti on my plate, while my cup of chai was never allowed to get below half full. (*Note: whenever someone in India asks, "Chai?" the answer is always, unequivocally "Yes!" "More chai?" "Yes, please!")*

It later struck me that these ladies did not have a vehicle. They likely lived here, day and night for the season, which typically runs May to October (when the snow is gone). I found myself wondering what their life was like—if they had family far away in Leh or some other town, and if so, did they ever see them? They were essentially stranded here, in a tent with dirt floors, no electricity or running water, until supply trucks brought in items each week, which usually consisted of drums of water (for cooking, dishes, and bathing), Coke, bottled water, rice, lentils, and ingredients to make roti. These ladies were constantly singing and always had the biggest smiles on their faces. For a moment I thought, *wow, their life is really hard*. Then my focus shifted. Maybe they think *my* life is hard in America? Theirs is a very simple existence, and they appear so happy, without so many of the self-induced stressors that we westerners (Americans) create for ourselves.

When I was finally topped off and about to burst at the seams, the ladies, still smiling, still singing, took my empty plate and showed me the room in the back. It was a twelve-foot by twelve-foot common area with rugs laid out covering the dirt floor, surrounded all around by more heavy yak blankets. It was essentially a dorm and was as clean as could be expected given the high alpine, arid environment. The price was Rs300 (about $4). Three other Indian men arrived a few minutes later and began to settle into the dorm. All three had strong, deep coughs, an indication that they were either ill or suffering from some altitude sickness—neither of which made me overly interested in sharing a room with them. Instead, I opted to pitch my tent outside at the back next to an abandoned bombed-out jeep that looked to have been there for a decade. But it provided a great shield from the escalating wind and gusts that were ripping down the valley.

I had been above 15,000 feet for four days and above 11,000 feet for nearly two weeks. A great way to combat altitude sickness is hydration. Drink water. A lot—which I had—and this night was no different from other nights. After three days of exposure to these extreme elements, it was even more critical. As a result, I had to get up and go pee on several occasions each night. This night was especially interesting since it was my first night camping in India.

The first time I awoke, I lay cocooned in the warmth of my down sleeping bag, unwilling to get up. I looked at my watch and it was only 1:30 a.m. If it were 6 a.m. or at least some time close to morning, it wouldn't be a big deal. I would just get up and start my day. If I didn't get up now, I knew I would never be able to sleep for the rest of the night, so I reluctantly pulled the zipper on my sleeping bag, sending shards of thin ice fluttering into the air, and poked my head outside. The wind had subsided as I opened my tent to a perfectly still and cloudless night, and in that moment, nothing else mattered. All around, the faint silhouettes of the towering peaks released their grip on a million stars extending just out of their grasp. They seemed so close that I felt I could simply reach out and grab a handful. After several moments of peaceful awe, I crawled back into the warmth of my sleeping bag and drifted back to sleep. I got up twice more that night to pee, but didn't mind a bit.

I awoke the next morning to a bone-chilling cold, the result I suppose of camping at nearly 15,000 feet without the blanket of cloud cover to hold in the previous day's heat, or a yak blanket. Only my nose was sticking out of the sleeping bag to breathe, but as I peered out, I saw the layer of glazed water vapor crystalized like mini stalagmites on the ceiling of the tent. I pulled out my arm and discovered that my water bottles were frozen. The sun had yet to hit the valley, and it was simply too cold to go out yet. Grudgingly, I crawled out of my sleeping bag and went into the *dhaba*, quickly noticing that the heavy coughers had already rolled out. It was only 7 a.m., and already the younger woman was boiling water for chai and rolling out fresh dough for roti. After finishing her morning prayers, the mother proceeded to sweep the dirt floors and fold up the blankets from the night before.

Each day thus far had brought a mix of stress and excitement. Excitement—to see what the day would bring, who I would meet, what the terrain would look like, and where I would sleep and find food. Stress—at the same time, for the same reasons. Sometimes it was a little daunting to leave a place of comfort and security, even one as simple as a *dhaba*, to venture out into the unknown.

I was at 15,000 feet, in one of the most remote parts of India, and my phone did not have a signal. What would I do if something happened? What did we do before we had cell phones, anyway? As kids, we had that silly plastic device screwed to the wall that allowed us to talk to people, but it was screwed to the wall. People born after 1995 probably have never used, nor have likely even seen, a non-cordless rotary telephone.

Growing up in the 1980s, my friends and I would regularly disappear for an entire day deep into the Michigan woods while our parents would fleetingly yell, "Be home by six for dinner!" at the back of our heads as the screen door slammed behind, eagerly launching us into the adventure of the day as we disappeared into the woods. There was no way for others to find us or for us to call our parents if we got lost or hurt. And yet, somehow, everything worked out fine.

Here I was, more than thirty years later, engulfed in another adventure (to be fair, on a much grander scale), far removed from anything familiar, in a place so remote, with nobody knowing where I was and no way to find me should something go sideways. I should have had that same excitement, that anticipation of impending adventure. As kids, we have no fear, but as adults, we read the news, and we listen to stories about bad things that happen to people. Many times, we let that fear infiltrate and lay siege to the adventurous part of our brain. I was at times guilty of letting my mind visit there too, but once I pushed through the initial trepidation and need to feel safe each morning, I stoked the flame of that insatiable curiosity and felt my intrinsic childlike sense of adventure resurrected. Though the arrow would regularly bounce back and forth between the extreme poles of *excitement* and *stress*, gradually it skewed considerably more to the *excitement* side.

A day later, I made it through the wind tunnel of the Moray Plains, a road that otherwise benignly meanders through a valley at 14,000 feet, framed in by towering peanut-butter colored walls, down the snaking three miles on a blown-out, rutted descent into Pang, another *dhaba*. In familiar fashion, I coasted in on fumes with nothing left in my tank. This time it was only 11:30 a.m., but I was done. I never even considered continuing on to Lachalang La, another not so benign 17,000-foot pass that awaited me immediately as I would be leaving Pang. I had been living above 14,000 feet for a week, and although each day brought increased stamina and higher red blood cell counts, my legs were still pissed about the climb over Taglang La at 17,500 feet two days earlier, and would absolutely not let me forget about Khardung La at 18,500 feet the day before that. I couldn't argue. They made a strong point.

Unlike Debring, Pang sits at just above 15,000 feet and is actually a permanent structure made of stone, with wooden-framed windows and the word "HOTEL" etched into the flaking white paint. I wandered my way inside the roughly eight-hundred-square-foot box and was surprised to find such an elaborate interior. Instead of dirt, ornate rugs were covering the concrete floor, and lime green walls peeked out from behind kitschy Indian art. Wooden benches covered with pillows and more rugs lined the perimeter of the main room, while a single lonely light swung from the tapestry-covered ceiling.

The woman who ran the *dhaba* offered me a private tent out back for Rs500, about $7.50. It was made of white canvas that subtly revealed the abuse of the sun and wind but was otherwise flawlessly clean and boasted a comfy bed and rugs covering the dirt floor. It was paradise. I dropped my bags, dumped my bike, and quickly went out back to find a bucket to bathe with before dissolving onto the bed.

Over the next few days, I crested a handful of mountain passes over 15,000 feet that would make the highest mountains in Colorado look like speed bumps. I was lost deep in the chalky canyons, squarely in between Leh and Manali in what felt like the driest and harshest terrain on Earth. Weathered cracks across the road were like the aging wrinkles chiseled by time and wisdom on the face of an old man. The wind had scoured this place for centuries, carving out jagged spires and conversely smooth peaks—almost as if some master sculptor had molded them. Although I was in awe of these features, I was quickly snapped back into reality one day when I noticed a delivery truck that had rolled off the single-lane road and down the embankment several hundred feet below, crushing its body, ripping off its axle, and scattering its contents—most of which had already been scavenged.

Each morning, the sun cautiously peered over the dusty peaks, once again dripping a honey color into the valley while bringing life and warmth to the frozen valley floor. The sounds of nothingness were almost deafening. I think of my dad regularly, the emotion and inability to speak he would experience when we hiked on paths together back in Colorado. "How do you describe mountains to someone who has never seen mountains?" he would always ask me. I don't know, Dad. I really don't. India had left me speechless since I first arrived here much the same way my dad is when he visits me in Colorado. I wish I could share this emotion with him. It reminds me of the pop-up books he would read to me when I was a kid. Each time he would flip the page, a cardboard insert would unfold and explode out at me, providing wonder and amusement, and unknowingly an inquisitive passion that would stick with me my entire life.

In spite of this overwhelming beauty, there is one thing about being on a bike that infuriates me, however. One thing. Wind. Nothing else. Just wind. It blows through my skull, scrambles my brain, and shatters my psyche the way a wrecking ball demolishes a once-formidable building. And today it didn't let up until I was smashed into rubble. I could feel it picking up as I descended the Gata Loops, a series of twenty-two hairpin turns and switchbacks meandering down nearly 2,000 feet to the valley floor. But it wasn't a crosswind. It was a direct hit, square across my chin. The rumors of wind in this region were indeed true.

At one point, I was ten miles from Sarchu, a *dhaba* where I planned to sleep that night. Through this desolate landscape, I could see the glimmer of shiny buildings in the distance. It was tangible. As the crow flies, it was at most three miles. I came around a bend, but the road retreated three miles back into the canyon and three miles back out in order to cross the river. As I pedaled deeper into the canyon, I could see Sarchu fading in the distance, and with it went my composure and optimism. I came out of the canyon, back into the blunt force headwind, with no place to hide. I saw Sarchu again. Three miles away. It was right there, but I couldn't reach it. The same way a toddler tries to reach candy on the counter until he finally collapses and cries in frustration. It was futile.

I pressed on into the pummeling wind that was scouring my skin, but mostly, my mind. Regardless of how hard I pushed the pedals, I just wasn't getting anywhere. The two trucks that did eventually pass me were both full and thus had no space for my bike. The final insult was that they both responded, very kindly, in broken English, that Sarchu was only three miles away, as they pointed helpfully at the glimmering candy still out of reach in the distance.

Four hours later, I arrived in Sarchu. I wasn't just fried, I was wind burned, salty, and sandblasted. Unlike the previous *dhabas*, the accommodations were essentially corrugated steel boxes. As I approached, I saw a sign that had the words "Private Room, Hot Water" scratched into it. My room actually had the word "Room" painted on it, which was helpful in my dilapidated state.

I walked around outside and glanced at the sign promising hot water, hoping it wasn't just my wind-scrambled brain playing tricks on me. I had taken several frigid yet refreshing bucket baths, and it was better than nothing, but I had my hopes pinned on something that seemed too good to be true. I anxiously asked the woman who ran the *dhaba* for a bucket of her advertised "hot water," which turned out to be just a bucket of water sitting out in the sun. So, it was *warmish.* With another piece of candy swiped from my grasp, I went around the side of the building, since there wasn't an official washroom, stripped down, and dumped the first cup of tepid water over my head, sending rivers of salty water cascading down my face and into my mouth.

From the outside, my room looked like a shed to store a lawnmower and a few rakes in my dad's back yard in Michigan. However, upon entering, it was far more luxurious and accommodating than the exterior facade was masking. Elaborate yellow tapestries were hung from the walls and ceiling, buffering the sounds of the wind lashing sand against the corrugated metal exterior. The bed was a four-inch piece of foam laid out on a wooden frame with more colorful blankets spread out, almost daring me to lay down. At the head of the bed were six more heavy blankets, foreshadowing how cold the night would get.

It was apparent that this woman, like the others I had met along this route, took immense pride in her business, which is interesting because there is no competition. There is no better place across the street that travelers can opt for if the offerings are not up to their standard. This is it. The floors inside this *dhaba* were hard-packed dirt and were constantly being watered to keep the dust down and then swept with makeshift brooms made of sticks and straw lashed together with twine. In the middle, there was a small stove that vented through the roof, with a charred smoke ring encapsulating the tin shaft. Somehow, she and her husband were able to scavenge pieces of shrub from the otherwise barren moonscape, although I'm not sure where. I hadn't seen anything other than rock and sand for five days. What they did find was incredibly dry and burned fast, and the heat they created, even for ten minutes, was a nice reprieve that evening before crawling into bed.

Throughout my travels in Vietnam, Zimbabwe, Madagascar, Bolivia, Peru, and now India, I have experienced an odd paradox. I'm anonymous because I'm a foreigner in a far-off land, and nobody knows me or my story. I don't speak the language. I'm a stranger, and I love it. It's where I'm most free; like that young boy in the woods in Michigan. Conversely, I'm not anonymous. I stick out, and I hate it. No matter how tanned my skin gets from the sun at this altitude, regardless of what color I paint my bike, I'm not from around here.

In almost all of the places I have visited, especially the remote Himalayas, they see very few western travelers, far fewer on a bike and fewer still who are alone. Those looks of curiosity that quickly give way to ear-to-ear smiles, warm my soul and get me out of bed (or sleeping bag) every morning. I witness the irony of the hospitality of traveling here in this otherwise inhospitable landscape. The kindness and generosity of everyone I have met has been incredible. It is a simple life, and each day that I spend here, I am convinced that people really are just people.

As a culture in the western part of the world, we are so good at making our lives more complicated, usually with things that we *need*—a new car, a bigger house, new clothes. I've been traveling with two pairs of socks, one pair of underwear, some bike clothes and one "outfit" for when I'm not on the bike and want to look *normal*—as if that's even possible here. Initially, when I set out on bike tours several years ago, I carried more. More options. More *backups*. More, *just in case*, but essentially just more *stuff*. Now, after being in India for a couple of weeks, I look in my bag and wonder what else I can let go of, and somehow this feeling of *less* leaves me with a feeling of *more*.

I had been on this route for over a week and had begun to notice subtle changes. The altitude was lower. Nights were warmer (evidenced by the fact that my water bottles didn't completely freeze). But mostly, I was noticing changes inside of me. I was less anxious each day and more curious to see what was over each incremental, physically debilitating mountain pass. I had no internet access, and the separation from what might be happening in the rest of the world, or my own world back in Colorado, was liberating. But I was going too fast. The further south that I traveled, the closer I got to more densely populated regions, to other tourists, to the tourist city of Manali (and the endpoint of this route), and easier living. And with that thought, my anxiety crept back in.

In prolonged times of internal and physical struggle, while clawing my way up one of the ubiquitous soul-crushing mountain passes that each day stood in my way as I traversed this region, there were fleeting moments when I thought to myself, *yes, a soft bed and hot shower sound amazing*. But then I would crest that pass, arrive at a *dhaba*, and be greeted by the personification of true kindness, given a hot meal, a bucket to bathe with, and shelter—and everything was right again. With my longing for an easier passing immediately vanquished, I found happiness and contentment in the simplicity.

So then, how do I slow down time, appreciate that the suffering and hard times are part of the ride and should be celebrated and cherished as well? This is not exclusively a lesson about cycling, but rather a metaphor about life as well, and I was taking notes. I thought back to the Alan Watts quote tucked in the back corner of my brain that seeps out from time to time: "You don't go to a concert just for the encore. You want to hear and experience the show in its entirety."

One day, without notice, the road improved. Cars, other than military vehicles, whizzed by. But then: Pow! Boom! Just like in the old Batman cartoons, the words were seemingly etched into the sky. Peaks were exploding all around me. Gone were the dry, brown, eroding sandstone sculptures, replaced by craggy granite spears with centuries-old glaciers perched atop, dripping down like the whipped cream on top of a melting ice cream sundae. I saw trees, their vibrant green slowly turning to gold and beginning to give way to autumn. There was again a lushness. Water flowed lovingly from those same glacial peaks, bringing life to the valley.

I was below 11,000 feet, the lowest I had been since I arrived in Leh. After living above 15,000 feet and summiting numerous climbs above 17,000 feet, my lungs were the size of watermelons. I had perfected the art of holding my breath while pedaling up those 17,000-foot passes as a truck would chug by me, spewing diesel exhaust in my face. Here, I could flippantly denounce the modest *hills* that stood before me now, guarding the gateway to Manali. Around each bend and over each rise, I was moved to emotion with the overwhelming and paralyzing new beauty of this part of the Himalayas.

I slept in a modest hotel with clean sheets and hot water in the quaint village of Sissu. I felt strangely out of place in this opulence after having slept in *dhabas* the past week, but I suppose it was a subtle teaser to what likely lay ahead in the ultra-touristy town of Manali the next day.

The sky was clear, the road was battered and full of switchbacks, the kind of road that would make a local shock and muffler repair shop rich simply by the carnage that it inflicts. It was once again my perfect cocktail. Because Rohtang La is the closest and easiest accessible pass to Delhi, it is quite touristy. I received numerous honks, thumbs-ups, and general encouragement as I churned the pedals like a machine around each incremental switchback. Everyone was ecstatic for the opportunity to experience this tiny slice of the Himalayas, and I couldn't argue. Around each bend was a different and somehow more enthralling view of the daunting peaks that were drawing nearer with each pedal stroke. The crowds of people became denser, and I felt like I was climbing Alpe d'Huez in the Tour de France as fans lined the road, separating as I churned through, startled to see this strange guy on a green bike scaling a road that they had driven up.

Immediately after cresting the summit, I pitched off the backside of Rohtang La, and for some reason, I had the Lumineers cover of the old Talking Heads song "This Must Be the Place" in my head. I whizzed down the swerving, meticulously paved roads, rocketing me closer to Manali, filled with absolute euphoria. Somewhere along the route, a few faint tears escaped from my eyes, possibly from the warm wind sneaking around my sunglasses, but likely from the emotion bubbling up inside of me. I began belting out the lyrics at the top of my lungs as I descended the undulating curves without once grabbing my brakes. " . . . *I guess we must be having fun. The less we say about it the better . . . make it up as we go along. Feet on the ground, head in the sky, I know nothing's wrong. Heeeyyy! I got plenty of time."*

Slow down! It's going too fast, I tried to remind myself as I descended thirty miles past cascading waterfalls, through two climate zones, and more than 6,000 vertical feet to the bustling tourist city of Manali, a permagrin plastered across my wind-burned face as I skidded into town.

Manali has a population of about 8,000 full-time residents but felt much larger and suffocating due to its influx of tourists, and I seemed to be arriving at peak season. Ice cream shops and pizza places lined the narrow main strip, while paragliding and 4x4 companies hocked their excursions from every street corner. Cows, dogs, and even monkeys lounged around in the warm pink sunset that drips into the chaotic streets, while tourists outfitted with North Face backpacks tromped around gushing about their upcoming adventure. After where I had been for the previous ten days, I fell into sensory overload and instead reluctantly deferred an intrinsic ice cream craving and quickly scurried up a steep alley to find a quiet haven for the night.

CHAPTER 4

I've Got Worms

I awoke the next morning feeling—off. My stomach gave the impression that I was five months pregnant but the smells emanating from my body indicated something far worse. Unfortunately, these symptoms weren't unfamiliar to me. After coming home to Colorado from Madagascar, I found myself battling two rounds of a very clingy giardia parasite, during which my friends came up with the nickname, "Jerry-ardia." They're so clever. Fortunately, the symptoms were quite mild: mainly a grossly distended stomach. But the smell—wow. That was the ringer. Imagine an opossum roadkill that had baked on the highway in Alabama for three days in July, then crawled into your small intestines to fester and make a home. Yeah. Many nights I actually woke myself up simply from that smell.

I guess it should not surprise me that something happened to my health in India. It's all part of the experience, I suppose. The way I looked at it, by the time I had traveled through India *and* Africa, I would have bikepacked my way through the two largest petri dishes in the world. Things are happening there that scientists don't even know about, and if they do, they don't have names for them yet.

So thus began giardia, round three. It was kinda like *Rocky III*, and this giardia was Clubber Lang (remember Mr. T?). It was bigger, meaner, and just as arrogant. Fortunately, I was in Manali, a recognized tourist hub with an established medical facility that caters to ill-equipped foreign immune systems.

So that morning, I pedaled down to the Lady Willingdon clinic at 7:30 a.m. It's an inviting, single-story wooden building, painted white with green trim, and rows of potted flowers line the walkway where patients queue up. On the front of the building are hand-painted stick figures of the various ailments that someone seeking medical attention might suffer from. They ranged from a man on crutches with only one leg (not me), a pregnant woman with three children clinging on to her (nope), and a man in a squat position with an odd grimace on his face (ding!).

Unfortunately, the clinic did not open until 9 a.m., but I was told I could go to the 24-hour ER instead. The ER cost would be Rs500 ($7.50), or I could wait until 9 a.m. for a regular consult for Rs50 ($0.75). I didn't feel that my situation justified occupying the ER team, so I waited until 9 a.m. and then put myself on the list.

At 9 a.m. I was promptly called into the doctor's *office*, if you could call it that, where I met my doctor. He was an Indian man, approximately 35, wearing a crisp white lab coat, and spoke excellent English. His office was just through the main door of the clinic, where he sat behind a very worn wooden desk in front of which was a rickety wooden stool for the patients. The people waiting for their consultation stood in line, two feet behind the stool until it was their turn. When it was my turn, I simply took one step forward and sat down. I guess HIPAA is not an issue in India. I explained my symptoms and shared with him what antibiotics I had taken for this problem before.

"Yes, yes. We have this medication. Let's get a sample first," he responded.

I went to the front desk, picked up my sample cup, which was the size of a shot glass (and no plastic bag to return it in), and went to the sample room. The sample room was a steel box, marked "gents" with tiled floors and walls. It was simply a bathroom with nothing more than a squat toilet in the floor. However, there was no light, only a tiny window and a bucket in the corner to wash with. From the smell, it was not a clean space, which perhaps made the lack of light slightly more comforting? Kinda like, if I can't see it, then it must not be that bad. I went back to the front desk and asked for some toilet paper. The lady sighed and came back with four squares. Yes, she counted them out. Four squares—apparently the foreigner allowance. I guess I should have been happy since paper really isn't used in India and was thus hard to find, but perhaps since Manali is a tourist hub, they have to cater to foreigners. A few minutes later, I took my sample back to the front desk and was told to come back in forty-five minutes. I had this same test two months earlier in Colorado, and it had taken three days.

Forty minutes later (they were early), I was called in to talk to the doctor again. "Ascariasis. Roundworm. Very common in India," he calmly explained to me in a way that I'm sure he has explained to thousands of patients before me.

His prescription? Albendazole. The same med my doctor in Colorado suggested and for which I had paid $400. I went across the courtyard, picked up my prescription and was on my way.

- Total time spent from consult to departure: 90 minutes.
- Total cost: Less than $4.00.
- Consult: Rs50 ($0.75).
- Lab: Rs190 ($2.87).
- Albendazole. Rs30 ($0.45).

The following day, I stopped at a pharmacy in another town and bought two more pills for Rs18 ($0.27), though the pharmacist only charged me Rs10 ($0.15) because he didn't have change for Rs20. Lesson learned from this: if you're going to get sick, do it in India because it's inevitable anyway. If you can deal with the *sample room*, then it's a win.

CHAPTER 5

Mind if I Sleep Here?

Shortly after my visit to the Manali clinic, the dead opossum that was living in my gut had gotten the eviction notice, and I was antsy to get back on my bike. Manali is a comfortable tourist town with all the accommodations one could need: good food, clean hotels, and, as I found out, impeccable health care. However, I was beginning to feel claustrophobic from the inundation of western tourists, droning on about their adventures. Sure, they may have looked like me, but for some reason, I didn't see myself as a tourist and surely not like "one of them." In my mind, my travels were more pure, more authentic. It's interesting the stories we create in our minds.

I walked into several tourist adventure shops intent on getting a feel for the route out of Manali. A dozen shiny red bikes lined the sidewalk in front of each shop, and inside, the walls were plastered with the same glossy stock photos. On one wall there was a blond girl, likely from Connecticut, in her early 20s, launching off a cliff with a parachute while strapped to a guide. On the opposite wall was the ever-popular photo of the family of four, probably from San Francisco, getting popcorned around the inside of an open-air jeep, all with seemingly artificially enormous smiles on their faces. This definitely wasn't me. After seeing the same eye bulge and hearing the word "crazy" followed by warnings of my impending death enough times from all the shop owners about my cycling ambitions, I climbed aboard Kermit and continued my way south.

The road out of Manali turned out to be a single lane, newly paved, thirty-mile descent through a snaking canyon, passing tiny villages along the way. It was a welcome introduction to this region, a stark contrast from two weeks of cycling the barren moonscape of Ladakh. Children in tidy blue uniforms on their way to school. Men walking to work. Shop owners opening their doors for the day. Everyone greeted me with a warm smile and a "Namasteeeee!" This wasn't so bad.

As I was mindlessly zooming down this single-lane road, I careened around a corner and locked up my brakes rather than careen into the approximately eighty long-haired sheep, stretched from one side of the road to the other, migrating their way downhill, completely shutting down the road. The herder was a sharp-dressed man who looked about my age, with short brown hair, a thick mustache, and wearing sandals, grey slacks and a grey hoody. I was quite surprised by his appearance, instead expecting someone more "herder-looking" with tattered clothes and an overall shabbier appearance. He seemed quite calm and aware of the fact that his flock was occupying the entirety of the road, while oncoming cars were uncharacteristically patient, likely because they were familiar with this phenomenon. This wasn't a traffic jam, more like a traffic *lamb*.

"Namaste!" he shouted, unfazed by the screeching of my tires as I blindly came upon him.

We exchanged a smile as I rang my bell and attempted to carve my way through the sea of lambs.

The peaceful meandering route down from Manali continued its gentle caress of my senses until Kullu, and the *Tunnel of Doom* (remember that?) Maybe this is what the eye-bulging was all about? After surviving one of the most terrifying roads that I had thus far experienced in India, navigating through total darkness as lumbering trucks and busses that were oblivious to my presence threatened to end my life, my heart slowly began to settle back into my chest. I now found myself back in the world of light on a paved road that climbed gently along the rushing but murky Tirthan river until I arrived in Banjar. It was a narrow mountainside town with a little over a thousand residents, built along a steep road—a grade punishing enough that I had to push my bike through town for about a quarter of a mile until I found the first guesthouse, where I walked inside to inquire. The shiny, white tile floors were immaculately polished, and a smell of curry permeated the air.

"Hello, I am the receptionist," said a young Indian boy with terrific English, dressed in a clean, white, collared shirt, his youthful voice cracking and echoing off the tile.

"How old are you?" I asked in a confused manner.

"I'm 11 years old. Would you like to see the room?" he responded matter-of-factly, completely discounting the angle of my question. "The room is 1,000 rupees ($14). It is the only room available at this price. All others are much more expensive. This one over here is our VIP room and is 1,500 rupees. I would not lie to you."

A pleasant smile stretched across his face, displaying his bright white teeth. This was clearly not his first day on the job. It is common in India to barter for rooms, so I offered him Rs800, about $11. He never flinched. That's what I get for trying to barter with an eleven-year-old. Following an awkward staring contest, I didn't have the energy to do anything other than have a shower and lay down, so I paid the kid $11.

After cleaning up, I wandered down the street to a small restaurant. It was owned and run by an older man, likely in his 70s. He was stocky and had heavy, droopy eyelids that reminded me of Yoda. And like Yoda, his eyes also likely carried with them the weight of years of experience and wisdom.

"Mind if I smoke?" he asked as I entered *his* restaurant, the wall behind him prominently painted with the words "No Smoking" in three-foot letters.

Perplexed, I chuckled. "No problem." I appreciated his irony.

He promptly served me up a hearty plate of what I have come to expect and crave: bottomless rice, dhal, mixed vegetable curry, chapatti (local Indian flatbread), and chai for Rs60 (about $0.90). After making quick work of his offering, I bid him a "Namaste" and promised to see him in the morning for breakfast before leaving town.

"Tomorrow, road very steep," he warned in broken English (or Yoda-speak), with his hand pointing up at a seventy-degree angle—

leaving me with the feeling that I was being sent off to face Darth Vadar in the morning.

Each day on the bike is a new battle, a new curiosity, a new high—or sometimes a crushing new low, and thus far in India, at least a hundred happy new smiles. I had been going downhill for three days straight, barely pushing a single pedal stroke. From my high of 18,000 feet in Ladakh to 8,000 feet in Manali and now 2,000 feet lower in Banjar, the difference in climate, oxygen, and concentration of people was—noticeable. A further departure south from the mountains meant even more people, even hotter weather, even more traffic—everything that I was bracing myself for. In a couple of days, I would arrive in Rishikesh for a week of yoga to reset not only my body after a month into this journey, but mostly my mind after the prior year (wow, that last bit really reeks of western cliché).

As promised, I stopped in Yoda's shop for breakfast, and on cue, he smiled, welcomed me, and asked if I minded if he smoked. I once again laughed and nodded. He promptly loaded me up with a belly full of greasy fried eggs and three cups of chai.

"Namaste!" the old man jubilantly encouraged me, his arm pointing up in the air, up Jalori Pass, Darth Vader awaiting.

"Namaste!" I returned. The road couldn't really be that bad?

It was 8 a.m., and all the children on their way to school giggled at me as I passed by. The boys were dressed in their uniforms of crisp long-sleeved blue button-up shirts and pressed grey slacks, and the girls were wearing knee-length pink dresses with flowing white slacks underneath.

"Good morning!" they all screamed in broken unison. It was the perfect start to my morning.

Almost as soon as I had yelled "Namaste," the smile was quickly snatched from my face as the road launched up into the sky, meandering its way almost drunkenly into a dense forest. Up into the lush canopy of trees that filled the canyon, the road climbed, first kindly, then gradually, then unforgivingly, finally—mockingly. Although I had a map on my phone, due to the absurdity of the pitch, I had no idea where it would end or how long. I was beside myself. Actually, I was beside my bike because I couldn't pedal it. I had never seen a road this steep before. A path, yes, but not a road. Not in Vietnam. Not through the Andes in Bolivia and Peru. Not in the Ladakh region where I had just been. This was absurd.

Over the next fifteen miles, the otherwise pleasantly paved road gave way to a busted, eroded by water, death march as I dug deep within myself in an effort to battle the Dark Side. Four hours in, I simply sat down on the side of the road, knowing that I still had probably another couple of miles to the top. A family in a shiny Toyota Hilux truck coming from the other direction stopped to check on me, no doubt because they saw the dejection in my face, the salt ring on my jersey, and the sweat pouring profusely down my temples. And, of course, the truck was black.

"I am altering the deal. Pray I don't alter it any further," I initially heard this line in my head from Vader to Lando Calrissian just after Han Solo was put into *carbon freeze*. But actually, the driver rolled down his window and, with a generous smile, called out, "Hello! *Lassi*?" I could feel the air conditioning blasting out the window toward me, taunting me with its comfort, while the allure of his creamy beverage offering made my mouth water. "Never see cyclists on this road. Need help?" My heart rate was spiked, and I could barely hear him over the flow of blood drumming through my ears.

"How far to the top?" I inquired rhetorically, already knowing the answer.

"Close. Maybe four kilometers," he said in an encouraging manner. By my math, that was at least another hour—two if I was walking. In times like this, all I could do was laugh because the absurdity of the situation felt like I was in a comic strip. I gratefully accepted his chilled lassi (traditional Indian drink that is a blend of yogurt and spices), dusted myself off, and *pushed* on.

I tried singing some Sinatra because it seemed more productive than battling the taunting voices of Vader in my head. Honestly, I was willing to try anything to find a reason to keep pushing pedals and not simply tip over from lack of inertia. Two hours later, and just after 2 p.m., I reached the summit and continued over the top. The cool air at the 8,500-foot pass dried my sweat and wiped away the agony of the past five hours, and like a dry erase board, I had a fresh start. I was left with a two-hour descent in every way mirroring the road that I had just come up, ultimately depositing me in the rugged, muggy, truck stop town of Luhri. It was the kind of place where people only stop for necessities, but otherwise continue on through. A small town at the confluence of three roads along the Sutleg river; it was the first town I had been to in India where language was a problem. All the signs were written in Hindi, which made finding a place to sleep even more challenging. There were no blatant "HOTEL" signs like the ones scratched into the sides of the buildings in Ladakh. I garnered more than a few stares from people clearly perplexed by the foreigner who, for some reason, had appeared in their village.

I wandered around for about an hour, seemingly aimlessly. In a village the size of Luhri consisting of a single dusty street spanning four blocks, it didn't take much time for people to notice. Finally, a man in his early 20s wearing a Michael Jordan t-shirt and skinny jeans came up to me and asked if I needed a place to sleep. Apparently, I had *that* look. He spoke only a few words of English but led me down an alley and up some stairs. He opened the door, and it was not what I was expecting. Clearly, it hadn't been cleaned and in hindsight, I'm quite certain it wasn't even a hotel room. The Dora the Explorer sheets, while whimsical and reassuring, *seemed* to have been changed. However, there was laundry hanging in the bathroom, along with a used toothbrush, a razor, and freshly shaved whiskers in the sink. *Does someone live here?* I wondered to myself as the man was showing me the room. There were no other choices and, if there were, I didn't have it in me to explore them. No sooner did I give him the Rs1,400 (about $7) than he vanished. Was this his room that he was renting to me for the night, in an attempt to make a few extra rupees? Or did it belong to some other person, possibly unaware that their room just got rented for the night? At that point, I really didn't care.

I laid in bed, shirtless, on top of the Dora the Explorer sheets, under the rickety ceiling fan, earplugs wedged in, dreaming of cold weather and once again being nestled in my down sleeping bag somewhere else, high in the Himalayas. Even though I was exhausted from the day, I could never fully relax because the entire evening I lay wondering if the resident of the room would come back. The answer, I found out shortly thereafter, was "yes"—at about 9:30 p.m., just as I was finally drifting off to sleep.

I heard a knock on my door but declined to answer. Through the half-opened window, I could hear a man make a phone call, likely to the person who had sublet his room. He hung up, pounded on the door, saying something to me in a language that of course I could not understand, though the tone was unmistakable. I didn't dare answer. I pictured myself in a similar situation. I had gone out for dinner with some friends. I had a great evening, and all I wanted to do was take a shower and go to sleep. However, when I came home, I was locked out of my own house, and someone was sleeping in my bed. I'm sure he wasn't too happy, but at this point, I wasn't super motivated to get out of bed in the middle of the night and sort this out. I jammed my earplugs further into my ears as fatigue from the day overcame me. The knocking and yelling eventually subsided, and I drifted off to sleep peacefully.

CHAPTER 6

I'm Still Gonna Shine

For the second day in a row, I found myself entrenched in a gladiator-esque battle to the death, a familiar theme thus far in India. The road clawed its way up the mountain, intent on busting a hole in the sky, ascending in a twisting, serpentine manner along the horseshoe-shaped canyon. Steep, but still rideable. Challenging, yet not crippling. Almost before I pushed my first pedal stroke, my shirt was already wet and clinging to my back like plastic wrap. After being in the arid region of Ladakh, my skin gratefully sucked up the moisture the way a desert floor drinks in the rain after a storm.

Here, the beauty of the state of Himachal Pradesh conjures up lucid memories of Colorado in the spring. It reminds me of home, and even though I'm 8,000 miles away, I never want to leave here. Ladakh, in the Jammu and Kashmir state where I began, had been spectacular for sure. The true beauty of it was simply the all-ness and the nothingness, simultaneously. The sheer magnitude of the towering, peanut-butter peaks literally took my breath away, while not seeing a person or town for days allowed me to completely lose myself. It was like being on another planet.

Himachal was different. Cycling through a dew-dripping canopy of trees while waterfalls cascade down the slopes and across the road, there was a lushness surrounding me that I hadn't felt in several weeks. Monkeys called from the forest and scurried across the road moments before I pedaled by. The vegetation was so dense that on one side, I could step five feet off the road and completely vanish. Five feet off the road on the other side, and I would tumble down a ravine dropping 3,000 feet to the valley floor below. Guard rails? Right. There were some. The ones I had seen were mostly mangled and twisted metal, splashed with a rainbow of colors taken from the vehicles they saved from launching off into the abyss. Safety is an illusion here.

For six hours, I methodically churned pedals, a continual flow of sweat pouring through my helmet as I anemically crawled my way into the sky. At 2 p.m., I reached the small mountain top village of Bahli and stopped to refuel. Maybe six buildings were lining the narrow dirt road with a few other homes sparsely scattered further up the hillside.

Immediately, I was surrounded by seven very curious local men who appeared to be in their 40s. They saw me grinding up the road and adjourned from their afternoon chai to quickly trot out and greet me. Before I could even stop, I was offered a chair to sit while someone else promptly put a steaming hot chai in my hand, only moments before overwhelming me with the usual gauntlet of questions that I had come to expect—an indicator of genuine curiosity and a desire to connect. I'm left shaking my head when I try to imagine this scenario taking place in the US, envisioning a foreigner rolling up on a bike in a small town in Michigan, only to have a bunch of people immediately drop what they're doing and rush across the street to give him a chair and a beer, eager to meet him and hear his story. Probably not.

"Why you do not speak Hindi?" one man asked me in a very serious tone as if to imply, how is it possible for me to travel in this country, or any country, if I don't speak the local language? It did indeed seem like a fair question.

"I have only been in India for three weeks and have been trying to learn as much as possible, but I need more time! Hindi is a very difficult language," I tried to explain with a laugh. They all laughed and nodded in unison.

The serenity of this tiny village, caressed with a cool mountain breeze, was a welcome reprieve from my previous night in Luhri. This would be my last mountain pass, and three long, yet mellow and progressively warmer days of mostly downhill awaited me before I arrived in Rishikesh, a spiritual mecca for yoga and meditation along the holy Ganges river. As I was about to throw a leg over my bike and continue on down the road, I realized that I just wanted peace. No blaring horns. No barking dogs. No stifling heat. Nobody trying to get into my room at night.

I asked if there was some place for me to sleep, and my seven new friends quickly whisked me across the street to a guest room inside an old government building, which really looked more like a cottage that one of my friend's parents had on Lake Michigan. It was a white, concrete structure, with a green roof and covered patio, and wrapped in a profusion of wildflowers. My room was cavernous, with a fireplace, private bath (with hot water), and wall-to-wall burgundy carpeting. There was even a separate prayer room. In total it must have been nearly a thousand square feet. For Rs550 ($8.33), how could I say no?

The views of the valley were stunning as the sunset created a hazy pink silhouette over the surrounding peaks. The cool mountain breeze was blanketed by the warmth of that now-familiar Indian kindness as I felt a reminiscent calm flow over me as I watched the sun setting. From my patio, I could see the faint twinkle of village lights more than 4,000 feet below.

Three days later, my mountain top oasis was a distant memory as I was approaching Rishikesh. I had put on my iPod to drown out the incessant horns of hundreds of cars, buses, and other vehicles screaming by me, bringing with them, ironically, a barrage of other serenity seekers to this holy place. Jason Mraz's "The Remedy" came up on my iPod: *You can turn off the sun, but I'm still gonna shine . . .* The song's lyrics felt eerily appropriate.

I was close to breaking. After being in the mountains for three weeks, all the serenity I had stored up was being obliterated by the rising temperatures and blaring horns smashing through the once formidable walls of my now crumbling psyche. As I entered Rishikesh, the place of all things spiritual, it was anything but—and I nearly kept going. My sun was being turned off.

The city was not what I had expected. For whatever reason, I had romanticized this holy place, one as peaceful and tranquil with monks and yogis in flowing robes, meditating in parks. Ashrams flung open their doors to travelers who were eager to embark on a spiritual pilgrimage. I was a bit off.

Rishikesh is a small city built along the sacred Ganges river and has a rich history in Hinduism. The Ganges, 1,553 miles long, rises in the western Himalayas in the Indian state of Uttarakhand and flows south and east through the Gangetic Plain of India and Bangladesh, eventually emptying into the Bay of Bengal. It is named after Ganga, the Goddess of Purity and Purification. She is worshiped by Hindus who believe that bathing in the river causes the remission of sins and facilitates Moksha, liberation from the cycle of life and death. She is represented as a fair-complexioned woman, wearing a white crown and sitting on a crocodile.

Moving water (as in a river) is considered purifying in Hindu culture because it is thought to not only absorb impurities but also take them away. Hindus consider the waters of the Ganges to be both pure and purifying, and that nothing reclaims order from disorder more than the waters of the Ganges. The swiftly moving water, especially in its upper reaches—where a bather has to grasp an anchored chain in order to avoid being carried away—is considered especially purifying. What the Ganges removes, however, is not necessarily physical dirt, but symbolic dirt. It wipes away the sins of the bather, not just of the present, but of a lifetime.

I had tritely anticipated rolling into this storied, holy place, finding an ashram, and spending two weeks in yoga and meditation practice and *purifying* my past. I guess maybe I had read the book *Eat, Pray, Love* too many times. There were countless ashrams and hotels, and I stopped at too many. They were either full, in busy areas, too expensive, too dirty, or some combination thereof. What I wouldn't give for a *dhaba*, locked away, high in the mountains right now. The sun was beginning to set, both literally and, to me, figuratively in Rishikesh as my disenchantment with the city grew.

After countless wrong turns and dead ends, I followed a recommendation from a woman on the street, around the corner and veered up a steep, narrow, broken path that lumbered up nearly three hundred yards into a jungle of trees. However, there were no signs or any indication of a guesthouse. As I stood there tired, sweating, dirty, and hungry, a woman walking down the path smiled as she approached me.

Before I could say anything, she said, "Hello. I don't have any water."

I guess three hours of cycling and three hours of looking for a place to sleep had left the distinct appearance of defeat on my face. I chuckled, having recently downed a liter of water. "Thank you. I'm just looking for a place to sleep."

We chatted for a few moments. She seemed to be about my age, with a reassuring smile, and dense, curly black hair that probably was even curlier as a result of the humidity. She was wearing a pink sari and her thick Hebrew accent easily gave away her Israeli heritage.

"There is a guesthouse at the top of the hill, but believe me, it is too far to push your bike," she calmly shared, apparently making a judgment solely based on my appearance. But she was right. I didn't have the strength to push my bike up the cobbled walkway, the pitch perhaps better suited to a ladder. "I'll watch your bike. You can ask, but I know they are fully booked."

With nothing to lose, I slogged up the broken, narrow path lined with cows and cow byproducts until I reached a clearing in the forest. Almost immediately, I saw monkeys swinging from the trees, birds were serenading me, and dogs actually had collars on them. People were eating fruit and drinking kombucha. I could hear the river but none of the rest of the city. It was a small wooden building with a metal roof covered in moss, with at most eight rooms, an oasis in the middle of a maniacal frenzy. Even if they were booked, I was committed to sleeping on the covered wooden patio.

I walked into the reception office and inquired about a room, fully expecting them to be full, which they *were* until I met a lovely Canadian couple who was checking out as I entered.

"We're leaving today, so you can have ours. It's the private bungalow in the back. We've been here for two weeks. It's quiet, clean, cheap, and the food is terrific."

At first glance, the bungalow was a simple, unassuming square concrete structure, painted a deep brick red with a green metal roof.

At most, it was 150 square feet. However, without ever stepping a foot inside, I took it, then scurried down the path to retrieve my bike, filled with renewed optimism.

Even though I was still in cycling clothes, filth plastered prominently all over me, outwardly presenting as something just shy of repulsive, inwardly, my sun was coming back out. I was starting to shine again. It was 3 p.m. and my bungalow would not be ready until after 4 p.m., so I sat outside and enjoyed a bowl of curry and a glass of fresh beetroot, carrot, and ginger juice. Over my shoulder, I heard distinct, unbroken English. It was the most I'd heard in nearly a month. I think my ears might have actually twitched. While I loved the solitude of Ladakh, I didn't realize how much I was craving regular conversation without having to clearly enunciate each syllable and combine it with a hand gesture or game of charades. I just wanted to be myself and have a personality again, to engage with people *normally.*

With my blood sugar and shine restored, I walked over and met two English-speaking women: Laura from Spain, and Laurie, from—Colorado—whose sister I learned just happened to live three blocks from me in Boulder. They were both in their early 40s, wearing brightly covered saris and were in Rishikesh for yoga teacher training. We quickly hit it off despite my glaring disheveled appearance.

"English!" was the first word that blurted out of my mouth, like a child learning his first word.

"American!" chuckled Laurie, recognizing the familiar delivery. "We saw you come up the hill on your bike. How long are you in Rishikesh?"

"I just arrived today." (As if that was not obvious.)

I sat down with them and just began blabbing, the words flowing from my mouth the way the Ganges flows through India. Before I knew it, an hour had passed, and the sun was beginning to set, but my hut was still not ready.

"We are going down for the *aarti.*" Would you like to join us?" offered Laura.

"Of course! But I haven't showered, so . . ."

"It's no problem. Just come," replied Laurie in a very welcoming way.

I was too embarrassed to ask *what's an aarti?* Too late. Even the dirt and sweat still smeared upon my face couldn't hide my ignorance.

"The idea of the *aarti* ceremony is that all day long God offers us light—the light of the sun, the light of life, and the light of her blessings. *Aarti* is a time when we offer back the light of our thanks, the light of our love and the light of our devotion," offered Laura.

Ganga *Aarti* means "prayer for River Ganga," and it is a ceremony to honor the River Goddess Ganga. Every day at dusk, hundreds of people gather to play music, pray, and burn incense at the *ghat*, or embankment along the riverbank. The ceremony is a devotional offering to show gratitude to the Ganga River. It involves the circulating of a lit candle centered on a metal *aarti* plate and is generally accompanied by the congregation singing songs in praise of that deva (divine being). In doing so, the plate is supposed to acquire the power of the deity. The priest circulates the plate to all those present. They cup their down-turned hands over the flame and then raise their palms to their forehead. This purificatory blessing, passed from the deva's image to the flame, has now been passed to the devotee.

We approached the *ghat*, and I could hear the melodic hymns emanating up from the Ganges. There were easily three hundred people standing shoulder to shoulder, singing and clapping. The closer we got, the more I felt pure joy and grace washing over my tired and salt-caked body. We joined in the crowd and without ambitions of our own, we were swept into the sea of flowing devotees who were swaying and singing aloud, drowning me in the emotion of the *aarti*.

Laura, Laurie, and I filed out of the ceremony an hour later, none of us uttering a word. Perhaps we were all too overcome by the weight of the experience. Although we were all walking back to the same guesthouse, I smiled back at them, a look of gratitude as I opted to walk home alone. They smiled back with a look of understanding. Gone was the initial frustration that I brought with me when I rolled into Rishikesh, a feeling that seemed a lifetime ago.

The air was heavy and warm, and the night was peaceful. As I blissfully entered my hut and flipped on the window fan next to the bed, hundreds of ants immediately came flooding out of it, fleeing with their eggs. Apparently, nobody had turned on the fan in quite some time, and they had made their home there. I had now unleashed an earthquake, and they were packing up the kids and getting out! I watched the steady exodus for about ten minutes, wondering how many more there could be, before giving up and going to the front desk to ask for a spray. The idea of ants next to my bed, where they would (in my mind) be crawling all over me in the dark, was just not going to work.

"You have disrupted their home, and they are moving. Give it a half-hour for them to find a new home, then no problem," I was told by the man at the front desk.

Reluctantly, I walked back to my bungalow and patiently watched as the steady stream of ant refugees finally dissipated down the wall and into a crack.

"Dammit!" A flood of not-so-clean water came blasting out of the back of the toilet, flooding the bathroom moments later. I had forgotten the only advice from the Canadian couple who had the bungalow before me.

"This is important: when flushing the toilet, hold onto the main pipe from the tank to the bowl. It is loose and sometimes falls off."

I didn't—and it did. And instead of flushing 1.6 gallons of water into the bowl, it instead unleashed 1.6 gallons of water directly onto the cracked and moldy tile floor. I stood there helplessly, cursing myself out, the water drowning my previously zen-like state. Fortunately, in India, the toilet is in the same place as the shower, so all the water eventually flowed down the drain. After I was done cursing, I took a deep breath and started to laugh out loud and enjoyed a warm shower.

The next morning, my two new friends invited me to a yoga class. The sun was just creeping up, casting a glimmer across the Ganges. It was muggy yet serene as we walked down a quiet alley. I barely remembered what it had felt like to cocoon myself in my sleeping bag in Ladakh, suppressing any urge to go pee outside in the frigid temperatures, only to wake up each morning to a frozen water bottle and then hover around the morning stove in the *dhaba*, a desperate attempt to revive any circulation in my freezing limbs. Instead, I was in flip-flops, shorts, and a t-shirt. My thermal clothes had been packed away for two weeks now, deep in the recesses of my bags.

Even without speaking, there was a tangible feeling of levity and joy as we approached a nondescript building, down a random alley, far off the main street and nowhere near anything. There were no signs, or any indication that yoga was happening. Every building in Rishikesh has blaring signs for yoga, yet we apparently had found the *secret stash*. We walked up the stairs to the second floor and into an already packed class at 6:00 a.m. Every mat was touching another. Normally back home in the US, this would send me immediately fleeing out the back door, craving my space. However, in India, for some reason it was different. I was here, and I was once again practicing *being*.

As I was unrolling my mat, the instructor walked in. Although he was Indian, he was not what I expected. Instead of what I visualized as the quintessential *yogi* with long, lean muscles, he was quite stocky with a thick, mangy beard that extended at least 6″ beyond his jaw, while his coarse black hair was swept back into a somewhat tame ponytail. Despite his rather frumpy physical presentation, he was wearing white linen pants and a similar white long-sleeved linen shirt. Both were flawless. If I had to guess, I would say he was 45, but it was difficult to say with any certainty because his beard covered so much of his face. Beyond that woolen facade lay deep-seated brown eyes that conveyed a timeless wisdom and spirituality.

As we all settled onto our mats with our knees bent, sitting on our heels, our palms facing up while the backs of our hands rested gently on our thighs, the instructor began to speak. Initially, it was in Hindi but also in English for the benefit of the class that was clearly a mix of many diverse nationalities. He spoke of three renunciations that we must do in order to make room in our lives to achieve true happiness: physical, mental, and emotional. *Physical* items provide only fleeting glimpses of happiness, so do not attach any value to them. They will leave you feeling empty, yearning for the next fix. Free yourself of *mental* negativity, cognitive dissonance, and other things that clog up your mind and prevent happiness from having the space to flourish. Finally, make peace with and release the *emotional* scars and traumas from the past so you have space to cultivate new highs.

My eyes were closed, but it was clear that the instructor was speaking directly to me, as a tidal wave of emotions flooded over me. I choked back a tear and gasped desperately for air. My heart began to thump so loudly that I was worried that the person on the next mat might hear. There were so many things from my recent past that were still clinging to me, weighing on me, not wanting to let go. I thought that I had dealt with all of them. The hospice had been gone for ten months, and Emma just slightly longer, but obviously they were still hiding, tucked away someplace dark, and now newly released. They were anchors, holding me in place, threatening to drag me under and drown me. I needed to fully set them both free to make room for all the new beauty I was experiencing.

Although I was at most a few inches in every direction from waving arms, and flowing legs, I found peace in the choreographed symphony of the movement. At the end of a yoga practice, the final pose is *shavasana*, meaning "corpse pose," where each individual lays flat on their back for usually between five to ten minutes, completely still in a meditative space, feeling your body completely at rest and in contact with the earth, the flesh dripping off your bones. At that time, my pulse was calm and my breathing barely noticeable. This is why I came to Rishikesh, and why I stayed. *You can turn out the sun, but I'm still gonna shine . . .*

CHAPTER 7

Let Me Go

Leaving Rishikesh, I found myself back in the mountains—if only for a moment. There are few things I have experienced so captivating as seeing the sun rise each morning over the Himalayas, casting its hazy, pinkish spell over the valley below, and waking the stillness with its cool kiss. In the mountains, it's different up here. Life is quieter. It moves slower. There is a calm in the crispness of the air. I was nearing the border and would soon be crossing into Nepal, leaving India behind.

"Good morning, morning!" Indian men called to me as I set out each day. The sun was barely cresting the horizon but already people were stirring about. "Come here! Chai!?!" they would often say in a declarative and simultaneously interrogative way, almost demanding yet asking for me to join them. They would sit next to me and stare, sometimes unknowingly awkwardly. I'm used to it and would simply smile back, inspiring a smile in return. It is amazing how powerful a smile can be. It's as if they were seeing something (me) that they had only seen on television. They try to talk to me in broken English. Each time I would politely nod back and smile.

Children, both boys and girls, dressed in their crisp and tidy school uniforms walk for miles each way to school up these steep mountain passes, always singing and always with unfakeable smiles affixed to their faces. They would run along beside me through their small remote villages, simply eager to touch me as I slowly passed by. "Hello! How are you? Where are you going?" they beckoned to me, with the extent of their English. When I replied with the town that was that day's destination, they smiled and giggled, partly because they were able to interact with me and partly because they likely had not traveled that far from their village and thus had no idea what village I was talking about. I'd patiently answer the same question a dozen times each day. Throughout my travels, it became clear that life is about connection, and the human experience. After Rishikesh, it had never been more clear.

For two hours, I coasted peacefully down the single-lane, paved canyon road without ever pushing a pedal, wondering if I had ever been more relaxed. In this pristine slice of time, there was no traffic as the sun continued to crest the distant peaks, electrifying the dense green mountainside. From above, the trees looked like endless heads of broccoli, hiding the road and anything else below. There were no buses to run me off the road and no trucks to choke me out with their toxic diesel exhausts. Instead, the sounds of the roaring river below, monkeys screeching at me from their perch on the side of the road, and birds singing overhead brought about a calm that I had been missing on the bike since before arriving in Manali. The gentle ambiance and meandering of the road offered to rock me to sleep like a baby in his cradle, and I wasn't fighting it.

Slowly, almost without notice, the road crept upward. It was sneaky. But then, it changed, and it wasn't so subtle. It made a hard 180°switchback and vaulted up into the woods. A couple of weeks had passed since my bike pointed uphill at that angle. My breath deepened. My heartbeat quickened. My senses awoke. I remembered this feeling. The road dove back and forth, steadily climbing into the forest. Time slowed down, and although my heartbeat was racing, I was at peace. My body knew what to do and responded appropriately. Before I realized it, I had been climbing for three hours and over 4,000 feet when I popped out of the trees at the summit. "Pssst . . ." Nonchalantly, I veered to my left to see what was beckoning me. I locked up my brakes. Sweat was dripping from my brow, but in an instant, I had chills. Those weren't clouds. In the distance, above the densely covered green mountains, far above rose the snowcapped peaks of the high Himalayas in Nepal, piercing the tranquil blue sky to say hello. They were still hundreds of miles away, yet seemed very much tangible, almost beckoning.

After Rishikesh, the towns were once again becoming smaller, and a few days later I rolled down a mountain pass and arrived in the town of Lohaghat. It was a sleepy, forgettable place, not unlike any of the other villages that I had passed through over the past week, and I walked into the only hotel in town.

The first room I was shown had no window. Truly. It was a box. Fortunately for $1.50 more, there was another room, a double for Rs500, about $8.00. There were two windows: one to the outside courtyard and another with a different vantage. Initially, I wondered why I could hear every word from the next room, verbatim. Indian hotels have tile floors, so the sound unsurprisingly echoes and carries. But this was different. I went to the bathroom and peered through the window. At first glance, it just went to a space that looked like an internal shaft, and I didn't look any further than that. However, when I stood up after using the squat toilet, through the *window*, I saw a head. Startled, I squatted back down, then slowly peered back through again. I was looking directly into the room next to me where two men were sitting and chatting. But it was not the adjoining bathroom. If it were bathroom to bathroom, that would seem to have made more sense, but instead, it was a clear line of sight to two men conversing on the edge of the bed. I was glad to end up with this room because I would have felt differently if I was lying in bed and could see someone in the next room on the toilet. But, it's India, and I'm sure they thought nothing of it.

The next day came early with a somber optimism. I was within sixty miles of Nepal, and this very likely would be my last day in the mountains—and in India. I began reflecting back on the past five weeks. There is magic here, and I was in no rush to leave it. While I was excited to experience Nepal, there was a part of India that just would not let me go. But I had to wonder . . . with the punishing climbs over the past week, was India trying to crush me and send me off to Nepal, a broken, shredded semblance of myself, or was she simply trying to keep me and not let me leave?

Starting out that day, I took a quick glance at the map, knowing that I had one more climb, one more battle in India before she would let me pass. However, this ascent had a far different feel. Each pedal stroke resurrected feelings of my first ones when I landed in India more than a month ago. They were effortless. I felt playful and exuberant like a child just let out for recess. The pitches were steep. The road was curvy. It was no matter. Emotions from the prior day of suffering were scarcely recallable, replaced instead by eager curiosity for what lay ahead. But this day, each pedal stroke I knew was bringing me closer to the end. I momentarily lapsed back to those final moments in Madagascar. Emotion started to overcome me but was chased by the comical relief that this time I wasn't bleeding from a nearly broken hand.

I reached the summit by 11 a.m. and pulled over to sit and just *be.* This was it. All around me was beauty. From the simple and rugged kindness along the Leh Manali highway, to the growth and perspectives achieved in Rishikesh, it was easy to be emotional over a place that had been so generous and welcoming, a place that I had called home for nearly six weeks. After twenty minutes of vivid recollection, I wiped away the emotion that was flowing down my cheeks and made my peace with India, threw a leg over Kermit, and began my final descent. I looked off to the east. I could see the Mahakali River separating India from Nepal, and I knew I would be there in a few minutes. I'll admit that I used my brakes a bit more on the way down—if only to savor the experience a bit longer.

As in typical Indian form, I came upon a bus. Even though the drivers careen them wildly up and down these mountains, on my bike, it was still easy to catch them on the descents. I followed the bus down the pass for about ten minutes. He was handling the curves remarkably well (though I had no idea what it felt like *inside* the bus), yet it was still not as fast as I wanted to go. However, we were on a one-lane, winding road that was etched into the side of the mountain, with simply no place to pass. It was not how I would have chosen my final Indian descent, but it seemed appropriate, and maybe it was just India's way of telling me: "Not yet. I'm going to hold on to you as long as I can."

But then, in unprecedented fashion, something I'm certain has never happened in all of Indian history, the driver pulled over, put his arm out the window, and waved me by. Gleefully, I was once again that child who got let out to recess. I plowed through the rocky shoulder on the left, popped back onto the pavement and whizzed by as the driver and all the passengers gave me the thumbs up. It was as if India had finally conceded and was letting me go.

Lobzang and I in Leh

Top of the world!

Cycling down the back side of Khardung La

First night in a dhaba. Well, sorta. I camped behind and used the truck as a wind block.

Pang.

"Room". A dhaba along the Leh Manali highway

Lonely, uncompromising roads along the Leh Manali highway

Climbs that last all day.

Bikes always win! A transport vehicle in India.

PART 4

Nepal

October 24 – December 2, 2016

*"Rivers know this: There is no hurry.
We shall get there some day."*

– Winnie the Pooh

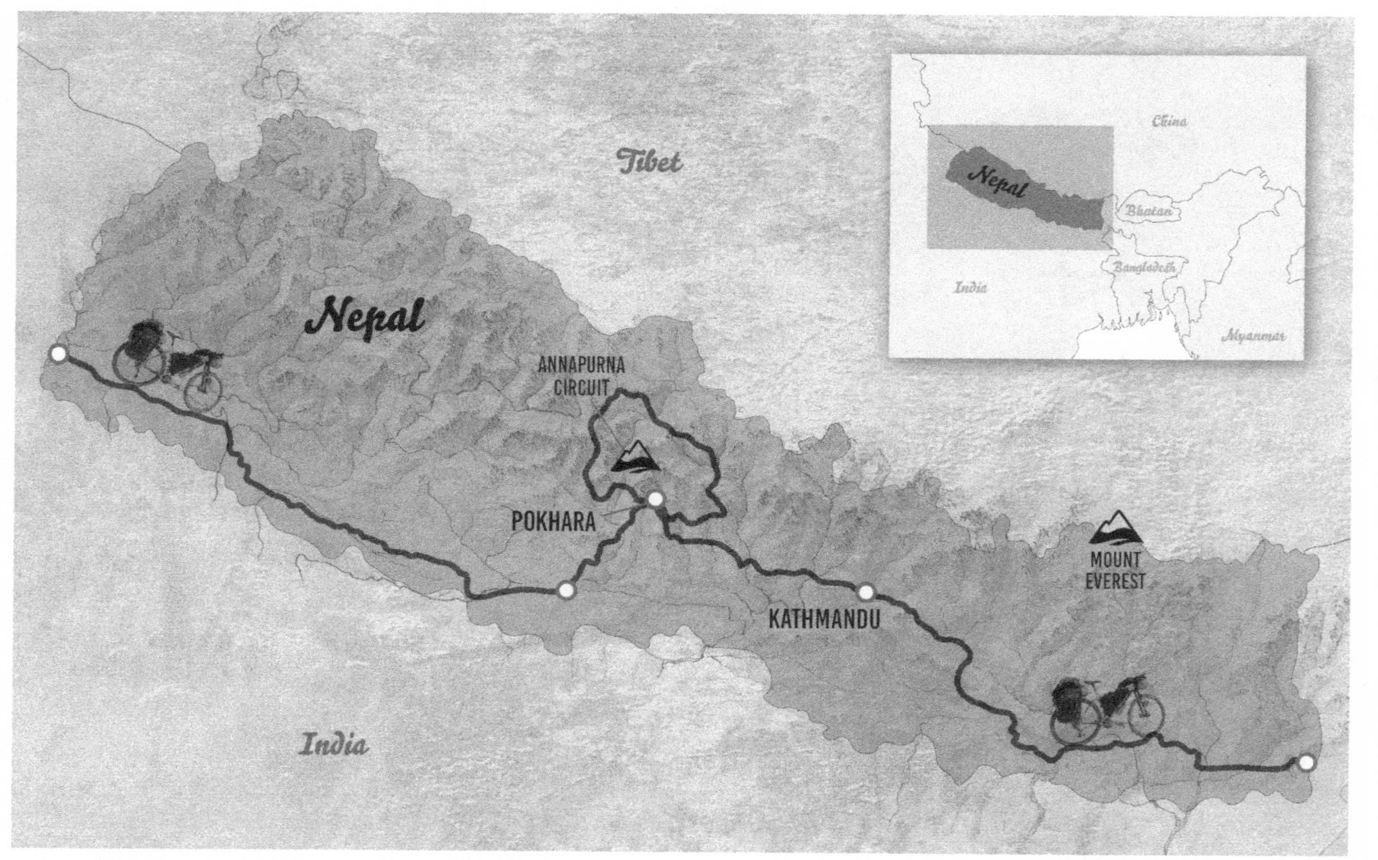
Tibet
Nepal
ANNAPURNA CIRCUIT
POKHARA
KATHMANDU
MOUNT EVEREST
India
China
Nepal
Bhutan
Bangladesh
India
Myanmar

CHAPTER 1

You're Going the Wrong Way!

Ssshhhh . . . Just like that, as I crossed the border, it all stopped. All of it. Buses blaring their horns traveling through narrow busy streets at speeds unsafe on a four-lane highway. Cars weaving in and out of those buses, also blaring their horns, somehow traveling even faster. All gone, almost instantly, at the border. Instead, as I looked around, I saw bicycles, and they were everywhere. I heard the clanking and grinding of squeaky chains, and it was a symphony to my ears. I could actually hear myself think. I could ride *with* traffic. I had only been in the country for five minutes, but already Nepal felt right. *What took you so long?* I rhetorically chuckled to myself, no longer lamenting the feeling of cheating on India with a new love.

As I quickly passed through immigration and was welcomed into Nepal, a sense of excitement and anticipation immediately flooded over me. "Namaste!" people called to me as I slowly pedaled across the narrow baby blue metal bridge spanning the Mahakali river that separates the countries. I began passing dozens of women who were also crossing the border back into Nepal, their bicycles loaded from the market in India. Only they weren't actually riding them as much as using them as a mode of transport, almost like a loaded wheelbarrow. Some were stacked seven or eight feet high with heavy, brown, nylon sacks stuffed with clothes, vegetables, or whatever else they were selling. A few, however, were actually pedaling them, a feat that was nothing less than astonishing since their bikes had to weigh far in excess of 150 pounds. And I thought I was traveling a bit heavy?

It had been a continual roller coaster down from the mountains when I left India, but now I was officially at sea level, the lowest I had been since I was in Delhi. And it was noticeable. The emotions of being in the mountains from only a few hours earlier were already a distant memory, and the high passes of Ladakh felt like a lifetime ago. Although it was nearly November, here in the Terai, a farmland region that covers nearly 17 percent of the land area of Nepal, the climate was oppressive. It felt like Michigan in August. Over the next four days, in what was every bit a mental as well as physical war, I methodically slogged my way nearly four hundred miles to the village of Butwal and the turnoff to Pokhara, where the road again began to climb back into the Himalayas.

Pokhara is a picturesque city nestled along Phewa Lake at the base of the Annapurna mountain range and is the launching pad for all things adventure (climbing, mountaineering, trekking, rafting, etc.) in Nepal. Need a new North Face puffy? Got it. Crampons? Yup. Expedition pack? No problem. Pizza and hamburger shops line the main street and cater exclusively to the influx of western tourists, and here, unfortunately, the local Nepali population felt like the minority. Even the dal bhat was fancy and cost $8. It's just rice and beans, man! Fortunately, over my time in Mada and India, I had become an excellent sleuth, able to covertly follow the locals down otherwise overlooked corridors to tiny clandestine restaurant nooks finding not only the best food, but a genuine local experience. Each time I would discover a new spot, I was given unsolicited directions from locals back down the alley to the main strip where all the rest of the sheep flocked. They assumed I was lost when in fact, I was exactly where I wanted to be. In Pokhara, my sleuthing had paid off, and I once again found the secret stash, providing a much-needed respite from the smothering tourist crowds. After the same awkward pointing, a few mutual smiles, followed by some hand gestures directed at my stomach, I was served up a heaping portion of dal bhat and surrounded by four new friends.

And still, in all the time since I had first landed in India, I never saw myself as "one of them," a tourist drunk on the magical weirdness of these faraway places who then returns home with a legion of Instagram followers, claiming to have seen the world. I selfishly and egotistically viewed my journey as more raw, pure, and authentic, a claim based on nothing more than my own myopic, even self-serving ideas of what adventure is.

I cringe thinking about simply bussing my way through the Lonely Planet checklist, snapping a selfie at the top of each peak while throwing my arm around the nearest local, somehow validating that I was there. I wanted to fit in, to be looked at as an equal, and instead, be one of *them.* As a white man growing up in the western world, privilege gifted upon me at birth, I'll never know what racism feels like, or what it's like to be looked at as different. I suppose this is likely as close as I'll ever get. In Nepal, and previously India and Madagascar, people came running out of their huts, chasing me down the street, just for a chance to look at me, talk to me, and sometimes, touch me, which of course is better than people fearful, and running from me. The attention is flattering, and no matter where I went, the reception was always the same. Yet still, I longed to walk down the street in a village or town of any size and go unnoticed, sit down in a local's restaurant with no looks of confusion.

In a different mental state, perhaps a different chapter of my life, I could have stayed in Pokhara for a month and have been completely content. Maybe longer. However, in this place, where I should fit in the most seamlessly with fellow adventurers, I felt the most out of place. I was suffocating, craving simplicity, and this wasn't it.

The *circuit* or *APC (Annapurna Circuit),* as it is commonly referred to, is about 145 miles and rises from near sea level to an altitude of 17,769 feet over Thorang La, touching the edge of the Tibetan plateau. The Annapurna range includes the Annapurna Massif, which is a compact yet segregated group of peaks. The highest peak, Annapurna I, is the tenth highest mountain in the world at 26,545 feet. Collectively, the Massif includes one peak over 26,000 feet, thirteen peaks over 23,000 feet, and sixteen more over 20,000 feet. This place will put a kink in your neck, a smile on your face, and literally take your breath away.

Most trekkers approach the route counterclockwise. This makes the daily altitude gain more gradual, and the crossing of Thorang La easier and safer, lessening the chances for HAPE (High Altitude Pulmonary Edema, the accumulation of fluid in the lungs) and HACE (High Altitude Cerebral Edema, the accumulation of fluid on the brain). Both of these can occur in otherwise healthy mountaineers at altitudes usually above 8,200 feet. For HAPE, early signs include shortness of breath, cough, fatigue, and chest tightness or congestion. The symptoms for HACE are marked by confusion, loss of consciousness, fever, rapid heartbeat, and an altered mental state. Both are caused by ascending to high altitudes before one is adequately acclimatized, with the potential for coma or death if left untreated. Fortunately, the treatment in most cases is simply to descend from the high altitude at the earliest onset of symptoms, something that is not always so simple, depending on how deep you are in the mountains.

In October 2014, at least 43 people were killed as a result of snowstorms and avalanches on and around the Circuit, thus resulting in one of Nepal's worst trekking disasters. People who were not killed in avalanches were snowed into the various small tea houses (like hotels) along the route for several weeks, while others died on the trail, unable to get to shelter. It was November, and I was officially entering the region even later in the season. The combination of traveling this late, on a bicycle, at high altitudes meant I needed to pay attention and not fall victim to my own hubris.

I've never been a hiker; instead, I had a different plan. *Just hear me out, Dad,* I said to myself one night in my hotel room as I poured over this caper and once again envisioned Big Jer shaking his head at another one of my wild ass ideas. I had heard that it was possible to cycle the Circuit, which I learned from countless tour operators in Pokhara was not the best idea—to put it mildly. *Shut up, Dad.* But unlike so many other adventurous concoctions I found myself chasing, they didn't say it was "not possible."

Prior to leaving Boulder nearly two months earlier, I had reached out to a local guide in Nepal about the possibility of cycling the Circuit. "Do you have experience in high alpine terrain?" he asked. Almost arrogantly, I replied, "I live in Colorado," assuming that answer alone would suffice. "Those are hills. Not mountains," he quipped, even less subtly arrogant.

The generally accepted route is counterclockwise. The last base camp of Thorang Pedi sits at 15,748 feet and is much nearer to the summit of Thorang La at 17,769 feet, thus lessening the chances of HAPE or HACE. However, in the direction I was traveling, I would first reach Muktinath whose summit is at only 13,123 feet, but has a much longer and greater ascent, thereby increasing my exposure to altitude issues. *Shut up, dad. I know what I'm doing.* The trick would be to either go slow and spend a few extra days as high as possible in Muktinath...or get up and over quickly, which is what I planned to do.

For trekkers, there are recommended stopping points along the way to aid in acclimatization. Not many people cycle the circuit, so my stopping points were a bit more interpretive. All along the circuit are "tea houses" which, while they do serve tea, also offer food and lodging to the trekkers (or cyclists). Most of the time, the cost is about $5 per night but can be negotiated down to as little as nothing if you agree to take all your meals there, which of course everyone does because where else are you going to eat? The rooms are private and simple, with a bed and a blanket and a shared bathroom outside. Electricity is common, but running water is not, so I was quickly back to my favorite: ice-cold bucket baths. The first cup over the head is shocking but serves as anesthesia as it numbs the body before subsequent dousings. However, the first night, I found myself in the village of Tatopani (translation: "hot water") and eagerly took advantage of the natural hot springs, knowing I would not feel hot water on my skin for the next two weeks.

Early on in the circuit, there is a road that was built less than a decade ago. It allows people to take a bus higher up if they want in order to shorten the trek. Almost immediately the term *road* became fodder for my internal discussion as it relentlessly pounded, twisted, and clawed its way into the sky. The bus drivers are quite adept at handling this route and do their best to shuttle passengers up the track as quickly as possible. As a result, many people on the bus get sick, and thus there are a plethora of exploded vomit bags that have been jettisoned out the windows, littering the road like a thousand jellyfish washed up on shore.

Nearing 2 p.m. on my second day, I was feeling the weight of the day's effort finally supplanting my enthusiasm. My check engine lights were blinking, so I stopped for lunch in the village of Gasa, where I saw three cyclists pinballing their way off the loose rocks and rubble down the trail at me. After hearing from everyone how crazy I was cycling the Annapurna Circuit, I was pleasantly surprised to see three cyclists on only Day 2. (Although they technically were going the *right way.*)

The crew consisted of a local guide and a German couple. "Namaste! You're going the wrong way!" the guide yelled out to me as we collectively stopped in front of the tea house, a cryptic laugh in his tone. His name was Sonam Gurang, and he was 62 years young, but appearing not much older than me. I would later learn that he is the Godfather of Nepali mountain biking and is known to have pioneered the sport in Nepal some thirty years ago. He's a jovial guy with the spirit and enthusiasm for cycling that easily surpassed my own.

Over lunch, Sonam told me that he actually laughed when he saw me coming up the road and made jokes about the foolishness of my endeavor to the Germans. While not known for their sense of humor, the Germans laughed. "Very hard. Leave at 4 a.m. Six hours to top of Thorang La. Too long. Too much altitude. Very dangerous," he said sternly over lunch. Great. So now, not only was I going the opposite direction of every trekker (and biker), but also counter to what the Godfather says. Had the Godfather talked to Big Jer? *Dammit!* "What we have here is . . . failure . . . to communicate."

But even after my scolding, I laid in my sleeping bag that night, my mind at peace, once again in the gentle cradle of the mountains. There is stillness here and inside, a quiet anticipation for each day that I would climb higher. I was only at 7,000 feet, but I could feel the change. All around, I was surrounded by peaks so jagged that they were either seething with malice or harvested from dreams, depending on my mental state at the time.

In many places, the original trekking path mostly parallels the new road, continually tempting me to get off the tourist *highway*. However, I had been warned not to veer from the road because the alternative trekking paths were typically seeded with extended sections where steps had been hacked out of the rock—not ideal for a loaded

60 pound bicycle. However, I was getting tired of dodging hurled vomit bags lobbed from bus windows while inhaling their toxic diesel and dust cocktail as they sputtered by, so I went for it.

Across a quarter-mile ravine, there was a suspension bridge connecting me to freedom. It was made of heavy-gauge, rusted steel cabling which bounced and swayed precariously the moment I set foot—or wheel—on it. The bridge was barely wide enough for my handlebars and the height on the sides slightly above my waist, which was just high enough to flip me over, headfirst, two hundred feet to the river below if I caught one of my bars on the cable, which would not be so difficult to do. (Pretty sure this happened in one of the Indiana Jones movies, which is why it had me so rattled.) What better way to challenge my lifelong fear of heights than essentially riding my bike on a tight rope?

"Don't look down," is what people always tell those of us who are height phobic. Sure. The bridge swayed with increasing violence with each pedal stroke, stirring increased tension the further out I ventured. *Just keep your eyes out toward the end of the other side, toward the solid ground,* I reminded myself. Slowly and methodically I ticked off the pedal strokes, and a few minutes later landed on the other side of the gorge and in that moment, I wondered what I was so worried about.

I looked around and immediately discovered a loamy single track, buried in the dense forest. It meandered along the edge of the gorge, winding its way through the trees. I veered across to see a cloud of dust billowing into the sky as the next bus went chugging up the road. *Suckers,* I thought to myself.

Thirty minutes later my luck ran out, and the trail spiked up into a series of tight switchbacks, nearly too steep to even hike, and surely too steep to ride. I quickly understood why all the guides had told me to "stick to the road." More concerning, since they were clearly right about the route, were they also right about the direction? With renewed skepticism, I reluctantly retreated back and crossed the same bridge, joining the suckers on the other side. The next day I would arrive at the final base camp village of Muktinath before attempting Thorang La, and a decision would need to be made.

—

Muktinath is a dusty tourist village that is the end of the road for the parade of buses. It sits at just under 13,000 feet, a daunting climb already from Pokhara, and even more so from the hot and muggy Terai where I originally began. Over the three days I spent on the Circuit, I had encountered at least a dozen trekkers who suffered from altitude sickness, many of whom needed to be evacuated back down to Pokhara, further casting doubt on my plan and shaking my confidence.

I learned that just above Muktinath, there was a very basic guesthouse before reaching the summit, so I pressed on, hoping to not only escape this tourist mecca, but ideally to let me sleep a bit higher, cut some time off the final ascent, and lessen any potential for HAPE or HACE.

The path from Muktinath to Thorang La climbs 4,600 feet in less than ten rugged miles, and within the first few minutes, I got a very sour taste of what the next day would be like. The ambition of pedaling was abruptly snatched from my lofty, romantic fantasy of cycling the Annapurna Circuit and replaced with the dark realization that if I was going to cross Thorang La, my bike would only be coming along as a medium to transport my gear.

Two hours later, after trying in vain to convince my bike to climb the rocky hillside, I collapsed at the guesthouse, aptly named the Paradise Hotel. I looked back at Muktinath, expecting it to be but a speck in the distance but was deflated to see that it was easily still in view, with droves of tourists congregating on patios, drinking tea, and basking in the dipping afternoon sun, some likely wondering what that guy was doing up there this late in the day.

I peeked my head in the front door and called out for anyone who might be there. A few minutes later, a woman in her 40s came out of a room where she was apparently napping. She flashed a delighted smile of gold and white teeth as she led me down a dimly lit concrete hallway while a single light bulb dangled helplessly when the winds gusted through the drafty corridor—which was often.

From the outside, the Paradise Hotel looked like a quaint, whitewashed villa, the kind you might find in the Alps. It was all a façade. On the inside, the Paradise Hotel was no more than an empty bomb shelter, a haven from the exposed high alpine war conditions that awaited me tomorrow. The dirt floor was covered by intermittent blue tarps, which I assume were used to keep the dust down. There was a damp chill inside the concrete building, instantly reminding me of the musty basements in so many of my friend's homes growing up in Michigan.

My host opened a door and showed me to my room, which was equally utilitarian and resembled a prison cell. On the floor were more blue tarps, while the walls were covered in a similar clear plastic, presumably for better insulation. My bed was a 3″ piece of foam draped over a wooden frame, perched directly below a window facing due north and thus giving me the opportunity to gaze up to where I would be going tomorrow.

Because the temperatures dip so violently overnight, I was told that the pipes supplying water from the melting snow would freeze, so I filled up all my water bottles, then put on all my clothes and hunkered down in my sleeping bag at 6:30 p.m. I drifted off to sleep as the evening winds began to batter the single-pane window in my room while the lone hanging light bulb turbulently churned in the hallway, its dim rays filtered like a strobe through the cracks in my door.

Unlike most of my nights in India and Nepal, there was an obvious and welcomed absence of roosters at this altitude, so I awoke before my alarm at 5:30 a.m. and made my way to the kitchen to warm myself over the wood stove, where I discovered my hostess was already preparing tea and chocolate pancakes. Contrary to its appearance but true to its name, of course, the Paradise Hotel makes chocolate pancakes!

Outside, it was still dark, but the howling winds had quelled their fury leaving a brilliant yet frigid, starry sky, making me feel that I was alone at the edge of the universe. I was presented with two paths. One was a loose, sandy single track, far too steep to drag up an uncooperative, 60 pound bike. I know because I briefly tried, but quickly slid backwards with both brakes locked up. The alternative was a slightly lower grade double track, covered in a sea of loose, pointed, granite marbles the size of grapefruits. Each step for the next two hours, my ankle would roll on the frost-covered stones, subsequently kicking up one of these projectiles, either into my ankle, shin, or bike. Intermittently I would glance back, expecting to see the Paradise Hotel fade obscurely in the distance, only to be callously reminded of my nearly immeasurable progress.

By 8 a.m. I passed my first trekker coming down, and the look from her guide was telling—more confirmation that I was *possibly* going the wrong way. "Five hours to top. Very steep! This way more difficult!" he shared unsolicitedly, almost barking in unison with the voices of Big Jer and the Godfather already clamoring in my head.

I crossed the first ridge at 9 a.m., ankles now bruised and shins bloodied after absorbing three hours of abuse since leaving the pleasant accommodations of the Paradise Hotel. The terrain had changed from marbles to loose sand, and with it, a new challenge: I now had a pretty direct line of sight up to the next ridge, and it wasn't close. "Fuck!" I yelled, hoping that the trio of naysayers didn't hear me.

Step, step, push. Step, step, drag. Breathe. I alternated hand grips, positions, pace, anything that would create any type of efficiency. It was all the same. This was hell, and there was no getting out.

By 10 a.m. I began seeing more trekkers coming down the pass, but instead of bewilderment, they looked at me with amazement and offered support and encouragement. "How long since you were at the summit?" I asked each trekker as they passed me. It seemed reasonable to double their *descent* time to arrive at my hopeful *ascent* time, assuming, of course, that I could sustain this pace, which I couldn't. Step, step, push. Step, step, drag. Breeeathe.

Finally. There were prayer flags and I could see the summit! It was right there. "How far to the summit?" I eagerly asked a trekker and her guide again trying to gauge my timing.

"For you, maybe an hour and a half, two hours." My eyes bulged as my jaw dropped, the visual effects of a virtual stomach punch, the disappointment unmaskable.

I was nearing 17,000 feet, and the air was indeed thinner. My breathing was shallower and, as a result, my muscles began to revolt at the lack of oxygen. Unfortunately, the summit wasn't as close as it looked. Well, it was, but I was just going so slow. Step, step, push. Step, step, drag. Breeeaathhe . . .

Just under ninety minutes later, and with one final groan, I arrived on the summit of Thorang La, at 17,769 feet. It was slightly before noon, and most of the trekkers had already descended off the summit for fear of afternoon storms. Immediately, like amnesia, the grind of the past six hours was washed away when I dropped my bike and laid beneath the welcoming canopy of weathered prayer flags. I felt as though I was at the top of the world, but with a euphoric inertia, almost like laying in the center of a merry-go-round, and everything was spinning around me. But the world was still, if only for a moment, and the sky was that same blue—that indescribable, bluer than the truest blue. It was the kind you only see in cartoons and comic books—that I could still never fully describe to my dad.

After a few minutes, I sat up from beneath my canopy of prayer flags and noticed that I was inside a shark's mouth. All the way around me, there were menacing, jagged white peaks. I glanced to my right and saw a narrow ribbon of single track carving a squiggly line down the ridge. No longer concerned with HAPE or HACE, I threw a leg over Kermit and prepared to point it downhill, all downhill, for the first time in a week. I let go of the brakes and descended over the first roll, almost recklessly, like the first time I learned to ride a bike, with no fear of injury or repercussion, only that natural Mountain Dew high.

The path, which was not much wider than my handlebars in many places, was rocky and loose, and seemingly stitched to the side of the canyon wall. At the speed I was descending, and with the weight I was carrying, one loose stone could kick my front wheel out and send me careening 1,000 feet down a rocky embankment into the icy river below. My breathing slowed, my pulse quickened. I was a four-year-old again, blasting down a dirt road in Michigan.

"Mountain biker coming down!" yelled a girl to her friend just below and around the first corner.

"Whoop, whoop!" I shot back while ringing my bell. They giggled and cheered as I zoomed by, my face plastered with an ear-to-ear comic book grin, stolen directly out of the pages of the surreal comic book landscape I was pedaling through.

I arrived an hour later in Thorang Pedi, the high camp for people making the final push over Thorang La—from the correct direction. It sits at 15,748 feet, almost 2,000 feet higher than Muktinath, and the three hotels were spilling over with western trekkers preparing to make their push the following morning. By 3:30 p.m., the sun had retreated behind the peaks, plunging the temperature immediately below freezing and sending me and my exhausted body, happily to my sleeping bag wearing every item of clothing that I had.

After nearly twelve hours of motionless sleep, I awoke at 4 a.m. to dozens of darting headlamps, reminding me of the brilliant array of fireflies on a muggy Michigan summer night. Instead, this was the Himalayas in mid-November and, even inside my hotel room, a layer of frozen crust coated my sleeping bag near my nose, the only exposed part of my body. Everyone was getting ready for their ascent and jockeying for use of the outdoor squatty potties, which were dangerously frozen over from the night's prehydration flurry, making using them almost as daunting as the ascent up Thorang La.

Two hours later, I crawled out of my bag to a ghost town of empty hotel rooms—doors flung open like someone had pulled the fire alarm. I walked into the kitchen, which was empty and cold, and littered with dirty dishes, the cook expecting, of course, that everyone had left two hours earlier. He smiled and whipped me up a couple of chocolate pancakes (which apparently is a thing up here) as I waited for the sun to peek over the ridge, warm the canyon, and more importantly, thaw the ice in the squatty potty.

I rolled out of Thorang Pedi, knowing that even though it had taken me five days to get here, the story would play out much quicker on the way down. I heard a clanging of bells. "Namasteeeee!" a porter called to me, with seven donkeys loaded with supplies making their way up the pass.

"NAMASTEEEEEEE!" I called back, more euphorically as I zipped on by. I began passing groups of trekkers making their way to where I had just been. *Slow down. Breathe. It won't last forever*, I continuously reminded myself.

Almost without notice, I had descended down to Pisang at just over 10,000 feet, a far cry from the gasping, head-pounding oxygen deprivation of Thorang La. I could taste the richness of oxygen in the air, almost as if I could drink it with a straw. Once again there was green on the hillside and a rushing, unfrozen river, telling me that I was nearly down, and that this chapter, like those of the past, would soon come to an end.

The razor-sharp, snowcapped shark teeth that once beckoned me forward with each agonizing pedal stroke were now bidding me a slow, but still too hasty, farewell. They were still there, daunting and magical as ever, but effortlessly slipping away. I was traveling slowly, trying in vain to stave off the inevitable; I knew that Nepal was coming to an end.

CHAPTER 2

Unchecked Baggage

"Will it rain today?" I apprehensively asked the hotel owner prior to rolling out of Pokhara early the next day. It was a crisp morning, and for the first time I could remember, there were clouds, which gave me pause. He assured me that it wouldn't. Inside, I was passively hoping that it would, giving me an excuse to stay in Pokhara another day, or three, and extend my time in Nepal. The truth is, I would be back in Kathmandu in less than a week and likely on a plane back to Colorado shortly thereafter. Although I had not purchased a return flight home, the finality was becoming tangible.

In an effort to lighten my load, I had left about 20 pounds of gear and other nonessential items at the hotel before embarking on the Annapurna Circuit—things like my tent, extra clothes, and even the hair clippers. I needed the bare minimum since I would be sleeping in tea houses and only gone slightly more than a week. I had carefully laid everything out on the bed, as though I was taking stock of my needs not only for this side trip, but my life as a whole.

At the trip's very start back in June, I had naively made the mistake of bringing more, simply because I could. There was plenty of room in my panniers, so I brought along "backups" and "extras", things I probably would never need, just in case. As a result, my bike was carrying too much stuff, and it was weighing me down. But this revelation exposed the important metaphor of my life: *I* was carrying too much stuff, emotionally, and it was weighing me down.

In addition to the extra physical items, I did my best to leave the aches inflicted by the losses of Emma, my mom, and the hospice back in Pokhara. At least for that week. The resulting levity, while fleeting, was noticeable. It had never been more clear that all that "stuff"—both physical and emotional—wasn't serving me. It was only weighing me down.

When I returned to the hotel in Pokhara after the Annapurna Circuit, I loaded up my bike with all the gear that I had left behind. It was all there waiting for me, but somehow along the way, I had lost a little of the emotional stuff. I'm not sure how or where it had gone, but maybe time has a way of doing that. Although I wasn't ready and thus hadn't consciously confronted those demons, I knew they would still need to be faced at some point, but maybe they would be a bit less scary by then.

This experience had gone by in a blur, and it seemed like only last week I had been sleeping in a *dhaba* in Ladakh, India. But now, I was suffocating under the weight of a reflective stoicism, flipping back through the emotions and experiences of the two months since I had departed Colorado. Paralyzed with indecision, I sat on a stool outside my hotel as the sun was beginning to rise, struggling to find the ambition to get on my bike and head back to Kathmandu, because I knew what was waiting for me there.

From the moment I had arrived in Nepal, I felt that I had checked off a lot of the boxes, including cycling the Annapurna Circuit, but now as I rolled out of Pokhara, I wanted to see the Nepal that was not in any guidebook. I planned to get lost on some secondary roads and experience the simplicity of the rural villages along the way. Sure, there was a main road connecting Pokhara to Kathmandu, but it was heavily patrolled by overcrowded, air-conditioned luxury tourist buses. I had seen plenty of those as they zoomed by me. I wanted to see the real Nepal.

Before setting off, I was told by countless locals that the roads are "very bad." Almost immediately before arriving in Gorka, the former capital of Nepal, I learned that, just like there is subjectivity to the idea of a "bad road," so too is there interpretation to the term "flat road." I suppose when compared to dragging a bicycle over Thorang La for six hours, everything is a "flat road."

The route from Gorka to Arughat was indeed a bad road, and far from flat. In fact, if I hadn't seen so many SUBs (Sport Utility Buses) come sputtering by me, I wouldn't have even known that I was actually on a road. These SUBs (as I named them) were seemingly normal local buses, however, they were anything but. On some parts of the "bad roads," the ankle-deep, soul-crushing sand was so fine that it was the consistency of chalk. Each time a SUB passed by, it left in its wake a cloud of this fine chalk that immediately bonded to anything with a hint of moisture—my skin, my clothes, and the drive train on my bike. The road was either layered in this chalk or slathered in two-month-old mud left over from the monsoon season that would never dry. But, no matter how debilitating the road was to cycle, it had to be far more enjoyable than being tossed around in an SUB like the inside of a popcorn popper.

In many places, the road was just two troughs, carved out from the runoff of the monsoon season, and made worse bus after bus, year after year. As the buses approached behind me, I could hear the suspension clanking, axles twisting, and frames moaning under the stress as they heaved from side to side through and around the troughs, sometimes up on three wheels. Many times they would have a spotter jump out to instruct the driver where the best line was. The bus would then back up and get a running start just as the spotter jumped back in through the open door.

"Namaste! Where are you going?" people would shout out the window as the lumbering SUB bounced and sputtered by. They had already passed around a corner before the cloud of chalk settled, and I could pull down my facemask to reply. This was likely their daily commute and was a further testament to what is "normal" and how people adapt.

Each day along this route had been a familiar storyline and took me to places where the guidebook dropped off: up and over countless ridges, down to the river, through knee-deep water, and up again, through tiny villages—some not even on the map. There were periods when I would cycle for hours and not see anyone. However, just when

I needed something, an oasis that wasn't on the map would appear with samosas and dal bhat to rescue me.

"Namaste!" said the adult men and women, as I slowly rolled into their village in search of a hotel or food. "Cycle, cycle, cycle!" yelled the small children chasing behind me as I spun down the dusty main road. This is the Nepal that I wanted, that I yearned to see, void of any North Face backpacks, yet overflowing with kindness. Here, life slowed down and was simple. The bucket showers were cold, but the smiles were warm, welcoming, and seemingly everywhere.

It is easy to be in awe of the Annapurna area, a region with paralyzing beauty. But I found just as much happiness in the *ordinary,* however that is defined. Off the well-beaten tourist track, there is beauty in the simplicity of a warm smile, a random act of kindness. If you are ever feeling glum or down, simply say "Namaste" to any Nepali person. The smile that immediately ensues is the most genuine you've ever seen and is guaranteed to pull you out of whatever funk you might have been wallowing in.

One day, while stopping for tea, a man likely in his early 40s, invited me to his home. He enthusiastically pointed at the chicken that was pecking around our feet and told me with a chopping motion of his hand that we would have dinner together that evening. It was the first time that someone offered to "off" a chicken for me, and I was humbled.

Ten months earlier, I had diligently planned and researched this trip. I had scoured guidebooks and connected with people from around the world, inquiring about different aspects of this route from Leh to Kathmandu. I had examined weather patterns and road conditions. I modified my bike, changed tires, added gear and got rid of others. It was way beyond my comfort zone. But even with all that planning and trepidation, it was ultimately the people, not the landscape, that provided the ultimate reward.

Here I was now, cresting the final ridge before dropping down into Kathmandu. I joined a one-lane, mostly paved road that ground slowly and sternly to the top of a pass before gently descending into the melee of the city. Just as summiting the final pass departing India felt bittersweet, I was stricken with overwhelming emotion and reminded of all the people and places I had seen. Another chapter was nearing conclusion.

After a few minutes of emotional recollection, I summoned the courage to finish my journey and plunged down the pass. Stealthily navigating my way through the harrowing congested alleys like a local, weaving around the familiar barrage of taxis, tourists, and lounging cows, I arrived back at my hotel where I was immediately greeted with familiar smiles and hugs by the same staff that had seen me off—nearly two months ago to the day. I felt like I was already home. But first, I had one more thing planned.

CHAPTER 3

The Illusion of Randomness

I had been messaging with the race promoter of the Kathmandu Mountain Bike Festival ever since I arrived back in Kathmandu three days earlier. I had fortuitously come across this event before I left Colorado and thought it would be a fitting end to my trip. I pored over the website to try and make sense of the directions to the event. Even the narrowest of congested alleyways had names, but of course were not marked, so as an outsider trying to follow directions and navigate them, it was impossible. It was like being physically dropped into one of those old-fashioned paper mazes I used to do with my grandma before bed. It had been frustrating then. It was futile now.

According to the event website, there was also a ten-mile group ride up to the event in the hills just outside of Kathmandu, leaving at 8:30 a.m. It was now 8:15 a.m. I was geared up and ready to go, but frustratingly stuck in the hotel lobby, unsure how to decipher the cryptic directions. The hotel staff could offer no assistance. As I was dejectedly wheeling my bike back to my room, a young Nepali woman dressed in spandex rolled up on her mountain bike. She was barely five feet tall with a lean build and a beaming smile. Her name was Laxmi, and she glanced over and noticed my bike. Laxmi apparently was friends with some of the hotel staff and just stopped by to drop off something for them.

"You go to Kathmandu Mountain Bike Fest today?" Apparently, she could see the mounting frustration prominently displayed across my face. "I'm going there now. You can cycle with me," she said in her soft-spoken, near-perfect English.

Laxmi led me through the dizzying maze of cobbled Thamel alleyways, jousting with motorbikes and dodging cows, until we connected with a group of ten or so other Nepali locals and made our way into the hills. She was initially quiet and shy around me, but quickly warmed into a gregarious and joking caricature as soon as we met up with her friends.

"You racing today?" Laxmi asked me.

"Maybe?" I said without conviction. I told her that I had been touring for two months but did not offer any further details for fear of coming across as bragging.

"I'm not racing today. I don't do local races like this because if I do, sometimes other girls don't come and I want to promote women's cycling in Nepal," she said humbly. This seemed like an odd comment, but I thought little of it until a few minutes later when we parted ways, when I was approached by an American guy.

"Did you ride here with Laxmi?" asked Tyler. He was about my age, with an athletic build, his face buried in a furry beard. He was originally from Colorado but moved to Nepal and started a water filtration company, something essential in a country where clean water is far from common. "Were you able to keep up?"

"Huh?" I replied.

"She's the Nepali national champion. I've ridden with her and the crew you pedaled up with. She's fast!"

So there it was. The Nepali national champion rolled into my hotel, out of all the hotels in Kathmandu (and there are thousands) and gave me a tour of the valley.

Tyler and I continued talking, and we quickly hit it off. We knew some of the same people in Colorado and had done many of the same mountain bike races. I told him of my travels in India and Nepal, and he immediately said, "There is a couple that is also bikepacking a similar route as you. You should meet them."

We cruised down the dirt road and in the grassy field I met

Zbednek and Zusanna, a Czech couple in their mid-30s. They were sprawled out in the grass and had just broken down their camp from the night before. Zus was making porridge on the camp stove while Zbednek was doing yoga. They had matching crew cut hairstyles, likely for the simplicity of long-distance traveling. Tyler introduced us and then handed me off and went to get ready for his race, a race I apparently wasn't doing. Instead, ZZ (as they called themselves) and I spent the next hour sharing adventure stories over tea.

"We're having dinner with a Swiss couple tonight back in Thamel. They are also bikepacking all of India and Nepal. You should join us."

The next evening, I met "the Swiss." Ivo and Brigitte were schoolteachers also in their mid-30s who had grown sour on the rigors and structure of their chosen life path, and four years ago embarked on a different one. During that time, they had cycled nearly 40,000 miles to every place I could think to ask about. "Have you been to . . ." I would ask, and the answer from Ivo was almost immediately, "Sure, of course," in his very literal, black and white Swiss demeanor. Throughout my travels, I had met countless people from dozens of countries, but never anyone from Switzerland until now, so I didn't have a preconceived stereotype in my mind, the way many people have for say, an American. The only thing I knew about Switzerland was the precision and simplicity of their watches. After meeting Ivo and Brigitte, they were definitely very—Swiss.

Over dinner, we shared stories about the Andes through Bolivia and Peru, Madagascar, the Leh-Manali highway and of course the Annapurna Circuit. Places that I had recently been to, they had done them all, and it didn't stop there. They had pedaled from the south to the north in South America, from the north to the south in Africa, all through Europe, the Iditarod dog sled race in Alaska, the Mongolian steppes, the Tibetan Plateau, deserts in the Middle East, and even through Siberia in the winter. I was in awe as they humbly recounted highlights of their adventures, making the trips I had done feel like kindergarten recess. They lived a life of simplicity and adventure, void of structure and the conformity of societal expectations. They valued experiences over *stuff* and counted passport stamps instead of holiday bonuses and promotions. They were truly *free*. I had met my people.

If I closed my eyes and simply listened to their tales of exploration,

I would not visualize the actual people in front of me telling the story when my eyes reopened. The Swiss looked like they belonged in a laboratory doing chemistry research instead of exploring the world on mountain bikes. Ivo and Brigitte were very modest and soft-spoken, of a slim, almost unathletic build, and not at all the sculpted physical specimens I would have imagined after hearing of their extraordinary journeys. They were both probably 5′8″ and 130 pounds, and also had the familiar "bikepacking" haircuts as ZZ. They wore similar wire-rim glasses, the same puffy coats, shoes, pants, and seemed to seamlessly finish each other's sentences.

"So, you just finished the Annapurna Circuit?" inquired Ivo. "Where to next?"

"Back to Colorado," I replied with mixed emotions.

"Why are you going home?" Ivo quickly fired back.

"Well, I planned this route, and now it's finished, so it's time to go home."

"Do you have a job?" Ivo shot back again.

"No. It's the first time in my adult life that I can say that, which sounds odd to say," I replied.

"Do you have a wife? Kids? Dog?" Ivo continued to interrogate me.

"No. None of those things actually."

"Okay, so, I'll ask you again. Why are you going home?" Ivo prodded with a subtle smile.

"Wow. I don't know? What else is there?" I appealed to the living personification of a Lonely Planet book.

"We're leaving next week and cycling through eastern Nepal into India, near the Bhutan border. It's a restricted area so you have to purchase an Inner Line Permit, but you can book them online. It's pretty easy. Do you want to join us?"

This was an idea that had never crossed my mind because this part of Nepal wasn't in *any* guidebook. Everything that I had done up until this point had been carefully researched and planned. I didn't know anything about this part of the world, nor did I know anything about these two people whom I had just met less than an hour ago. I had gotten so used to traveling solo that the idea of traveling with another person, let alone a couple wasn't very appealing.

I started imagining all sorts of scenarios. What's the worst that could happen? If I didn't like it? If we didn't get along? What if we annoyed each other or cycled at a different pace? I felt guilty that I was already passing judgment simply based on their physical stature as my mind was spiraling down the rabbit hole of all the potential things that could go wrong and wandered nowhere near any optimistic thoughts of how potentially amazing it could be. Worst case, I could always catch a ride on an SUB and be back in Kathmandu. And besides, as Ivo pointed out, what was I going home to?

—

"That's so random . . ." I would have mused if this chain of serendipitous events had happened to me a year ago—meeting Laxmi in my hotel, then Tyler, then ZZ, and finally the Swiss. And what about meeting Jenna and all those connections, too? I now know that the idea of *random* feels like an illusion. A fallacy. These *random* events had been poking at me far too frequently to attach such a label or mentality, but it was only recently that I have peeled back the shutters of my awareness to them. Throughout my life, I had always defaulted to saying "no" either out of fear or because of my innate need for control. But throughout Africa, India, and now Nepal, I was learning to relax my grip, live with the mindset to "always say yes," and step through doors that opened, into these seemingly *random* connections.

My grandma was a religious woman and would always say to me, "The Lord works in mysterious ways." I have always wondered—do things happen for a reason or are we simply a product of the choices that we make, and thus our lives are shaped by the outcomes and connections that come from them? Even though I'm not religious, the Serenity Prayer has always resonated with me since I was a kid.

> *"Give me the serenity to accept the things I cannot change, the courage to change the things I can, and the wisdom to know the difference."*

It was now crystal clear that my world was changing. This was particularly challenging for me because, as a purebred, Type A control freak who could will myself through any situation regardless of how daunting or grim, I was powerless to stop the unavoidable landslide that was coming. The year 2016, my 42nd year, was the hardest and most emotionally savage *shit show* year of my life—the end of Family Hospice after ten years and the subsequent hemorrhaging of my family, splitting up with Emma, and the death of Cynthia. That year's events had stripped me of everything I knew and could confidently stand on and had thrown me into a drunken tailspin—and in its void were left grief, frustration, and even a little anger.

I've replayed all of these situations in my mind—frame by frame with dozens of scenarios like the old *Choose Your Own Adventure* books that I read as a kid. Could I have done something differently, chosen a different response or action? Yes, of course. Would it have changed the outcome? Unlikely. Just like in the Serenity Prayer, in life, we can't always choose what happens to us, but we can choose how we deal with it, how we respond. We all have that choice. With all the adversity of my 42nd year also came the veiled opportunity for growth and clarity. A perspective shift, and although disguised in pain and uncertainty, it was an opportunity.

After just over a year since our break up, it was clear that Emma and I weren't the perfect couple that I wanted to believe, that I tried to will to fruition. And we weren't going to work it out. A family business is hard and my mom was stuck with the impossible decision of choosing between her son and her dream and the man that she married. And Cynthia. That was just shitty. All of these were beyond my control.

I had now been cycling through the world for nearly six months. *This experience won't change me,* I foolishly told myself before I began. *It will just be a fun two-month adventure, a diversion, before heading home and getting back to normal life.* By leaving, I had chosen to disconnect from everything that was familiar, to distance myself from all the pain in an attempt to find clarity—to slow down, find peace, and figure it out. Sometimes you have to be knocked down, flat, to discover how resilient you actually are. Absorbing all three of those losses in a four month stretch, did just that.

After dinner with the Swiss, I went back to my hotel room, my computer still open to Google Flights, just waiting for me to click the "purchase" button and complete my journey back to Colorado. There was a very palatable, insatiable taste in my mouth to see more, not just of Nepal or the world, but of myself. I was once again reminded of that thought I had before leaving for Africa: *what would you do if time was not a factor?* Right now, I had a gift of time. Instead of booking a flight to Colorado to try and grasp for my old life, I booked an Inner Line Permit for India, then closed my laptop and went to sleep.

My first friends in Nepal. (Renu and Bikash on the right)

The chaotic alleys of the Thamel district in Kathmandu

Cycling up the Annapurna Circuit

Conquering my fear of heights

Bikes always win? No cyclists on the Annapurna Circuit

Getting warm in the kitchen before crawling into my sleeping bag for the night.

The Paradise Hotel

Worth it!

Cycling down from the Annapurna Circuit

SUBs

Hitching a ride to meet the Swiss along the Midland Hills Highway

PART 5

India – Again!

December 3, 2016 – February 23, 2017

"There's not a word yet for old friends you've just met."

– Jim Henson, Creator of The Muppets

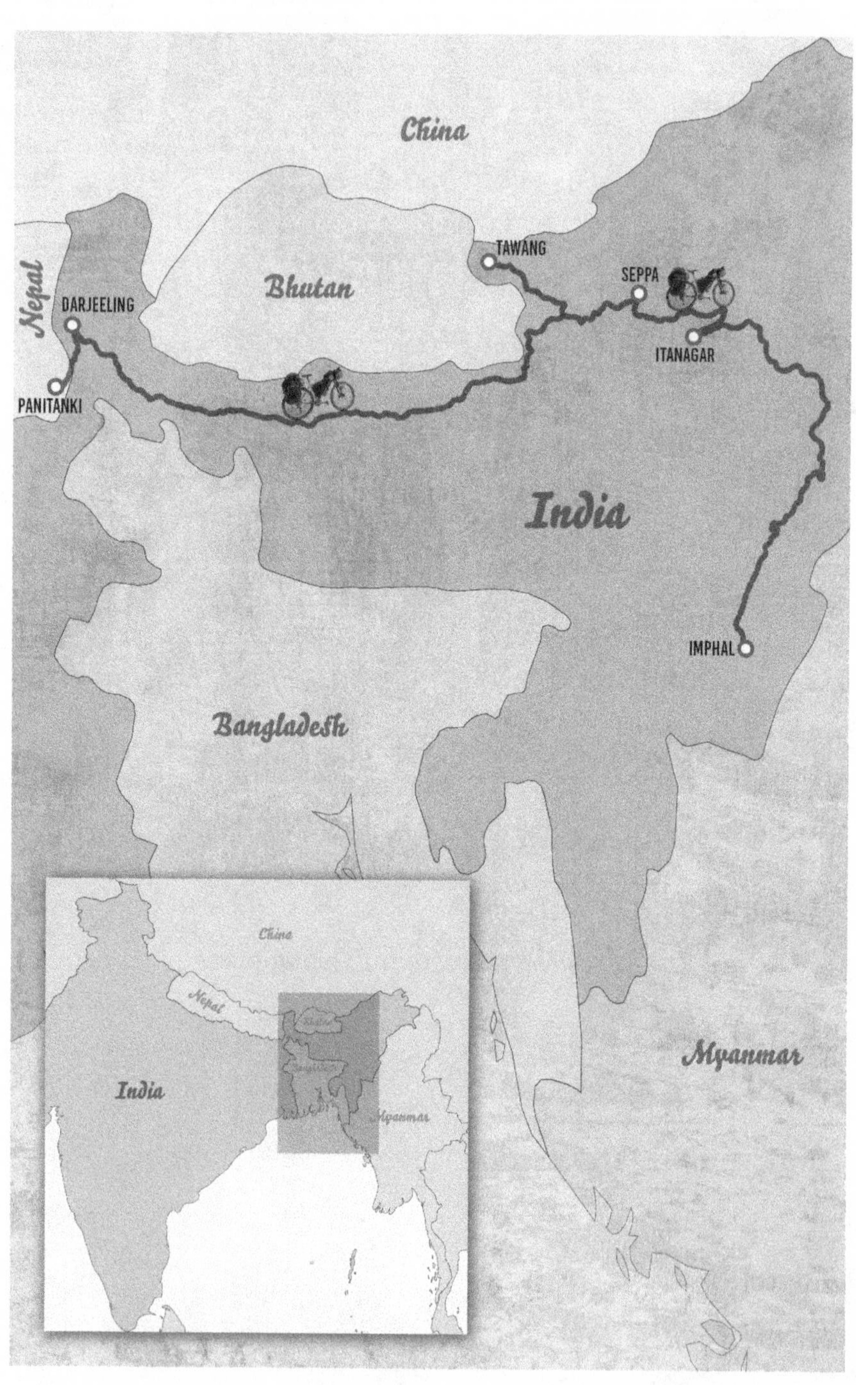
China
Nepal
DARJEELING
PANITANKI
Bhutan
TAWANG
SEPPA
ITANAGAR
India
IMPHAL
Bangladesh
Myanmar
China
Nepal
India

CHAPTER 1

Counting Salt Rings

I think back to when I was probably 12 years old and got my first road bike. Back then, we just called them "ten speeds" because well—it had ten speeds. Mine was a black and gold Schwinn World Sport and my dad paid $240 for it. It was by far the most expensive thing I had ever owned, and it retained that title until I turned 20 and got my second car (I only paid $190 for my first car. The friend who sold it to me wanted $200 but I was able to talk him down).

I remember the freedom I felt the first time I pedaled away from our small townhouse, heading out of town, the speckled gold accents of the frame sparkling in the late day sun. My first adventure was a five-mile ride down a narrow, paved, country road to my friend Bill's house. He lived "in the country" as we would say, which simply meant, in the woods just outside of our small farm town in rural Michigan with its 5,000 inhabitants. Rolling cornfields as far as I could see, framed by towering hundred-year-old oak trees made me feel like I was on some great odyssey. I was prepared for anything, armed with a water bottle full of Mountain Dew and a Snickers bar.

Even though my dad had driven me to Bill's house dozens of times, now it felt somehow magical and new, doing it by myself, on a bike, for the first time. It was only five miles, but it may as well have been five thousand. There were no cell phones, and no one to come save me if something happened. And that was the best part because in that moment, I was free. Barely fifteen minutes into my adventure, my legs were already exhausted, not yet trained for such an undertaking. Every hill that I crested, while benign from the passenger seat of my dad's Pontiac, tested me both physically and emotionally as the lactic acid bubbled up in my legs, causing them to burn and my lungs to wheeze. I took a swig of Mountain Dew and pressed on.

While on my bike, I began to notice things that had been simply a blur from that old Pontiac: the emerald color of the canopy of leaves overhead, the swaying of the corn fanned by the July winds, the lone red cardinal perched on a tree branch. Even the putrid smell of the dead opossum seemed more pungent and lingering at my pedaling pace while I swatted away the flies as I rolled by. I was doing it, on my own, and in that moment, I knew I would never stop. I had tasted the freedom that only a bike could offer, and my life would never be the same. If 12-year-old and gangly Jerry could glean any wisdom and share it with the now 42-year-old slightly less gangly Jerry, it would be simply that *bikes always win* because here I was now, thirty years later, craving more adventures on the bike, in Nepal.

Nepal had been amazing. Every day, I fell more in love with this beautiful country—the people, the smiles, the kindness—and of course the raw, inspiring (and sometimes unforgiving), landscape. Like a pair of old slippers, at first, when they are new, they are a bit stiff, but the more you wear them, the more comfortable they become. They take some getting used to but eventually begin to mold to the contour of your feet, and you wonder how you ever got by without them. This had been my Nepal experience. I continued to get more comfortable, and I wondered: *what took me so long to get here?*

I had been back in Kathmandu for over a week while I was figuring out what to do next. It was December and the temperatures were getting colder, which was a welcome reprieve from the suffocating humidity of the lower elevations in India. I spent time relaxing and soaking up the local culture, taking two hot showers per day, restocking needed supplies, and of course, catching up with friends and family back home.

Video calls with my dad were my favorite. Each time we would chat, he was always wearing his Korean War Veteran hat, his wavy greyish-brown hair poking out the sides around his ears. I'm still not sure how I got the bald head, and he's still rocking the flowing mane into his 80s. We talked about what movies he had watched recently or if Michigan had gotten snow yet. Honestly, I just wanted to hear how he was doing, but the conversation ultimately shifted toward me. He was so excited and made what I was doing seem like I was Neil Armstrong walking on the moon for the first time. I told him that I was just going for a bike ride, and it wasn't really any different than those times I rode my bike into the country when I was a kid.

My dad and everyone else that I spoke with approaching the end of my originally-planned two-month trip, was expecting to hear of my imminent return. Of course. I had been gone for nearly eight weeks and had not told anyone of my plan to continue on, because really, I didn't know what that looked like. I was just going to keep pedaling east until I didn't want to pedal any more, and then make a decision. Maybe it would be a week, perhaps a month. I didn't know, nor did I care to think too deeply about it. I was just following my "always say yes" mindset.

After traveling through the remote regions in India and Nepal, it was easy to get lost in the modern conveniences of Kathmandu, which is geared toward western tourists, even though "modern" was still a relative term. Hotels have clean sheets, hot showers, and even flushing toilets. It was clear that I was too comfortable in my *slippers*, and I knew that it was time to move on.

The next morning I got back on my bike and picked up the Midland Hills Highway, only to learn, unsurprisingly, that it wasn't much of a *highway*, even by Nepali standards. From Kathmandu to the border crossing into India, it is about four hundred fifty miles. My rough math put me comfortably at nine or ten days, and I couldn't have been more wrong, no doubt a function of my naive idea of the name Midland Hills *Highway*. The Swiss had set out a day before, and we planned to meet up in the next few days somewhere along the route.

The road, once nicely manicured, deteriorated in an instant into a series of landslides that had never been cleared, only compacted and driven over, resembling humps on a camel, in some cases six feet tall. This road leading out of Kathmandu seemed to pick up exactly where the road leading in had left off. At one end of the spectrum was once again that maniacal ankle-deep, soul-sucking chalk that bonds to anything wet, forming an instant paste. At the opposite end, on mountainsides void of any sun, the dirt turns to liquid cement that will never dry. Make the mistake of planting your foot in it, and you'll lose a shoe. This was the *good* road as I was told, and eerily foreshadowed what lay ahead.

Initially, the road danced along the river, close enough that I felt I could scoop up a glassful as I pedaled by. But before I could enjoy a cool drink, the road spiked up so viciously, causing me to aspirate as I searched for available air. This happened repeatedly, seemingly without purpose or reason. There were villages, if you could call them that, speckled along the way, but were nothing more than a couple of huts selling the same mix of Red Bull, instant noodles, and chips. And like that old pair of slippers, I quickly fell back into the familiar comfort of solitude, something I had been craving since I left Pokhara for Kathmandu; my thoughts (and physical suffering) were now my only company.

At the end of the first day, I arrived in the village of Ghurmi, which was at best a dusty truck stop at the junction of three roads. My entire body was covered in the familiar thin film of paste, compliments of the Midland Hills Highway, but at least I had both of my shoes. If nothing else, I looked like a local.

There were three *hotel* options, all equally grim, whose rooms followed a consistent theme: the bed was a three-inch piece of lumpy, well-used foam on top of a sheet of plywood built two feet off the floor, covered in what looked like a horse blanket, seemingly taken directly off the horse just before I arrived. The room, only slightly larger than the bed, sometimes had a window (an upgrade) and was typically accessed *through* another room and not a hallway, where someone likely would be sleeping. None of the rooms were cleaned, with the horse blankets casually strewn about on the beds as though someone had left just before I arrived. Even for $4 per night, I had other ideas.

Ghurmi was dug into a hillside, but there was a small patch of terraced ground behind the police station used for farming which seemed like a great place to camp. After getting the okay from the officers, I set up my tent, rinsed off my body with a hose in a field, then hung out with my neighbors which included seven police officers, a dozen goats, four cows, three dogs and a handful of chickens. One of the officers told me it would be cold overnight and offered me a blanket, but based on what I had seen in the hotels, I politely assured him that I would be warm enough in my sleeping bag. This was the simplicity that I desired, and it was a good thing that I didn't know it would be my easiest day for the next week.

Keeping with form, the following day, and every day for the next seven, the *highway* seemed to collapse abruptly, like an old man having a heart attack, and plummeting down to the river, before being slowly resuscitated and ascending the next ridge at a criminally, and almost comically (although not funny as in "ha ha"), steep pitch causing me frequently to get off and push—sometimes for several hours. The road conditions were volatile, depending on what aspect of the mountain the road lay on. The southern-facing aspects that got full sun were chalk, absent of any hint of moisture. Pedaling up was futile, however, it was *surfable* on the downhill, but at least I knew what I was getting. The northern aspects were far less predictable. Some of it was ridable, but I could never tell until I was in it. Early each morning when the temperatures were still cool, the mud was firm-ish, however as the day wore on and temperatures began to rise, it was a toxic mess. The problem was that just as I got used to being able to ride through the knee-high troughs with this congealed substance lurking at the base, the conditions would change and suck me in without any notice. There was simply no mental or physical reprieve.

On the rare unicorn sighting, when the dirt was compacted and the pitch lessened from "malicious" to "sinister," it was like a direct adrenaline injection into my legs, allowing me to seemingly, without effort, scoot my way up the next hill to the welcoming smiles and perplexed looks of local villagers who probably didn't see many forms of travel other than SUBs. Fortunately, this always seemed to occur just at the point when my soul was most crushed, and I was drifting off into a dark abyss. "Whoa, Superman!" yelled one local teenage boy just after I had crested another one of those absurdly steep pitches. If only he had seen me two minutes prior, cussing aloud.

Like a classical music conductor, the physical undulations of the

Midland Hills Highway were perfectly choreographed to match my internal turmoil. Every couple of hours I would pass a cluster of primitive huts (not to be mistaken for a village, however), and my spirits would lift. Young boys giggled and darted across the road. Every time they would change direction, a puff of beige smoke was sent billowing into the air as I slowly churned (or walked) by. It was dreadfully dry; the only moisture was from the sweat cascading down my forehead and damming up from the layer of paste seemingly permanently affixed to my brow.

At nondescript periodic intervals, I would inexplicably dive into an emotional abyss, either recounting turbulent events from the past year or simply cussing myself out for attempting to pedal an overloaded bike through this inescapable sand trap. Maybe this was good therapy, kinda like sweating out a heroin addiction? I have no idea what that is like since I've never taken a drug in my life, but I knew that I was sweating *something* out.

The further east I went, the hotter it got. By 9 a.m. each day, I had blown through a liter of water, my body already encased in paste. Putting on sunscreen seemed only to make the chalk more adhesive to my skin. However, each time I was feeling despondent, questioning this road and my actions, the *highway* would top out and give me a glimpse of the snowcapped peaks that I was once again pedaling towards, reaffirming my path.

At 3 p.m., on a dead calm afternoon, on the eve of a full moon, I crested the summit of a mountain pass just shy of 9,000 feet, the highest point of the route, physically shattered after climbing for five hours. It was the kind of calm where I could literally hear my own heartbeat, almost therapeutically thumping in my chest, and nothing else. Although there was no village, there was a simple guesthouse, run by a husband and wife who had a two-year-old son.

Technically it was a guesthouse, but that seemed like a stretch as it was almost a homestay since I didn't see any other guests or even any other guest rooms. The two-story structure was a combination of whitewashed concrete and corrugated steel, woefully showing the effects of weather and time that come with being perched at the top of a mountain pass. The kitchen consisted of a fire pit that was used to make the tea and dal bhat. At this elevation in mid-December, the temperature was diving, and I hopelessly wanted to stay in the kitchen for warmth, but was driven out by the poor ventilation, the lingering smoke burning my eyes and choking my lungs. I guess they were somehow used to it.

My room was a tiny concrete box barely larger than the bed, directly above the kitchen. The bed was the familiar piece of lumpy foam set atop a sheet of elevated plywood, with two horse blankets, one for padding and one for warmth. I opted to use both for padding and instead cocoon myself in my sleeping bag. There were wooden shutters that opened to the valley below. The scene was like an idyllic coloring book, and I flung open the shutters to witness the glowing sunset that lit the valley orange, shortly before turning the page to see the full moon replace it and continue the illumination.

I had been traveling along the Midland Hills Highway for over a week, and there was no disguising it. My cycling clothes had not been washed since I left Kathmandu. Each day I took off my shirt, a new salt ring had formed, clearly chronicling my time here like the growth rings of a tree. It would actually stand up on its own when not on my back. Every bolt on my bike and every muscle in my body had been tested, and both were beginning to fail.

I finally received a text message from the Swiss. They were staying in the mountain village of Birtamode, a two-day ride from the Indian border, one day from where I was—if I kept pedaling. As I plummeted down to the river after a now-familiar long day of battle, I arrived in another small, muggy village. The Swiss were waiting for me in the next village up the pass, but even the promise of a hot shower could not will my body or my mind to push another pedal that day—which sounded only slightly worse than another morning of putting on filthy clothes after a muggy night of restless sleep atop some very well-used horse blankets.

While enjoying a snack and pondering the lesser of my two options, I noticed some well-dressed Nepali men roll up in a Mahindra, a four-door pick-up truck made in India which is ubiquitous in this area. Along with SUBs, they seem to be the only vehicle able to withstand the relentless punishment of the Midland Hills Highway. Some bikepackers are purists, following an unwritten code to cycle every segment and never take a ride. Since I hadn't set out with any real plan, I began to entertain a third option.

Although the men were not speaking English, I overheard the name Birtamode, and through some well-choreographed charades, I found myself in the back of their truck, bound for the mountain village. There was actually room in the cab of the vehicle but based on the not-so-subtle disparity between my appearance and theirs, there was little debate about where my self-standing cycling shirt and I would be riding.

The sun was setting so I put on all the clothes I had, including a buff (thin neck scarf) across my face, and prepared for the impending one-hour sandstorm. I don't think they were intentionally trying to bounce me around like a pinball, but rather, they just had to keep up their momentum in order to make it up the pass, something I had seen dozens of times as similar vehicles had come blasting by me.

I had one hand on the roll bar for stability and the other on my bike, partially to keep it from flying out of the back of the truck but also to keep it from slamming into me. The men regularly looked back through the window of their air-conditioned cab to see if I had indeed flown out. Instead of an occasional cloud of dust and sand that would coat me each time a Mahindra or SUB would pass me by while cycling, I was now engulfed in that cloud as the truck churned, sputtered, and rallied around each blown-out corner. Fifteen minutes up the pass, I wondered if this was worse than pedaling. But an hour later, the dust settled as we hit the first tarmac I had seen since Kathmandu, and the Mahindra ground to a stop as we entered the village. I hopped out of the back, looking like the Tuskan Raider sand people from Tatooine in *Star Wars*, gratefully shook everyone's hands, and pedaled away to the hotel, where a hot shower, my new friends, and a new chapter, were waiting.

CHAPTER 2

Compromise, Shower Restrictions, and Resets

"It's my way or the highway," my dad would bark at me, his words still echoing in my mind. Growing up in Michigan in the 80s under his strict military regime, I hated being told what to do, but I was in *his house* and there was no negotiation. However, from when my parents divorced when I was four, all the way through high school, I didn't know anything else. In Colorado, however, where my non-military mom lived, I'm pretty sure my four brothers had a starkly different experience. "When you're under my roof," my dad would constantly remind me, "it's my rules. You can do what you want when you're 18 and have your own place." I assume this was a pretty common upbringing for other kids in my neighborhood during that generation?

When he was in the military and lived in the barracks, following orders and orderly living were understood, without compromise. Big Jer would tell me about the importance of making his bunk each morning in a certain way. If the sheets were not tucked tight enough such that he could bounce a quarter off his bed, his bunk would be *turned* by his commanding officer, and he would have to start over. I made my bed every morning under this mentality, and this is how I grew up, without compromise.

We lived in a two-bedroom, nine hundred square foot apartment that was part of a six-unit complex across the street from my high school. My dad had worked out an agreement with the property owner to act as a resident manager for the building, which also included maintenance of the outdoor areas. This meant shoveling the sidewalks in the winter and mowing the lawn in the summer. Both of these ultimately fell to me as part of my chores. I was paid $20 for the four-hour mowing job, which at the time in 1986, $5 per hour was pretty good money. It beat bagging groceries at the local Felpausch supermarket, which is what many of my other friends did. Don't be confused, however. Just because I was being paid, the job was not optional, but rather it was conditional for my residency under Big Jer's roof. The money was just a nice way to soften that fact.

In the summer, the grass grew rapidly. One mow per week seemed reasonable, but in the military mindset of following orders and orderly living, my dad believed the grass needed to be cut every four days, regardless of my plans or assessment. Like most 12-year-old boys in the summer, with no school to wake up early for, I often stayed up too late playing Nintendo and thus would routinely sleep until 11 a.m. One morning, while sleeping off a hangover of Zelda and a six-pack of Mountain Dew, I vaguely heard some muffled words seep in and out of my consciousness. Thinking nothing of it, I drifted off back to sleep. A few minutes later, I *felt* the angry, purposeful stomping of boots up the steps approaching my room, a sound I had heard plenty of times. Before I could get one eye open, the order came, "I said I want the grass cut, *now*!" exactly three seconds before my barracks was infiltrated and my bunk was turned. Big Jer grabbed the mattress, with me on it, and flipped it over, launching me onto the floor, the mattress landing on top of me. I'm sure he had told me about cutting the grass the night before, but I wasn't listening.

This battle of wills raged on until the spring of 1992 when I turned 18. I was playing sports and lifting weights. I had grown four inches and added about 30 pounds of muscle, even though I weighed only about 140 pounds with my soccer cleats on. I developed a prolific, yet undiagnosed case of what was known as "senioritis," a common affliction brought on by my upcoming high school graduation. I was cocky and defiant, and my dad could no longer flip me out of my bed. After another contentious standoff over something I'm sure I categorized as trivial at best, he turned and stomped down the stairs, only to return a minute later with a suitcase. I was being dishonorably discharged. He threw the suitcase on my loosely made bed and walked away. I called up my best friend to come pick me up (because, of course, I wasn't allowed to have a car since a car was too much freedom), and I moved to the couch in his family's basement for the final three months of school leading up to graduation. It was probably the most traumatizing yet liberating moment in my life.

We didn't talk about this incident until I was in my 40s, after decades of guilt that had built up inside him.

"Do you hate me for what happened that night?" he asked one evening over dinner in Colorado. "I just would hate to think I screwed up your life," he said while apologetically choking back tears, without actually apologizing. But I knew he felt bad, and I wasn't about to make him feel worse. The truth is, growing up under Big Jer's structured regime made me the focused, driven man that I am—something I will always be grateful for. And ironically, this structure and lack of choice almost directly launched me on this rebellious, curious journey that I now found myself on.

Since arriving in Africa in June, I had been traveling solo for nearly six months, and for what seemed like the first time in my life, all my decisions were made without any consideration outside of my own needs or thoughts. It was truly liberating.

That all changed the moment I walked into the hotel in Birtamode to join the Swiss, unsure exactly what I was walking into.

Where to go, how fast to ride, where to sleep, when to wake up and start riding, when to take a break, where to eat and when—all these simple choices were now going to be decided by committee, a committee whose majority vote was controlled by people I had met two weeks earlier over dinner and had barely talked to since. This should have been an exciting time for me, extending my adventure in Nepal and India with no concrete plans or limitations. It was complete freedom, sorta. Instead, it was causing me near-paralyzing anxiety. Ironically, traveling with the Swiss in a way felt like giving up that *freedom*, and would ultimately be a tremendous test for me. Could I continue to *always say yes*? How was this going to work, but more importantly, for how long?

"Ah, the American is here. It is good to see you, man!" exalted Ivo when I knocked on his door, temporarily burying my anxiety. They had arrived the day before and were freshly showered and rested, a stark contrast to my battered physical and mental state. "We have an awesome route planned. Go to your room and take a shower. We will tell you about it tomorrow."

The committee had made its first decision. Tell me about it tomorrow? How about I tell them about it tomorrow! It had been more than a decade since my last corporate performance review in 2005, and while I'd like to believe that I had grown both personally and professionally since then, apparently some of my tendencies still lingered. In that review, my manager had discerned my propensity for collaboration and had some choice words to share:

> *Jerry is outgoing and capable of contributing his ideas in a group setting. Just keep in mind that he may not be patient with those people who he perceives to be more tedious or needy, detracting from his ability to mentor or remain patient when engaged with some colleagues. Basically, there are times when rather than "partnering" with people, Jerry is more apt to start "telling" people what they need to do.*

Time would tell how well I'd "partner" with the Swiss, how patient I could be and, in my eyes, how tedious and needy they might become.

The next day was a much-needed rest day (or a *reset* day as I preferred to call them). Reset days typically involved laundry, cleaning the bike, cleaning myself, catching up with friends and family back home, and resting—a total *reset* of the system. After ten days along the Midland Hills Highway, both myself and the Swiss (the collective), needed a reset day before riding the final two days toward the India border and climbing back into the mountains.

Three days later, we entered India after about a hundred miles of mostly forgettable, flat, and muggy terrain, not dissimilar to what I had encountered as I entered Nepal. The instant we crossed the border, India came protesting back, and it was just as I remembered;

motorbikes, cars, and buses in ascending order of road seniority were screaming by, many times within inches of us, *welcoming* us to India. With their blaring horns and sputtering exhaust, they quickly reminded us not only that we were no longer in Nepal, but also of our place in the pecking order on the road—which was at the bottom.

Somehow, this time the organized chaos of India was comforting, if that's at all possible, and I relished being back. I felt alive in the mayhem. The distant peaks were just as I remembered, but to get to them, we still had to cross about eighty miles of the same flat, humid, mosquito-plagued, mold-infested, diesel-spewing monotony.

For all the beauty that resides in the mountains of India and Nepal, it's truly unfortunate how not a hint of that beauty exists anywhere near the borders. It has been my experience that border crossing areas are really the worst part of any country. I would expect them to be some of the best, kinda like, "Welcome to our amazing country! Come on in! This is only a taste of what you can expect here!" but once again, that was not the case here. Roads were broken, muddy, and potholed, and the only restaurants and hotels appeared to cater to a captive, undiscerning audience. Knowing this, we all agreed to tuck our chins and pedal as far as we could until it got dark in the hope of a better option.

After slogging along for most of the day, we were running out of ambition, and daylight. There were no hotels in an area where I would have expected at least one. The air was heavy and was weighing on me. Once again there was a prolific military presence and thus no place to camp, and even if we could, the saturating humidity had turned most of the fields into marsh. Surprisingly, English was much more sparsely spoken but after countless futile attempts to find a hotel, we were finally told that we could find lodging at the Nature and Wildlife Sanctuary, which sounded amazing.

We arrived at the Nature and Wildlife Sanctuary and were given two rooms in what they described as the "Holiday Bungalow." Their words, not mine. It was shelter, to be sure, and it would set the new baseline for which all future accommodations would be measured against. "Well, at least it's better than the Holiday Bungalow . . ." we could later joke.

The small, two-room concrete building was tucked back off the road into the overgrown woods. I assume it was once painted white, but now the walls oozed a toxic greenish-brown mold. An abandoned white van was parked out front, looking like it had been reclaimed by the swamp years ago, though realistically it had likely only been there a few months. In this environment, I have no idea how fast the jungle moves. Vines were growing through the windows while the same familiar mold crept up from the tepid stream that ran underneath.

Rooms in the Holiday Bungalow were given to visiting state officials in the area, and despite the conditions, we were grateful for the offering. Each room had a bed, which was the familiar, very tired, broken-down thin foam mattress. Fortunately, in contrast to the rest of the facility, the bed showed only mild suggestions of mold, and also came with a much-needed mosquito net to drape over it. Everywhere we looked, mold seeped up the once whitewashed walls from the musty concrete floors, a general smell of rot saturating the room. The common bathroom had a squatty potty that likely hadn't been cleaned since the Holiday Bungalow was built. There was a faucet with a moldy, cracked bucket that we used for a bath. I will say, however, almost without exception, I always find it better to take a bath and go to sleep clean after a long day on the bike, regardless of the bathing standards. Soap can clean away just about anything.

To be sure, if we could have found a place to camp, we would have, but instead, we blew up our air mattresses and camped inside our rooms. In the spirit of Indian kindness, the officials who offered us the rooms got us a takeaway curry which we enjoyed encased in our (mostly) mosquito-proof beds, before drifting off to sleep.

We left the Holiday Bungalow early the next morning going uphill, out of the jungle, before the mold had a chance to reclaim us. We were traveling through a region known as West Bengal, a spectacularly lush, mountainous pocket, snuggled deep into the elbow crease between Nepal and Bhutan. I'm pretty sure the board game "Chutes and Ladders" was modeled after the roads in West Bengal, adding new meaning to the term "steep." Hour after hour, turn after turn, they will crush your ego, your legs, and your will with a relentless, impossibly steep assault until you are decimated in a fetal position on the side of the road as the convoy of Indian tourists zoom by in their 4×4 vehicles blasting diesel exhaust into your already compromised lungs. Due to the ludicrous pitch, the government has driven steel spikes into the tarmac, seemingly by hand, to provide traction. The spikes, spaced approximately ten inches apart, stretch the width of the road and resemble pimples on an otherwise silky, unblemished face. I suppose the construction of switchbacks would translate into more tarmac being poured, so instead, let's save money and just pour the road straight uphill, and add steel spikes! In spite of the pitch, it provided a nice reprieve from the chalk I endured the past two weeks along the Midland Hills Highway.

We arrived in the mountaintop town of Darjeeling after two excessively long days of climbing the tarmac equivalent of an elevator shaft, while a constant parade of honking SUVs loaded with Indian tourists raced by. Our legs and psyches were still decimated from the Midland Hills Highway, and now West Bengal finished the job. We all agreed that Darjeeling was a good place to have a reset day, which seamlessly turned into four.

Darjeeling is a popular tourist destination with good food and clean hotel rooms. It sits at about 6,700 feet above the emerald jungle that we had escaped from, with panoramic views of the tea plantations that blanket the valley below. To the north were provocative views of Kangchenjunga, the third-highest peak in the world at 28,169 feet, behind only its better-known siblings, Everest and K2. Our guesthouse was a meticulously spotless building down a quiet alley, away from the droves of tourists and their commotion. For the first time in India, I actually used the pillows and sheets without fear for my health. In addition, there was Wi-Fi, sorta. But the kicker was that we were allowed a single hot shower per day. Yes, only one. How was that regulated? There was a separate power button located in the hotel owner's suite that controlled the hot water geyser (pronounced "geezer") in each bathroom. Each morning, at 6 a.m. she would turn on the power for forty-five minutes to heat up the five-gallon tank, then promptly turn it off. Just as some people get excited by the sound of coffee brewing, I woke each day to the seductive sound of my percolating geyser, almost like Pavlov's bell.

The hotel owner was an older woman of Chinese descent, and outside of the miserly shower policy, she had a heart of gold. She told us that her husband actually built the hotel several years prior.

Although the concept of one shower per day seemed a tad militaristic, almost like the one-child policy in China, I found it more comical than the Swiss. Apparently, they really like their hot showers and would take two or more per day, even on a reset day when they were just lying around their hotel room.

This was the most comfortable I had been since I was in Pokhara nearly a month earlier. I had taken for granted the trauma placed on my body and mind, the stress of constantly being on the go and not having a home. In the comforts of Darjeeling, I slipped easily into a normal routine of yoga and meditation in my room when I woke each morning, followed by my one shower for the day, using every drop of *my* hot water. After finding breakfast in the main market, I would return to my room to read for a few hours or sponge up some internet before meeting the Swiss for lunch around noon. While we both liked to wake up early on ride days and get a jump on the day, on reset days, I learned they slept until 10 or 11 a.m. and didn't come out of their room until noon for lunch.

"Relax, man. These are rest days," Ivo said to me the first morning in Darjeeling when I knocked on his door to get breakfast, his wispy blondish hair sticking up in the back. "We go back to sleep but will see you for lunch," as he closed the door and shooed me away.

It was all part of coexisting and getting to know each other. After lunch, the Swiss would retreat back to their room, and I would spend the afternoon in the market, filling my cup of extroversion while people watching and clowning around with the locals, before meeting up with the Swiss again for dinner.

I had been with my new friends for nearly a week now, and all my initial anxiety over giving up the autonomy of solo travel turned out to be unfounded. I was concerned that we either wouldn't ride at the same pace, or the same duration, or more likely would just eventually annoy the shit out of each other. But none of that happened. We had formed an unexpected partnership, one that was neither needy nor tedious, probably because all of us had a passion for mountains and an unquenchable curiosity for what lay over the next pass. Collectively, it was intoxicating. The only difference between us was their tendency toward introversion, which was either a byproduct of always traveling with a partner and thus having an established social outlet, or just being Swiss. I think it was a little bit of both. But after only five days, it felt like we had known each other for years. The best part (well, for me at least) was that I was able to have a personality again and just be me. The language barrier of the previous six months was now removed (mostly), although I'm not certain they always grasped my sense of humor, or animated clowning interactions with the locals. *Is it possible I'm not as funny as I think?*

—

Somehow, without my knowledge, Christmas had crept up on me, bringing with it mixed emotions. Being in India and Nepal for the past three months, where the primary religions are Hindu and Buddhism, there was no extravagant build-up to Christmas like in the US. Outside of the subtle hints around Darjeeling, including a Santa statue playing a saxophone located in the main square, which was draped with Indian tourists taking selfies, Christmas passed as just another day. Instead, we celebrated over dinner with a shared pizza from Pizza Hut. It was the first meal I had eaten since arriving that wasn't either curry or dal bhat, and while we all agreed to splurge on a $10 western meal, we walked away disappointed.

For me, this seemingly innocuous date on the calendar subtly churned up a bucket of suppressed emotions. Each year for the past decade, Family Hospice held a semiformal holiday party—a time for everyone to be treated to a special day when our clinical staff could dress up and wear something other than their scrubs. It was always a different venue each year, with dinner, games, dancing, and gifts—but mostly, gratitude. It not only brought our staff closer together, but also my mom and me. We had a shared pride in the organization that we built, and it truly felt like a family. Now, it had been one year since that company went away, one year since our last holiday party, and somehow, one year since I had last talked to my mom. I had never gone even a single day without talking to her in the previous ten years, and even before Family Hospice, it wasn't uncommon for me to see her a couple of times a week, either for tea or a bike ride. It all felt surreal that someone who had been such an integral part of my life was now not even on the periphery. Why hadn't she reached out to me like my dad since I had been away? Did she not care what I was doing, or wonder if I was safe? The void of my mom throbbed in my heart even more now on Christmas.

It also had been one year since I had spoken to Emma. Unlike my mom, I didn't expect Emma to reach out to me. Initially, when I returned home from South America after my trip with Taylor, I had hoped that we would find the space, but mostly the love, to talk through our frustrations and find our way back to each other again. Instead, she moved out the following week without even a hug or a goodbye, and outside of a few messages to coordinate the pickup of her things from the house, I hadn't heard from her since. Even though it's not uncommon to drift apart from a partner after a breakup, I always thought we would talk again and was slowly coming to grips with the fact that we likely wouldn't.

—

I woke up Christmas morning and went to the main square to withdraw some money from the ATM, only to find that it was empty, as were all the other ATMs in Darjeeling. I had thus far been using money that I had saved from my last time in India six weeks earlier, but now I was running low.

On November 9, the Indian government demonetized all of the old Rs1,000 ($15) and Rs500 ($7.50) notes and replaced them with new Rs2,000 ($30) notes. Prime Minister Narendra Modi claimed that the main objective was to eliminate "black money" which included income that had not been reported and thus was untaxed; money gained through corruption, illegal goods sales and illegal activities such as human trafficking, and counterfeit currency. The government estimated that ₹3 lakh crore (about $40 billion), or approximately 20 percent of the demonetized banknotes, would be permanently removed from circulation. The move was largely celebrated by Indian officials; however, it was short-sighted because it translated into an economic panic. If you didn't exchange your old notes by December 31, they essentially became cocktail napkins. Imagine having a bundle of cash that you had been socking away in your sock drawer, maybe for a few months, maybe a few years, only to find out that the government had decided that it was now worthless. Remember microeconomics in college? Here it was, on display. Scarcity affecting behavior.

Panic ensued and very quickly banks were wiped out of their cash reserves and simply closed down. The banks that did open had full day-long waiting lines snaking around city blocks. The challenge for us was that all ATM withdrawals were limited to Rs2,500 ($38) per day. Even in India, that was a paltry amount of money, which resulted in regular daily two-hour waits at every ATM until they would run out of money, which happened in about two hours. Even though many signs read "24hr ATM," they were always locked down overnight for fear that someone in their desperation would crack them open. Some ATMs wouldn't be refilled for days. At any minute I expected to see a riot break out. When we did get money from a generous ATM, we would get Rs2,000 notes, and most places, especially street food merchants, simply could not make change. It would be like buying a pack of gum from the newsstand with a $100 bill in the US. We spent a chunk of each day hitting up the various ATMs, ensuring we had enough of our own reserves once we left Darjeeling because we feared in smaller, less touristy towns, ATMs would be even more scarce.

After five reset days in Darjeeling, I think the Swiss had had enough of their shower regulation, so we eagerly pushed out of town on a crisp morning on New Year's Eve.

"Man, we need to stop," Ivo calmly yelled over to me after we had been descending down the other side of the elevator shaft for about a half-hour, the warm wind blowing in my ears like a hairdryer. "Brigitte's brakes aren't working."

The road, already steep, had just started to tip from *comical* to *comic book* as we noticed the first appearance of the traction spikes in the tarmac. Fortunately, Ivo had gotten my attention when he did, because while we climbed at a similar pace, there was a sharp disparity in our descending interests.

After slowly grinding to a stop, Brigitte's brake rotors seemed to be on fire, steam from the friction and also the late morning heat wafting from the serrated steel.

"Ah, here's your problem," I said with a chuckle while looking at her wheel, "her brake pads are shot."

The resin pads had worn all the way down to the metal, revealing the scorched steel underneath. After being on the road for four years, Ivo was a quick mechanic. Within two minutes, he had Brigitte's bike flipped over and was swapping out her front and rear pads, both having suffered the wrath of the West Bengal roads.

I took that time to sit on the mangled, metal guardrail overlooking the emerald tea fields below, to enjoy a snack and observe the monkeys that had taken an interest in us. Slowly and curiously, probably twenty feet down the road, three monkeys crept out from the overgrown hillside and ducked under the guardrail that I was sitting on. They were cautious but clearly not afraid of humans, having obviously interacted plenty of times with our type over the years. I engaged in a two-minute staring competition with one of the monkeys, and when I eventually lost, turned to walk over and check on Ivo's progress as the other two monkeys strategically came along.

"Almost done!" said Ivo proudly, as the two monkeys gazed on at his handy work.

"Bastard!" I yelled out, as I casually glimpsed back over my shoulder to see the third monkey pickpocketing Ivo's phone from the bag on his handlebars. I took off running down the road yelling and waving my arms, and seeing this maniac coming, he dropped the phone and escaped into the elusive cover of the hillside. I spun back around to see his accomplices flee the scene as well. I'm certain this was not their first ruse, nor their last. In my mind I can picture the three of them with a stick, drawing their playbook in the dirt. "Ok, Sanjay and Avee will follow along, looking cute, and distract the tourists, while I sneak around and raid their bicycle. There are three of them, so it will be difficult to keep their attention, but I only need a couple of minutes," as they all sat, chuckling with that familiar cultural Indian head wobble that not even the monkeys are immune to.

Later in the day, as the sun was beginning to set, we had managed to climb up to the small village of Lava. While looking for a hotel, we saw a newly constructed building with the words "Homestay" painted prominently on the sign out front. Technically it was a hotel, owned by a family, and on the outside, it didn't appear any different than a typical smaller hotel. Once we ventured inside, it was like walking into someone's home. The freshly painted white walls flowed into the separate bedrooms, shared bathroom, and dining room. Respectfully, we all removed our shoes before entering, and I immediately felt guilty. I had not worn socks in six months because I had been cycling in sandals, and my grimy feet were leaving a distinct funk silhouette on the shimmering white tile. "No problem. No problem," the young Indian girl who showed us to our rooms said to me, seeing my obvious embarrassment.

Technically they planned to open the next day, so we were their first guests. We were quickly shown to our rooms and given fluffy white towels. The beds were actual mattresses with crisp white sheets that had never been used. I made a dash to get the first shower, knowing the Swiss propensity for showers. If I didn't, I was certain there wouldn't be a drop of hot water remaining for me. There was even a western-style toilet instead of a squatty potty—the first one I had seen (and used) in nearly three months in India and Nepal—and our stay somehow cost only $15, including dinner.

"Are we in India?" I leaned over and asked Ivo during dinner, with a confused yet sarcastic tone that hopefully he picked up on.

"Shut up, man," he replied, clearly still not picking up on it.

After dinner, I quietly retired to my room with a hot cup of chai in a fancy, new, never-used mug. It was New Year's Eve, and again, another anticlimactic day. There was no party. No countdown, and surely nobody to kiss at midnight. It was only 8:30 p.m. as I pulled back the fresh white bedding, crawled into bed, and turned on some music on my phone. Fittingly, on shuffle, one of my favorite John Coltrane tracks came on: "I Want to Be Happy."

Although December 31 technically is just another day on a calendar, there is an inescapable symbolism that accompanies it, a mindset of "out with the old, in with the new." A time for rebirth and new beginnings. A *do-over.* Ask me a year ago where I would be now. Riding my bicycle through the Himalayas with two strangers? Not a chance. In hindsight, this had been an unforeseen and unwanted gift, but it was still a gift.

The Swiss had each other to celebrate with. Me, I had John Coltrane and a mountain of emotions. Alone in a hotel room in a rural village in northeast India, 8,000 miles from anything familiar, my carefully drawn out, and laminated road map for happiness had been jettisoned somewhere along the way. Gone was my company, my Emma, and my mom. I was alone without any direction, wandering through the world on a bike trying to figure it out. This was not the life I had pictured or sought. I had it all... or so I was led to believe. But sometimes, life happens.

I sat in my room, contemplative, poring over a year of exhilarating, unquenchable highs, but inevitably my thoughts drifted toward the crippling, heart-wrenching lows. I took a sip of chai and wondered what my mom was doing. Was she also feeling the same void in her heart carved out by our rupture? Was there any remorse or guilt, not just for the loss of the hospice, but more for the loss of her son? I was slowly moving on and getting over it, but would I ever forgive her? Would we ever talk again?

I thought about my friends back in Colorado making plans to go out and celebrate. New Year's Eve has always been one of my favorite nights to see my *important people*, the people closest to me. It was also Emma's birthday. I was finally making peace with our breakup, the realization that while we loved each other, we weren't meant to be, and maybe I would never see her again. With this acceptance, I tried to picture her with a smile on her face, and I hoped she was having a great time doing something that she loved. And I missed Cynthia.

Back in college, my mom had given me a jade plant, a symbol that now presented as another metaphor of my life. Over twenty years, mine had grown strong, with a thick, sturdy trunk and plump, rubbery emerald leaves. Occasionally branches would begin to wither and in order for the plant to continue to grow and thrive, those less healthy limbs needed to be trimmed away. If I didn't make those *cuts*, the jade would expend too much energy trying to revive the withering parts, detracting from the overall health of the plant. In order for me to heal, it was clear that I needed to cut away some of the withering parts of my life.

I was alone in a foreign country, and it was just another day. But maybe this is what I needed at this point in my life—to be able to process and make sense of things. To really sit with these inner battles, isolated in a far-off place, and finally cut away some of those unhealthy parts.

As I finished my chai, I thought back to the three renunciations I learned in Rishikesh, renunciations necessary to make room in our lives to achieve true happiness: *physical*, *mental*, and *emotional*.

- *Physical* items provide only fleeting glimpses of happiness, so do not attach any value to them. They will leave you feeling empty.
- Free yourself of *mental* negativity, cognitive dissonance and other things that clog up your mind that prevent happiness from having space to flourish.
- Make peace with and release the *emotional* scars and traumas from the past so you have space for new highs.

By 9 p.m., with a still mind and an open heart, I turned out the light for the day, the year, and this chapter in my life—eagerly anticipating what boundless opportunities the new year and next chapter would bring. Out with the old. In with the new.

CHAPTER 3

Connecting the Dots with Selfies and Smiles

It was New Year's Day, just another square on the calendar. Technically, it was a holiday in most of the world, but it wasn't like I had the day off from work. Yet somehow, things were different. I woke up optimistic for the year, feeling that a page had turned and that my life was beginning to smooth out. Paralleling that mental shift, we descended out of the jolting topography of West Bengal and crossed into the state of Assam, whose flat, featureless landscape invoked memories of growing up in Michigan with its dense forests flanking the sprawling farmland like the patchwork quilt that always draped across my grandmother's rocking chair, a gift given to her on retirement from the railroad.

I moved to Colorado in 1995 and since then have considered myself a mountain guy, at home in the thin, crisp air of the alpine. Down here through Assam, it was nearly four hundred miles of hot, flat, dry, and overall unnecessary existence. I already missed the mountains and yearned for their return. I've never been motivated to "connect the dots," so I planned to get on a bus and save myself the drawn-out monotony of six long, mindless days. Knowing that the Swiss were also mountain people, I dismissively expected them to simply join along in that plan, but clearly, we were still learning how to travel together. On this topic, the Swiss were hearing nothing of it, and we had our first route dissent. Instead, they were more traditional in their approach to touring and were committed to forging ahead, no bus, thus connecting the dots and not "cheating." Initially, I resigned myself to meet up with them in a few days, but in keeping with my "always say yes" mindset and not *break up the up band* in only the second week, at the last minute, I softened.

A modern four-lane paved highway stretches the length of Assam, west to east. More so than any place I had been in India thus far, in Assam there was a glaring, definitive wealth disparity. A shiny, black Mahindra SUV would zoom by me, the windows up and the air conditioning on high, just as I was pedaling by a man pushing a wooden cart full of rocks. He was barefoot, wearing tattered clothes. His skin was dark and weathered, showing years of hard work in the blazing sun. I think he is my age, but he looked much older. One of his sons was riding in the wagon while the other son guided a cow behind us. I guess they were maybe 7 and 10, respectively. Another man walking at a slightly swifter pace is carrying chickens by the feet, three in each hand. They all smiled and greeted me with a "Namaste" as I warmly returned the greeting.

By any economic measures, they are poor, even by Indian standards, and there really isn't another way to put it. But what if we removed the "economic" qualifier? How then do we define "poor?" From my view, their life is simple, but hard, without most of the modern conveniences that I take for granted. I wonder what it's like to walk a mile in their shoes. Would I be happier without all of western society's pressures, expectations, and definitions of success? But then I speculate that maybe they think the same of me, that my life is hard because it is so much more complicated, even though I have more money and the benefits that accompany it. Another shiny SUV zooms by us, the visual disparity unmistakable. Is the man driving the SUV any more happy or content with his life than these men?

Growing listless of simply ticking off easy, mindless miles along the black, pristine tarmac, I took one turn to the left onto a broken dirt road and was immediately transported back in time to a much slower, much simpler life. Gone were the shiny SUVs, supplanted by the more common site of men pushing wooden carts and boys leading their cows. People were plowing fields with oxen and picking vegetables by hand. Tiny villages dot the landscape where children rushed out from their homes, yelling: "Cycle, cycle!"

The women, with their silky, almost walnut-colored skin, starkly contrast against the vibrant pastels of their flowing saris, and despite the dusty environment, they are impeccably flawless. "Namaste," I say with a grin as I slowly pedal by. They return with their own "Namaste!" buried beneath their giggles.

Men of all ages pulled up next to me on their bicycles or turned around when coming from the other direction. Although their English was spotty, they did know one universal phrase: "Selfie, brother?" I was asked every time I stopped pedaling, and even times when I hadn't, but rather was beckoned to stop. Sometimes when I simply pulled over to pee. Immediately upon rolling through any one of the countless dusty villages, I felt like the paparazzi was chasing me. If I stopped to check a map, even for a minute along the spider web network of primitive roads, a mob of local villagers came out of their houses or the market, circled around me, and attempted to give me directions. "Come. Chai?" they would always say to me.

In the rural Indian state of Assam, people just wanted to stop and talk, to have a chai, to connect. In my western mindset, I'm just a guy riding a bike, but here, I was a celebrity. Anonymity was gone, and over the past three months, I had begun to slowly bring awareness to my status of being anything but "just a guy riding a bike."

It can be exhausting, and sometimes I just want to blend in, to be "one of them" and simply keep pedaling, but I know that's impossible, and even harder to shun such a genuine desire for connection. Which makes me wonder . . . what is the limit to how many cups of chai I can have per day?

Pedaling through Assam, I was once again resoundingly reminded that life is about the journey, not the destination. You can take a bus or plane and go see the Taj Mahal or Everest Base Camp, but you miss all the good stuff along the way. The people at those destinations are waiting there, expecting you. The people you meet along the way are not, and they are the ones that provide the most color to the story. Immediately I realized that if I had taken that bus through Assam, I would have missed this ordinary, yet extraordinary beauty.

After an hour of lazily meandering down some of the most remote roads I had thus far been on in India, my mind drunk off the kindness of the local villagers, I heard a *ping* and knew exactly what it was. I got off my bike and saw the broken spoke in my rear wheel, the first real mechanical issue of the trip. Up until now, I had not even had a flat tire, even through Africa.

The real issue, however, was that when I looked around, the Swiss were nowhere to be seen. We had set out in the morning and made a plan to ride at whatever speed that felt comfortable, and we would meet in a specific village at the end of the day. I knew that I was quite a bit ahead, but in the convoluted maze of single-lane dirt roads, it was unclear if they were actually following my same disjointed route.

"Hello! Where are you from? Where are you going?" a man from across the narrow dirt road fired the familiar greetings at me.

I'd heard and answered this inquiry more times than I could count, and honestly, I just wanted to get my bike fixed. It was getting late, I was in the middle of nowhere, and I was getting a bit frazzled. The solicitations were now an unnecessary distraction, and I began to sober up from my inebriated bliss. *Breathe*, I told myself. *Don't let your circumstances overshadow how you react to someone else. They have no idea what is happening in your mind.* I took several deep breaths, smiled, then crossed the dirt road and was immediately surrounded by six men, all wanting to meet me and take selfies, of course.

The man who called to me spoke quite good English, and I was able to communicate to him what I needed. He was 33 and worked at the bank in town.

"Ah, you have brawkin sprahk? Come with me. Best mechanic in town."

After a few more selfies, he hopped on his motorcycle, and I followed him to another shop across town, about five minutes away, only to find out that the mechanic was at lunch and would return at 5 p.m. While we waited, he invited me to his home, where his mother made us lunch. He shared with me that she had cancer, so he lives at home and spends his time and his money taking care of her. She stood at best slightly more than four feet tall with a body shaped like a lowercase "r"—a pronounced hunch, likely from years of hard work. She had frizzy gray hair tied in a bun, no teeth, and spoke no English, but had a glowing aura about her that radiated genuine kindness, evident by how much joy she derived simply by serving us a plate of veggie *momos,* delicious Indian dumplings.

At 5 p.m., we rolled back to the bike shop to meet the mechanic. Of course, he did not have a *sprahk* to fit. All were either too long or too short. And the idiot that I am, didn't bring any *sprahks* with me, blindly assuming that they would be easy to source in India. Glad I saved all that space in my bag, and those nine grams. Not to be defeated, he figured out that it was possible to bend the end of a *too-long* spoke so that it was the correct length, and whammo—wheel was fixed! I don't know who was more excited by this revelation? I would like to think it was me, but I think I would be wrong.

I glanced down at my watch and noticed that this stroke of genius had taken less than nine minutes. I eagerly extended Rs500 (about $7.50), which clearly embarrassed him. He smiled jovially beneath his push broom-shaped mustache, vehemently waving his hands and refusing any money. However, I was not to be defeated either, and he finally conceded to accept Rs50. I forced Rs100 ($1.50) on him, and you would have thought I handed him the winning lottery ticket.

It was getting dark, the Swiss were nowhere to be found, and I didn't have a way to contact them. We hadn't planned on separating, and they had not purchased an Indian SIM card for their phones. I was pissed at them for this because something so cheap and easy to obtain would have prevented exactly this situation. It was avoidable and in a momentary regression back to that 2005 performance review state-of-mind, I unfairly blamed them for this stupidity—even though it was me who chose to ride ahead. And clearly placing blame was pointless and solved nothing. But without an alternative, I found a hotel for the night and planned to continue riding in the same direction, with hopes of crossing paths with them at the end of Assam in the next few days.

The next morning I rolled out along the same patchwork dirt road system, feeling again relieved and humbled by my experience.

"Where are you going? Where you from?" someone called out to me just before lunch as I was lumbering down a dusty road along a stream. Only this time, there was a distinctly different accent.

"Shit! Are you kidding?" I said in astonishment, seconds before I burst into laughter. I had been pedaling for three hours and by some *random* luck (which I no longer believe in), I had caught up to the Swiss who had stopped in this village to have lunch. Countless route derivatives were crisscrossing the plains of Assam, yet somehow our paths crossed.

I joined the Swiss and sat down inside the small tea house for lunch when the *urge* hit me a few minutes later. I inquired about a "toilet," and although the actual word was universally understood in an otherwise persistent language barrier, the standards of said 'toilet' was anything but. Typically they were down some narrow stairs, out the back of the building, and pretty grim. It was always a simple hole in the floor, with varying degrees of hygiene and upkeep, and never a place to hang out.

This tea house was not unlike any of the others I had been in while in Assam. It was a small, wooden structure, with creaky, mostly swept floors, and maybe five plastic tables covered by red and white checkered vinyl tablecloths, with a jar of hot sauce on each. I had a pretty good expectation of the facilities as the man I spoke with led me down some familiar stairs and out the back door.

"Here!" he pointed proudly, happy to have helped me, before walking back to the kitchen.

I wasn't prepared for this. There was no squatty potty, or even a dedicated enclosed area. The back of the restaurant was elevated on stilts as he pointed to an area underneath the kitchen where they dumped their trash, among other things. The ceiling was barely five feet high, nearly tall enough to walk but low enough to preserve all the wretched stench. The ground was blanketed to the point that I felt like I was walking through a minefield, but unlike a minefield, nothing here was buried. I couldn't recalibrate. This was too much.

Seeing the discomfort in my face, I heard a man say, "Come this way, brother. Best bathroom. Open to all." He led me out to the tea field just beyond the back of the tea house. The sights and smells of fresh tea provided a welcome ambiance like no toilet I had experienced thus far in India. As I crouched down, another man who had seen the top of my head peeking out above the rows of tea plants, approached me carrying a water bottle, a smile as big as India stretched across his face.

"Here, sir. To wash," he politely offered.

"Thank you! Thank you! I'm fine! Just leave it! Thank you! No problem!" I repeated from my compromised position, imploring him to give me my space.

We made our way across Assam over the next four days and arrived in Udalguri, the gateway to Arunachal Pradesh where we would ascend back into the mountains. By this point, I had *almost* forgotten that I nearly got on a bus, and if so, I would have missed this ordinary yet extraordinary beauty.

CHAPTER 4

Why Do You Come Here?

We passed through a gate and were transported to another world. The road, once flat, in an instant vaulted up, into the rolling hills, a mere step stool precursor to the daunting peaks that define this area. Precipices that lay waiting for us in the coming days. In life, I'm learning that doors are continually opening, and when one does, simply take one step forward and walk through. After a week of traversing the flat, dusty roads, and featureless landscape of Assam, this was Arunachal Pradesh.

"Arunachal" means "land of dawn-lit mountains" and is home to twenty-six indigenous tribes. Much of this state remains beyond tourism's reach but new areas are slowly being opened. As foreigners, to travel here is an opportunity afforded to very few. Tucked in between Bhutan and Tibet, and feeling very much like both with its rich ancestral culture and punishing, exclusionary landscape, Arunachal Pradesh is a place that India, and the rest of the world, has largely forgotten.

As a result of its border proximity, there is a heavy military presence with frequent checkpoints. Our Inner Line Permits (ILPs) arrived via email, allowing us thirty days to traverse this rugged, uncompromising landscape, not a dismissive task considering we would be crossing Se La Pass at 13,680 feet, in winter. Once we flashed our ILPs at the military checkpoint, we were granted access to Arunachal Pradesh and began a four-day assault over Se La Pass, which is as close as foreigners can get to Tibet.

We finished our first day in a small village, after a long and abrupt climb on a newly paved two-lane road that aggressively clawed its way into the mountains, instantly reminding us that we were no longer in Assam. Villages in Arunachal Pradesh were small and the provisions basic, making it clear that we were in a region not highlighted in any guidebook—a snapshot of an earlier, simpler time.

Ivo walked into the only hotel in the tiny village and while he was inside, I was approached by a local man in his 30s. His name was Thuptan, and he was a doctor. He was well dressed in creased black pants and stood about 5′7″, lean, with facial features more Tibetan than Indian. He surprisingly spoke remarkable English, considering no one else we had encountered in the village spoke even a single word. With his lively sense of humor, we immediately hit it off.

Ivo walked out of the hotel shaking his head. "It's better than the Holiday Bungalow," he said with a subtle Swiss chuckle. Was my humor beginning to rub off on him?

"I don't know why I didn't think of this. I have a home with two apartments. My family lives on one side but the other apartment is completely open. You can stay there," Thuptan generously offered before even being introduced to Ivo.

Having known Thuptan for less than ten minutes, we all eagerly got on our bikes and followed him along a busted, muddy road for about a mile to his home outside of town. As we rolled up to the modest concrete structure, his parents and siblings greeted us out front with warm tea and even warmer kindness. But before we could change out of our cycling clothes, local regulators showed up. They had seen us roll into town and had followed us to Thuptan's house. I was immediately nervous. Were we supposed to check in someplace? The last thing I wanted to do was get Thuptan's family in trouble.

There were three men but only one who spoke English. He was a jovial, yet slovenly man in his 50s, with long, curly, unkempt black hair pulled back into a ponytail, bent, wire-rim glasses, tattered clothes, a fur hat and a bushy, full beard that threatened to take over his entire face. He resembled an Indian version of my neighbor in Boulder whom I affectionately (and secretly) call Hairy Gary. After making this connection, my trepidation eased.

Indian Hairy Gary (as I'll refer to him) was lacking any official interrogation forms, so he instead asked the family for a sheet of plain paper and a pen. In an effort to appear official, he fired off a series of standard rudimentary questions such as name, occupation, purpose of visit, which he methodically scratched down on the paper. Indian Hairy Gary next asked to see our permits and passports, then zoomed off to town to make copies. When he returned twenty minutes later, I sensed that this was not going to be a stern interrogation, so I proceeded to soften him up with some light banter. He spoke enough English to hopefully glean some of my humor.

"Shut up, man," Ivo whispered to me during the *interrogation.* Initially, I think this made Ivo nervous, evidenced by the glare he gave me. The Swiss have had much more serious encounters while traveling in China, so they were inherently more cautious.

"Happy journey!" said Indian Hairy Gary with a kind smile a few minutes later as he abruptly stood up and walked out, his two sidekicks in tow.

The next night, after a full day of chasing the elusive snowcapped peaks that peered invitingly over the lower, nearby broccoli-covered mounds, we arrived in a small village just before dark. Temperatures were plummeting, and the distinct smell of snow in the January air told us that a storm was imminent. I was excited to escape the suffocating heat of Assam and once again feel the biting chill of the mountains. This time however there weren't any hotel options or any Dr. Thuptan. There was however a school along the river, and after walking around town for thirty minutes, we found one of the teachers who allowed us to camp inside.

Surprisingly, we found three "stores" in town, which were merely small spaces attached to people's homes, all selling only the most basic of food options. We collectively settled on six packages of Maggi, a few potatoes, and some soya meat that we cooked on our camp stoves inside the classroom. The teacher was very concerned about us, and as he was leaving, gave us two bags labeled as "baby weaning food," a government-issued powder that, when mixed with water, formed a sweet and nutritious paste.

The school was a weathered concrete structure with cracks sprawling up the walls resembling a spider web. Half of the windows were either broken or missing, allowing the biting January winds to creep in. There were large metal cans in the center of each classroom to hold a fire, and a stack of firewood against the wall. The ceiling was charred black, indicating that it was easier to create heat than fix the drafty passages. Following a frigid bucket bath and a feast of instant noodles and baby food, we pitched our tents to protect us from the seeping cold, and by 7:30 p.m., we were sound asleep. We awoke the next morning to a frost-laden, frozen ground, slowly hardening us for the looming climb over Se La Pass, knowing that several long days of relentless climbing through unpredictable and deteriorating weather still awaited.

Around 3 p.m. the following day, the sun was setting behind the towering peaks and we were still 2,000 feet and likely three hours from the summit, which would not happen this day. As expected, the temperature was cratering, siphoning the heat from our bodies that we had been generating up the steep, winding, snow-covered road, and we knew that we had at most one hour to find a place to sleep before dark. We looked for a school, church, or any building to give us shelter from the night, or even a flat area to make camp, but the entire area was a sprawling military base, and it was clear that they didn't want anyone to camp there.

Almost immediately after I quit pedaling, I began shaking from the piercing cold. "Let's just ask," I said to Ivo, without a better idea between us. I didn't know what I was asking for specifically, but rather just looking for ideas, options, anything other than pressing on into the frigid night or turning around—both sounding dreadful.

I talked to several soldiers—and by "talk," I mean showing them my tent and miming the international sign for sleep, appealing to whatever angle I could. But each soldier waved his hands, without even a hint of a smile, indicating the same message—*go back down*. It wasn't that they were insensitive, but rather that this was a military base in a strategic location along a border. There's no way American soldiers would invite three dirty transients on bicycles to pitch a tent on any base, especially along a border. However, just as the futility of my efforts was starting to sink in, an officer who had heard about the three vagabonds showed up and offered us his personal home on the base, with a chef. Only in India.

We eagerly hopped on our bikes and pedaled behind the white military jeep a few hundred yards to an elaborate bleached white structure, which was nearly camouflaged against the snowy, mountainous backdrop, as the setting sun dripped orange down the walls. It was a two-bedroom, two-bath house known simply as the "White House," and for sure, it was not the Holiday Bungalow. Inside, ornate rugs adorned the walls, and soft, comfy couches and beds were the standard befitting an officer. Space heaters were immediately cranked on as chatter from our pre-hypothermic chill slowly melted away. An hour later, dinner was served to us in the formal dining room, and with full bellies, we climbed into our sleeping bags and marveled at our fortune.

Unfortunately, our stay in the white house was short-lived. At 9 p.m. we were rousted from our sleep, told that high-ranking government officials were possibly arriving later that night. We had to leave. In a foggy haze, we crawled out of our sleeping bags, picked our wet clothes off the heaters, and frantically gathered up the scattered debris that we had unpacked. We were hastily shuffled into the back of a military jeep and driven thirty minutes back down the mountain to a different base and given a private room in an army barracks. It was no white house, but it was shelter. Once again, I unpacked my sleeping bag and nestled back in. Within minutes, the exhaustion of the day wiped me out.

The next morning it was cold—a paralyzing cold like I had experienced in Ladakh. I didn't want to get out of my sleeping bag when I heard the knock on the front door from one of the officers. Reluctantly, I unzipped, after dismissing the fantasy that it was just a dream. Immediately I saw my breath, then ventured down the hall to the bathroom to find buckets of frozen water situated beneath frozen water pipes. Breakfast was served a few minutes later and afterward, we were taken back up to the White House where we had left our bikes.

The morning sun shyly poked its way through the wintery clouds and graciously offered to melt off some of the overnight ice on the road, however, turning it into a slushy mess. Last week I was dissolving away into the Assam tea fields, barefoot in sandals. Now I was plowing through shin-deep snowdrifts in Arunachal Pradesh (still in sandals but with socks and plastic bags over my feet), in a down jacket and Gore-Tex pants—just trying to generate enough heat to keep pedaling. Military jeeps zoomed by us every so often, each time with a honk and thumbs up, but naively drenching us with a stream of frozen crud.

Shortly before noon, the three of us crested the summit of Se La Pass and pedaled together under its red and blue archway. There was a seasonal restaurant that was closed for the season, but fortunately, there was someone inside who let us in so we could thaw out over several cups of hot chai as the winds thrashed at the windows. An hour later, we mustered the courage to begin our descent—the wind maliciously blowing shards of ice, raking across the only exposed portions of skin on my face. The sun was out, which helped mitigate some of the January sting, but it was still below 30°, and going downhill, I was no longer generating any heat.

The road was completely iced over and in places was drifting closed. As the cold seeped in, my body began to shake, making it difficult to steer my obese bike down the wintery mountain road. But by 3 p.m., we had dropped more than 6,000 feet and arrived in a lush green jungle and stopped to jam our thermal clothes back into the bottom of our bags, a faint memory of how we began the day. I was back to wearing shorts and sandals (sans socks and plastic bags) vaguely remembering anything related to being cold.

Cascading waterfalls were now part of the topography of the region, and due to this abundance of water in the lower elevations, around every corner, there was a landslide that had closed the road as crews struggled to keep up. Along these winding roads lay a graveyard of obliterated vehicles that had met their demise on this treacherous route, and like in Leh, another reminder that *bikes always win*.

We were misled on countless occasions by signs that read "hotel" which were for *fooding* as the locals told us, unless otherwise specified for *fooding and lodging*. Late one day, we arrived in another tiny, nameless village, and were duped into walking into a building labeled as a "hotel." It was immediately clear that it was for *fooding*, but with the sun nearly set and no other options of places to pitch a tent, Ivo came up with an idea. He walked up to the owner and asked if we could move some of the plastic dining tables and camp in the restaurant. There were still a few customers enjoying dinner, so of course, the staff was confused. However, after a little more explaining, an hour later we were setting up our tents for some indoor camping.

It was clear that this was the first time someone had asked to camp in their restaurant because the owners were concerned that it would be too cold. It was a small dining room, concrete floors, with maybe five plastic tables. Our tents would occupy two-thirds of the space. I can't help but think of the absurdity of three foreigners rolling into town on bikes, not speaking the language, and asking, through a game of charades, to camp out in the local Applebee's. I'm pretty sure the manager would be looking for the hidden camera, or worst case, calling the police. Instead, the owners of this local *hotel* felt guilty that they could not offer us a mattress or blankets, but we reassured them we would be okay with our camping gear.

Several days later, a foggy, dreary start to the day was combined with putting on wet cycling clothes for the fourth day in a row and set our moods on an uncommon downward spiral even before we pushed our first pedals. I'm not sure there is much worse than cold, wet, dirty cycling clothes adhered to your tired flesh. It had been nearly two weeks since we entered Arunachal, and we were all in need of a reset day. Seppa, the capital of Arunachal Pradesh, seemed like the place.

We arrived there a few hours later to find a shabby village that looked like a truck stop, hardly the vision of the capital we had anticipated. The one guest lodge in town was grim and not the place for the reset day that we were hoping for. Before arriving, we had met some people who lived in Seppa and exchanged contact info. A quick call to one of them connected us to someone at the local Baptist church, and an hour later we had two rooms at the church guesthouse, high up on the hill overlooking the city. Almost as soon as we checked in and unpacked our bags, the fog of the day, and our own fog, burned off with the warmth and kindness of the people of Seppa.

We had simple, adjoining rooms, with a shared washroom. It was quiet, clean, and perfect. Perfect, because the next day, I knocked on the door to invite the Swiss to lunch.

"Fooding?" I asked jokingly through their door.

"Brigitte has stomach (pronounced *stom-atch*) problems, so we stay here," Ivo told me matter-of-factly, his thin, dirty blonde hair matted and sticking up in a familiar way, indicating he too had just crawled from bed.

This was the first time that any of us had gotten sick, which was odd because we all ate the same meals each day. But the timing was perfect—if there was ever a perfect time to get sick in India—because this happened here, and not while sleeping in a drafty, musty schoolhouse or on the floor of a "hotel." It also meant that we definitely would not be rolling out the next day but rather would be in town for at least three or four days, something I was excited about. I was still refilling my cup of extroversion.

Motorbikes sputtered by, sending clouds of dust billowing into the muggy air, diffusing the already hazy orange light from the rising sun. There was a beauty in the rugged simplicity of Seppa as I strolled down the chalky main road in search of food. I found a great restaurant that served eggs and curry, while the owner's precocious daughter, who couldn't have been more than four, sat next to me and made pig snorts while I ate. Apparently, my reputation for mass food consumption had preceded me. She had creamy walnut-colored skin, shoulder-length curly brown hair, and a giggle that would make even an ogre laugh.

The owner, her father, asked me a familiar question: "Why do you come here?"

It was a logical inquiry that I had gotten dozens of times because, in India, most tourists go to see the Taj Mahal or other places in the guidebook. They definitely do not come to Arunachal Pradesh or Assam. As I pondered an original answer to this very unoriginal question, I realized that since arriving in northeast India nearly a month earlier, we had not seen any foreigners, or at least any people that looked like us. Before I could give my standard, default answer, he answered my question more perfectly and more simply than I had been able to thus far.

"To explore the beauty?"

I thought about that for half a second at most. "Yes! The beauty! Of the people, the culture, the mountains," I said gushingly, the words blasting from my mouth, almost like I was giving a sermon. I decided at that moment, this would be my new response going forward.

Eventually, on the third day, Brigitte emerged from their room, color slowly flowing back into her ashy, pale skin. It was great to see her smile as she was once again among the living. We had told the man who set us up with the rooms that we only planned to stay two nights, but when Brigitte got sick, we asked to extend our stay to five, and he happily agreed.

He lived with his family in a bamboo house just down the hill, not more than a hundred yards away. When he learned of Brigitte's recovery, he invited us to dinner with his family in their home. Excited for our acceptance, he patiently waited outside for over an hour for us to wash before escorting us down. We took off our shoes and stepped graciously into the large, open, bamboo-walled room. A fire was slowly smoldering in the recessed pit in the floor, warming the room from the dipping temperatures that seeped through the porous walls. We were invited to sit on cushy, red rugs that circled the fire pit. In the back of the room, four ladies were whipping up a feast. We were offered an ice-cold glass of Mountain Dew from the refrigerator, something I know was a treat, and that they were proud to offer. (It was a treat for me since my last Dew had been in 1991.) At the first sip, my teeth immediately stung as the sugary toxin flowed into my mouth, and my head began throbbing from the caffeine.

"It's good! Thank you!" I said reassuringly with an already hyper imposed smile, the venom coursing through my veins.

Our host was small and lean in stature, like most men in the region, likely in his early 30s with short, straight black hair parted to the side, squinty eyes, and a faint mustache that closely resembled the one I tried to grow when I was 15 (simply by refusing to ever shave it). The ladies tasked with dinner were his mother and three sisters. It was immediately clear that he was the only one in the family who spoke any English, so he spent the evening translating the flurry of questions from a group that by the end of the night included seven family members, four neighbors, and two other visitors from town.

Following dinner, the grandfather, dressed in traditional Nyishi attire, began singing traditional songs as the family joined in. The Nyishi community is the largest ethnic group in Arunachal Pradesh with a population of around 300,000. While the son and father were wearing short sleeve, polo-style shirts, indicative of the continual western influence, the grandfather's garb was more traditional tribal wear. We had seen elders dressed like this several times around Seppa but hadn't fully understood it until that evening. Clearly, it was not a costume. In the old culture, Nyishi braid their hair and tie it neatly at the forehead, with a brass skewer passing horizontally through the tied hair. Cane rings are worn around the waist, arms, and legs, and men wear a cane helmet surmounted with the beak of the great Indian hornbill. They also carry an *uryu* (machete) and a *chighi* (knife) in a bamboo sheath that is mostly covered with animal furs. He playfully swung his machete at me before gently placing it in my hands, sending the family into a chorus of laughter.

As the room filled with the rich melodies of the Nyishi, I melted into the bamboo floor, overcome by emotion. After a couple of songs, the grandfather turned and pointed to me, wanting me to sing a favorite American song. Never shying away from a social platform, I racked my brain to pull out something that I was sure they would know. There were plenty of songs that I had in my bag, but they were current and definitely had not yet made the jump to the hip music scene in Arunachal.

I have always been a Sinatra fan, so I began belting out one of my faves. "*Someday . . . when I'm awfully low. And the world is cold. I will feel a glow . . . just thinking oooooff you. And the way, you look, tonight.*" Crickets. The room was still, and it was not from my performance. How did they not know Sinatra? They smiled and clapped politely before turning to the Swiss who had, for the month I had known them, been more reserved in their social interactions. However, Ivo confidently took the stage. "*Country roads, take me home. To the place I belong. West Virginia, mountain mama. Take me home, country roads.*" Ivo, my introverted, calculated, Swiss friend, knew a John Denver song, and he sang it proudly. Crazier still was that several others knew the chorus and filled in even though they didn't speak English. I laughed aloud and filled in as well. Upstaged by a Swiss, singing an American song, in India. Go figure.

Following Ivo's performance, I looked over and noticed the mother laughing hysterically, whispering something to the translator, her kind, squinty eyes almost closed from emotion. "My mother watches Discovery Channel, and she loves *Man vs. Wild*. You look like Bear Grylls." (He's a former British special forces agent, and in each show, Bear gets dropped off in some remote part of the world and has to survive and find his way to civilization.) Apparently, she hadn't seen many, if any westerners and *maybe* we looked similar, and by similar we both looked like we had not shaved in a week and had been on some sort of adventure. But thus far I had not had to resort to drinking animal urine for hydration (a common theme in his show).

We had essentially been staying with this family for nearly a week, and as we were leaving that night, the mother looked at me with those unmistakable, kind, motherly eyes. In them, I could see a general concern, yet admiration. It was a look that I hadn't felt in far too long. Our time in Seppa was ending and she knew it. I felt an immediate connection with her, maybe because I was missing my own mom. I had not seen or spoken to her since our fallout last December, over one year ago—the feeling of hurt and betrayal still lodged in my heart. I could have reached out to her, of course. But I wasn't about to. Foolish pride, I suppose, and when I look back at it, was just foolish.

Regardless of Mom's side of the story, the story I curated in my mind was that this was her fault, and the longer that she took to reach out to me, to apologize, the more formidable the wall I was building. I felt justified in my obstinance and had fully rehearsed the full gamut of rebuttals to what I expected her to say, but ultimately, all roads led back to my feeling of betrayal. "You're sorry? What are you sorry for? For choosing your husband over your son? For choosing him over your dream?" Foolish.

For nearly six months, I had been experiencing mountains of joy since I first got on my bike in Nepal, and now India, slowly healing my spirit. But I had been intentionally suppressing those other emotions for a while. However, this night, surrounded by a loving family, picked the lock on that dark corner of my heart, and a sliver of light snuck in. This experience, although brief, had been the first semblance of a family connection, and it made me miss my mom even more. As we were leaving that night, I locked eyes with the mom. Unsure if hugging was normal or accepted in their culture, I decided I wasn't leaving without one.

I went to bed that night expecting, almost hoping to meet somebody, anybody, who was an asshole, so I could wake up from this dream. Never before had I felt such kindness with nothing expected in return. People who had nothing, but gave everything. Giving, just to give. Smiles so big that they were impossible to fake. This family was more honored to have us than we were to be invited into their family. And after our brief time with them, we felt like family.

A week later, we would leave this harsh, yet warm and mysterious land. I drifted back through the scrapbook in my mind, of the experiences and emotions I collected from one month in Arunachal Pradesh. As the sun shed its last rays of the day, with a smile, I recalled the interaction I had with the man in Seppa nearly two weeks earlier. "Why do you come here? Is it for the beauty?" Yup. This. This is the beauty.

CHAPTER 5

Riding on Faith

Racing daylight, I rodeoed my bicycle down the last few miles of broken road through the dripping, lush canyons in Arunachal Pradesh. The *road,* which was sheltered by an awning of overhanging vines, was littered with loose, fist-sized rocks, swimming in ankle-deep sand, trying desperately to buck me off. Below, once again, lay the flatlands of Assam and hopefully a clean, dry shelter to rinse away the battle from the day. The eight-hour ride was a familiar theme over the prior month, as we raced to get out of Arunachal Pradesh with just a single day before our permits expired. The road gradually smoothed out as I approached the Assam border. I could see the guard sitting at the gate, waiting to check me in, yet still unaware of my approach. I picked up speed, ducked my chin, and the gate, as I sailed coolly into Assam just under the setting sun. The guard never even looked up. Unlike in Zambia, I didn't intend to run the gate, but my mind was already fixated on a shower and curry. I was covered in a full-body paste, the same chalky film that I experienced in Eastern Nepal. My lungs wheezed. My eyes burned. My teeth felt gritty. I was smashed and just wanted off my bike.

As soon as we crossed back into Assam, the only thing resembling a hill—after a month of battling relentless mountains—was the speed bump in the road just after the military gate. We had seemingly entered another country, again. All of the foraging for food and shelter over the past month in Arunachal Pradesh was immediately forgotten. A new hotel with crisp white sheets, a fluffy, full-sized white beach towel and a hot shower, and actual curry, was waiting. Back in Assam, if only for a day before crossing into Nagaland, another great unknown.

We all slept late the following morning, physically but probably more mentally shattered from Arunachal; we all needed a *reset*. Pulling myself from the new, velvety cotton sheets that morning proved to be an unfamiliar chore. I had not slept in anything other than my sleeping bag and air mattress since we had left West Bengal more than six weeks earlier, so I gluttonously soaked it in. The fresh sheets with their strong smell of laundry detergent spread upon an actual (and comfortable) mattress created a potent tranquilizer, making it difficult to motivate. For the first time that I could remember, even I was mostly resigned to contently existing inside my hotel room. We stayed one more night before crossing the nearby border into Nagaland.

Although technically still in India, with a single pedal stroke, we entered a completely different country, definitively, at the border. The road was a mash of broken pavement and permanently set shale marbles the size of softballs that could shake the fillings from an elephant's teeth—if an elephant had fillings. In India they probably do—because India has elephants, and a lot of sugary snacks, and a surprisingly adept healthcare system. Any stretch of tarmac, even for ten yards, and I was immediately pointing my bike towards it, if only for a momentary reprieve. I was convinced that after my first day in Nagaland I would be effectively two inches shorter due to the repetitive, jarring, spinal compressions. Just as the Holiday Bungalow in West Bengal set the bar for substandard lodging, the roads in Nagaland became the very low bar against which all subsequent roads would be measured. In the distance there appeared a seemingly unlimited array of mountains running east to west, stacked one behind the other, like the folds in an accordion. Unfortunately, we were traveling north to south.

The temperature was noticeably hotter as we continued south, and in fact, it was just hot—about 85° of stagnant, suffocating humidity. At points, it felt like someone had put a plastic bag over my head. Within the first hour of entering Nagaland as we began our ascent into the mountains, we passed two broken-down trucks, a telling sign of what lay ahead. One had a blown axle, oil spewing out of the hub like water from a garden hose, the other a cracked radiator. Along the side of the road, I saw a woman in ragged clothes gathering water from a murky, dammed-up trough paralleling the road. I have no idea of the source, but by the color of the water, I could not definitively say that it wasn't coming from that truck with a blown axle. Looking around, however, it was obvious that there weren't many other options. It was quickly apparent that the development of Nagaland was far behind even Arunachal. Where Arunachal was striving for tourism and development, Nagaland made no such efforts, and it seemed its topographical harshness aimed to deter anyone from trying.

We stopped for a quick lunch on our first day. The family who owned the small eatery graciously gave me one bunch of bananas (seventeen total and about four pounds) that I gladly tucked into my bag, ignorant of what lay before us.

Be wary of any Indian who says, "Just a little up." Soon after leaving their shop, the road abruptly began to lurch upward, and I quickly regretted the extra weight. These primitive, spine-compressing roads did not go around any mountains or through any valleys. When we reached the top of the first ridge, without even a short plateau to claim a small victory, we immediately pinballed our way down the minefield of marbles, before clawing our way up the next, and each subsequent idiotic climb. By the time I dug into my bag for a banana, it looked like someone had smashed a case of baby food in there.

We made our way deeper into Nagaland, the relative plushness and hospitality of Assam already a distant memory. Children who appeared to be aged eight to thirteen walked the roads with rifles slung over their shoulders. Ancient villages sat atop the mountain peaks, likely to defend against invasion, yet making it difficult to obtain water for farming or even basic living. In fact, beside the woman gathering water from the roadside ditch, I had not seen any running water, only barrels of collected runoff. I was baffled by the distinct disparity in quality of life between Nagaland and its nearby neighbors.

It was getting dark. We had battled valiantly through seven hours and fifty miles, spread harshly over 6,000 feet of climbing, up and over a road that was seemingly carved out with a shovel. Physically, I was done. Drained. Empty. Destroyed. Mentally, I was far more destitute. I was the living embodiment of the road.

I briefly lifted my head to see a bus sitting idle several switchbacks up the road. It was the same bus that passed us nearly two hours earlier in the valley that we arrogantly scoffed when I jokingly had said to the Swiss that we should get on. That arrogance was gone, replaced by humility with a twinge of desperation. It was already 5 p.m., and the light was rapidly escaping, and in thirty minutes it would be dark. Completely dark. In our condition, there was no way that any of us would make the final six-mile climb to the next town, where hopefully food and lodging awaited.

As I approached, I expected to see a typical over-packed Indian bus, but instead, it was nearly empty. It was a dented box; the original robin egg blue paint having been taken over by orange rust many years ago. Underneath the front axle was a man, covered head to toe in grease, only the whites of his eyes remained clean. He was trying to work around the black sludge that was draining like a drinking fountain just above his reclined head. Evidently, the steering had gone out, not a good thing on this road, a winding chasm that had claimed another victim. I watched the driver turn the wheel side to side and give a thumbs up, indicating that it was fixed—a comforting sign considering the next six miles of this single-lane, snaking road clung desperately to the hillside that we needed to ascend in order to reach the next village. In our current state, hopping onto the bus seemed better than camping on the side of the road and eating banana puree, or worse yet, trying to cycle this same road in complete darkness for the next two hours. I had already narrowly escaped the Tunnel of Doom two months prior and was not anxious to go double or nothing.

We collapsed into our seats, relieved to be off the bikes, hoping to find a place to sleep at the top of the pass. The vinyl seats were smeared with dried mud, but only in the places where foam and the occasional spring weren't protruding. The bus roared to life as it squeaked and rocked around each precarious corner, hinting that at any moment, we might actually tip over. Dust began to waft in from the open windows, but we dared not close them because the heat inside would have been worse.

When the bus ground to a halt forty minutes later at the top of the pass, we exited and found a village that appeared to have already turned in for the night. There were a dozen or so dilapidated homes made from wood, all dwarfed by a prominent and much newer concrete church in the center, a large, flat grassy area surrounding it.

As we approached, we discovered that the entire town had not retired for the evening but rather was at the evening service. We waited for forty-five minutes, and when the local villagers were exiting, we found the pastor and inquired about lodging. He graciously showed us the washroom just outside of the church—which was a simple wooden structure the size of an outhouse, built over a pit, with a hole and bucket inside. He pointed at the two large barrels filled with collected water before kindly offering us the lawn to camp. After a quick bucket bath and a bowl of hot *maggi*, we all collapsed. It was only day one.

For the next week, we continued this familiar yet debilitating pattern of crossing two, sometimes three mountain passes each day, before willing our way to the final ridge in hopes of finding food and a place to camp, just as the sun was setting. Our bodies and our mental state were recovering less and less each day, slowly dissolving into an inescapable deficit, succumbing to the punishing environment. Nagaland was winning.

One day, we crested a ridge, and the once dense, forested jungle was gone; in its wake a vast, desolate wasteland stretching beyond the hazy horizon. The smell of charred wood saturated the air, while low-hanging smoke lingered, seemingly stuck between the ridges, unable to escape. The trees on the hillsides in Nagaland were being mowed down at an alarming rate. Huts previously hidden by the foliage now were visible against the black and tan hills. Fires raged constantly. We were told that the hills were being burned in order to be terraced and cultivated for crops. The sunset that night—and each night after—was a pink haze from the rampant fires that filled the canyons, while orange speckles, like lighters in a rock concert, dotted the slopes.

"What's that?" I asked Ivo as we walked up to a shop one day to buy some snacks. "It looks like someone was murdered here, and there, and over there. What the hell?" as I pointed at the red splotches coloring the road.

"It's *paan*," he replied simply.

Paan is a preparation combining betel leaf with areca nut and tobacco. It is chewed for its stimulant and psychoactive effects and in Nagaland had seemingly replaced cigarette smoking. The final combination is red in color and, when chewed, turns a person's mouth red, like it is full of blood—their gums, their teeth, their entire mouth. I never saw any women chewing this, only men, and when they smiled it looked like someone had punched them and tried to knock their teeth out. It is essentially the chewing tobacco of India, but instead of spitting out brownish gruel, it looked like large, fist-sized splashes of blood. There were signs in many places that read: "No Spitting," but were never obeyed.

A group of men began to congregate around us, mouths full of blood, and I decided to try a social experiment. Before they could launch into their familiar barrage of standard questions, I stepped to my podium and delivered what amounted to a campaign speech. "Hello! My name is Jerry. I'm from the USA. I have been in India for four months. I am traveling by cycle for tourism. I am going to Manipur."

Feeling confident that I had preemptively and effectively covered every possible question in their curiosity (and English capabilities), I smiled and began to eat my *maggi*.

"Where are you from?" someone in that same crowd called out.

"Noooo, no," I replied, wagging my finger with a laugh and smile. "I already told you. You didn't listen!"

"He is from the USA," another person chimed in while the group laughed. The experiment worked . . . sorta.

"Where are you going?" asked another man as he approached. Arrrrghhh! So close. He was in his early 30s, clean-cut, well dressed, and most importantly, no *paan* in his teeth.

"Here! I'm staying here!" pointing up to the hillside. "I purchased a home up there. Why would I leave?" I spouted out sarcastically. I never knew how much English any given person spoke here, so I took a shot at being funny, but really, I was the only person who could appreciate that humor, including even the Swiss.

"Oh, really? You funny guy!"

Busted. He spoke English. Good English, and he understood sarcasm. We exchanged a little more light banter shortly before he faded back into the crowd, but I was happy for the unique exchange.

It was getting late, and we needed to find a place to sleep, likely another church, which had been our familiar and reliable theme. I asked a man where the pastor was, and he pointed up the road. The three of us walked up to a concrete home, which was far nicer than the other wooden dwellings made from the slashed hillside, because, of course, he was the pastor. I knocked on the door.

"Hey, neighbor!" the man who answered the door bellowed. Dammit. It was the well-dressed man I had bantered with. We both laughed as I tried to hide my embarrassment. Fortunately, I don't embarrass too easily.

"It's getting late, and we're looking for a place to sleep for the night. We have camping equipment," I explained.

"You have camping equipment? There's the ground!" he said jokingly, mirroring my sarcasm as he pointed at the ground in front of his home. *Well played, sir*, I thought to myself. "But if you don't want to camp, you can stay in my home. Please come in and have tea," he said invitingly.

Once inside, we all sat and enjoyed tea and talked about Nagaland. There was a riot happening in the capital of Kohima, and as a result, the government had shut down the internet, which is, of course, the fastest and easiest way for protesters to mobilize efforts (Twitter, Facebook, etc.). He told us that the government in Nagaland is corrupt, and people were revolting. The highest-ranking elected official, the Chief Minister, had his house burned down, and three people had been fatally shot.

"Are you married?" *John* asked me, changing the subject. He had taken a new Christian name when he converted from Hinduism.

"I was, but it didn't work out. I'll try again sometime," I replied jokingly.

"Just like Naga government!" he jabbed back.

"How come with all your Kentucky Fried Chickens you are

vegetarian?" John fired back again.

Man, where was this humor the past six weeks?

John pulled out a history book, showing photos from sixty years ago. "These are our ancestors. They lived like animals," he said proudly, yet disparaging them at the same time. I laughed politely but was struck by this incongruous comment—that someone could talk about their heritage and the lives of their grandparents with such contempt and still be so generous to complete strangers. And yet, this had been the general sentiment from everyone we had spoken with thus far in Nagaland.

Forty years ago, Christian missionaries steamrolled through Nagaland, building megachurches, then slashing and burning the Hindu culture, much the same way the trees were currently being slashed and burned from the hillside. The churches in these villages were always the nicest structures, perched at the top of the hill for everyone to see, almost like a beacon of hope, while towering over a splattering of broken shacks, occupied by faithful Christian devotees. Prior to Christianity, there had been various local religions dispersed across villages and tribes. There were even headhunters in Nagaland. Yes, headhunters.

We were asked nearly every place we stopped, "Are you Christian?" It seemed a forward question, one that none of us had been asked anywhere in India or Nepal. The only religious edict I subscribe to is the Golden Rule, which I have simplified to "Don't be an asshole." I think if the world simply followed that rule, all beliefs could coexist in harmony. In Nagaland, we would meet countless pastors named John and sleep inside more megachurches than campsites—at times making it feel like we weren't in India at all.

A week later, we rolled through a small town. A festival was going on, and the narrow dusty street was abuzz. Music was blasting over a speaker and young women wrapped in elaborate pastel-colored saris smiled and giggled joyfully while posing for selfies. It was a welcome splash of color from the otherwise dismal, varying shades of *tattered,* through Nagaland. I once again felt like I was in India.

"It's your birthday, man. Do you want to stop here for the night?" Ivo asked. It was only noon, and normally we would never stop riding that early. But unlike Christmas or Thanksgiving, this day had always felt special to me.

We were in Nagaland, sleeping on the floors of churches, the internet was blocked, and I hadn't seen a mirror or bathed with anything other than a bucket in two weeks. I wasn't sure what day of the week it was, let alone which day of the month. Life was a blur and time a mere suggestion. This day, February 2nd, had been buried somewhere in my banana-coated pannier, and like that sweet, pungent smell, it had slowly, stealthily crept up.

Back in Boulder, I would celebrate with my *important people*, those who were closest to me, my inner circle. This would be my first birthday spent alone, even though I wasn't. Almost as covertly as my birthday had snuck up on me, my relationship with the Swiss had also done the same, slowly but steadily building into something much more than a convenient coalition of curious bike wanderers simply looking for company. They had joined the ranks of my *important people*. We had been inseparable since late December, something that I thought was impossible. I fully expected that we would ultimately travel at different speeds, have different habits, they would want their solitude to travel exclusively as a couple, or quite logically, we would annoy the shit out of each other. None of that happened. I even (unintentionally) gave them the slip in Assam when my rear wheel blew up, but somehow, they found me, and we had never been more than a hundred yards apart since.

We found a hotel for the night, our first actual hotel since the day before we entered Nagaland, nearly one month earlier. It was still a basic shack with creaky wood floors, only moderately cleaner than sleeping in the dirt, but with a private room and running water. It's amazing how much of a luxury running water had become, though it was something I never really had missed thus far.

After a quick (cold) shower, we made our way through the flowing sea of saris to a restaurant, but not before I found a place that served fresh yogurt. I quickly snatched two bowls of their largest serving size from the cooler, about two liters in volume, and gluttonously slurped it down. We had been existing almost solely on *maggi* for a month, so the tart taste of fresh yogurt sent my taste buds into a frenzy. Apparently, I had missed yogurt far more than a shower. When we finally sat down in the restaurant, we all ordered *dosas* (an Indian pancake with rice and curry wrapped inside) twice the size of our heads. It was my birthday, and I was gonna celebrate.

The next day, the buzz from my birthday high had worn off, leaving an unfamiliar hangover as we continued our journey through Nagaland. The tires, brakes, shifters, and shock were all wearing down on my bike—mirroring the state of my body and mind. I was also starting to see small cracks in the Swiss. They, too, were getting tired and joked about taking a bus out of Nagaland to the border of Myanmar, where we would part ways. Although they joked, there is always a little truth in sarcasm.

Then one day, without notice, it changed. Roads smoothed out, and so did my mental state. Both flowed easily without any hindrance or impediments. The relentless, idiotic climbs and debilitating armored roads of the prior three weeks were barely a memory. Miles began to click off, and were going by fast. The end was coming too quickly, and I wasn't ready. Getting out of Nagaland, something I had been looking forward to for over a week, I was now dreading. I had been wallowing in the doldrums of fatigue—physical, but mostly mental—and I thought that I was done with India, but when faced with the finiteness of this experience, it was clear that I wasn't.

Slow down, I said to myself. *It's nearly over. You'll miss this when it's gone.* I wanted time to stop, even if I had no idea what day it was. It wasn't just the awareness that India—and this bike trip—were ending, but more of what I was really losing. I should have already been back in Boulder in December, celebrating my birthday a week ago, but this, this was the gift—being in India with two of my *important people.*

A week later, we made the final climb to the town of Ukhrul. It's rare when you know something will be your last, and that awareness becomes tangible. This was our last climb together, but it was not the excitement of finishing a journey that I had envisioned, rather a gut punch. In a few days, we would go off in different directions, the weight of that inevitable event now securely within reach, although I did my best to push it away.

We tried in vain to prolong the inevitable, but two days later, after an emotional embrace, we parted ways. We had been inseparable for nearly two months and formed a bond so tight that tears were inevitable. Just as we began in Nepal back in December, we approached a dusty, broken junction in the road, only this time, the Swiss turned toward Myanmar, and I, I was done. I was going home.

The Holiday Bungalow

"Selfie?" (Ivo Jost @bikepackground)

Battling the snow near Tawang (Ivo Jost @bikepackground)

Warming up after crossing Sela Pass, near Tawang

Fooding with our host family in Seppa (Ivo Jost @bikepackground)

A tough goodbye in Seppa (Ivo Jost @bikepackground)

Camping at a school

"Keep Silence" (Ivo Jost @bikepackground)

Breaking up

PART 6

Thailand

February 24 – April 2, 2017

"I always get to where I'm going by walking away from where I have been."

– Winnie the Pooh

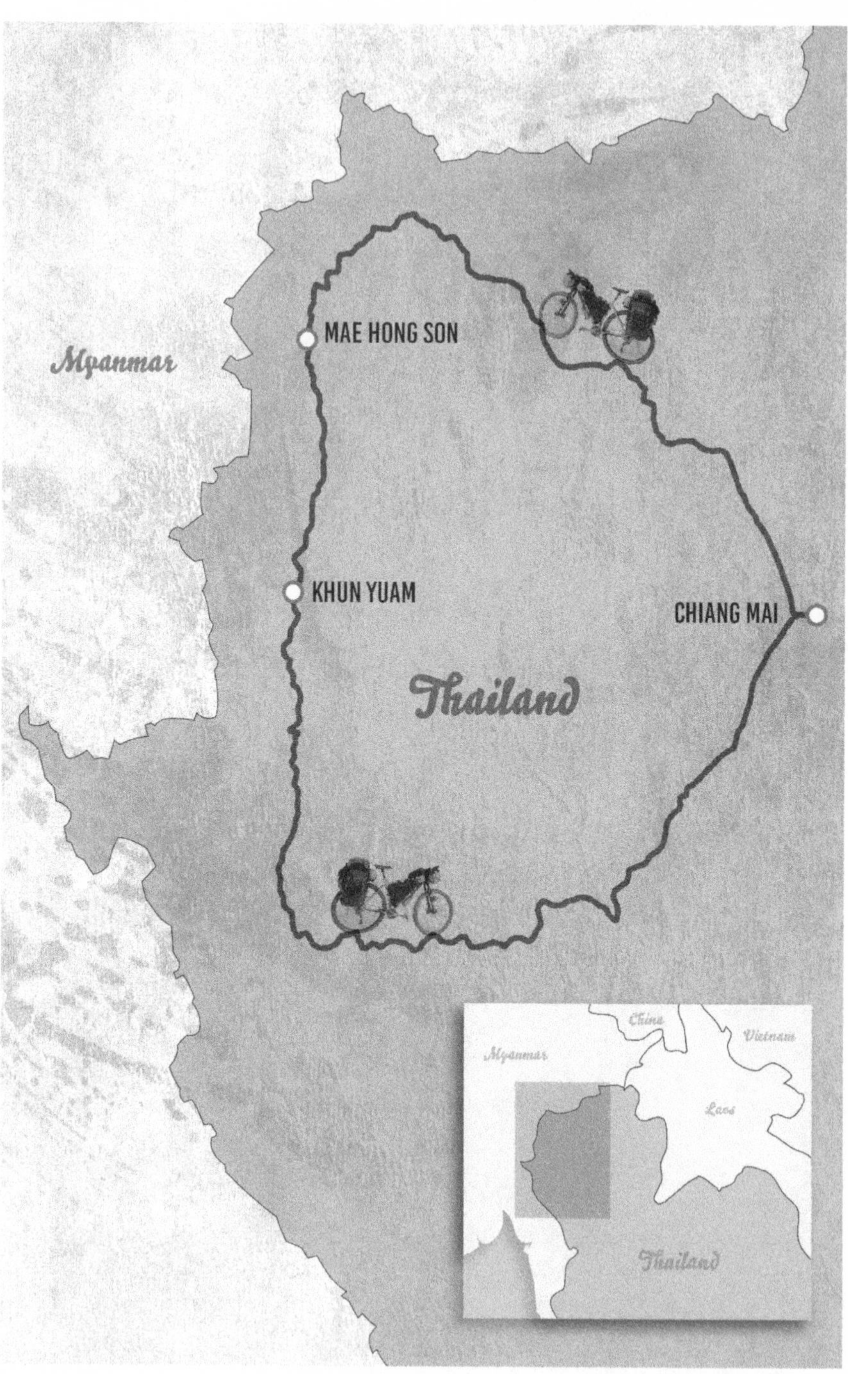

MAE HONG SON
Myanmar
KHUN YUAM
CHIANG MAI
Thailand
China
Vietnam
Myanmar
Laos
Thailand

CHAPTER 1

Barefoot, Beet Juice, and Cold Showers

"Where are you?" was the message I received from my buddy, Taylor, back in Boulder.

"I'm in a cush hotel in Imphal, India. I can't believe how nice this place is. Hot shower, clean sheets. It's pretty amazing," I beamed in a video call, covertly hiding my fatigue.

"What's your plan?"

"Looking at flights to Denver. I'll likely be back in two days."

"I'm looking at a map. Why don't you go to Thailand? It's right there. I toured through there for a month. It was unbelievable. But be careful of *Thai suicide.*"

Even though my journey with the Swiss had ended a few days earlier, I remembered our initial meeting when Ivo prodded: "Why are you going home? Do you have a wife? Job? Kids? Dog?" I had resigned myself to going home, believing that this had been *enough* and the smart thing to do after being gone this long.

While initially the thought of traveling beyond India and into Myanmar sounded unappealing, a couple of days' rest had renewed my curiosity. Two days later, I packed up my bike, hopped a flight from the Imphal airport, and instead of landing in Denver, arrived in

Chiang Mai, once again without a plan.

Stepping off the plane in Thailand from Nagaland was like an alcoholic leaving an AA meeting and going straight to Mardi Gras. Overload. The food. The conveniences. The *food*! Fresh fruits, juices, vegetables, curries—*Thai suicide*. I immediately understood. Could I actually gorge myself to death, I wondered? "Of course. You've been eating dirt for four months," scoffed Taylor.

After five grueling months of cycling through the Himalayas, my body and my mind were failing. I needed a reset. Cycling in Thailand hoped to be just that, but immediately upon pushing that first pedal stroke, I realized that Thailand is hot. Like volcanically hot, and I found myself yearning for the frigid mountain passes in the Himalayas again, wondering what had I done?

Even starting at 6 a.m. each day, the thermometer quickly exploded to 95° by 10:30 a.m., and with a slight breeze, felt like cycling directly into a giant hairdryer. My body and my brain were ill-prepared. One day, I made the mistake of leaning my bike against a building for a couple of hours while I attempted to rehydrate from the midday heat, only to climb back on my bike and have the rubber portion of my handlebar grips dissolve into glue on my palms.

I set out on the Mae Hong Son loop in the north, bordering Myanmar and Laos, which is more famously known in the area as "1862"—as in there are 1,862 curves in the road along its four hundred mile-ish route. The roads are walls, albeit perfectly manicured, paved walls without a speck of gravel or a grain of sand. I didn't know concrete could be poured that steeply. It was like climbing a ladder. There were road signs with the hill symbol and then "10%," but there were also signs showing a truck going uphill without a numerical quantifier. Those roads are *really* steep. I was out of the saddle, standing up and pedaling for sometimes two miles at a time at a pace that barely qualified as forward, over the top, then plunging straight downhill, and repeat. It was relentless. I couldn't even listen to earphones to distract from my suffering because I was sweating out of every pore in my body, including my ears. It was like lying down in the bathtub as a little kid, head fully submerged, and trying to make sense of the garbled sounds as my mom was talking. Sorta the way Charlie Brown's teacher sounds. "Wah, wah wah, wah." Or maybe that was just because my eardrums were also melting? I'm not sure.

Eager to find a more adventurous route, one day, I ducked into the shady reprieve of the jungle and encountered an older man, walking alone, who looked to be in his 70s. As I approached him, his eyes grew big as saucers. He busted out laughing, flailing his arms about, pointing in the direction that I was going, as if in total disbelief. If I could translate, I think he said, "What the hell are you doing out here with a bike? Are you crazy, man? Have you seen these hills? You're gonna die!" Yeah, I was thinking the same thing.

Ben & Jerry's, the ice cream maker, has a motto: "If it isn't fun, why do it?" I had punished myself enough the past five months through grueling conditions in the Himalayas. Honestly, I was just tired, unsure if it was the unending physical strain or the mental impact of being a nomad. It didn't matter. "Travel fatigue" is what Ivo called it when I messaged him. He and Brigitte were making their way through Myanmar and had a similar sentiment.

My bike was making noises that soon exceeded those emanating from my body. Noises that could no longer be oiled away or ignored. The wheels were falling off, literally. I recalled hearing a distinct creaking coming from the rear wheel the past few days. I wasn't quite sure what it was, but it wasn't indicating immediate peril, and I figured it would at least get me through Thailand. When I took the wheel off, the cassette (the round thingy with all the gears) literally broke off and fell in my hand. It isn't supposed to do that. Yet somehow the new *sprahk* from India was holding steady?

We (the collective "we," my bike, my body, my mind) were *officially,* broken. I put out a thumb and hopped in the first vehicle that approached. Sitting in the cab of the air-conditioned Toyota Hilux pickup truck and sipping a now warm box of soy milk, I laughed at each hill that the truck groaned its way up. I had survived five months in the Himalayas from India to Nepal, then back to India, but it was one week in Thailand that did me in.

—

Chiang Mai is a colorful, vibrant city overflowing with ancient Buddhist Temples (wats) dating back to when the city was originally founded in 1296. There are over two hundred in and around Chiang Mai, built by successive kings intent on leaving an enduring icon. The intricate carving and stunning hand-painted murals inside them are treasures. Beyond that, however, my initial impressions of Chiang Mai were that it was a nice place to reset and pass through for a few days but far too touristy. And it is, when you're living like a tourist. But then, I met Elizabeth.

When her friends asked how we met, we liked to think up the most obnoxious, cliché situations possible because that was just our sense of humor. "We met while scuba diving the Great Barrier Reef," Elizabeth would say with a straight face. Or, "We met at an ashram in India during an intensive silent meditation retreat," she would glowingly recount. Our favorite was, "We met at Everest Base Camp in Nepal." She was from Chicago and had lived for a spell in Boulder, so in reality, we could have met there. But actually, we met online.

My friend, Taylor, told me that when he was cycling through South America, he used a dating app to meet local people so that he could just feel "normal." Once or twice it turned romantic, but most of the time he just got invited to dinner parties or on local hikes and other adventures. Initially, I thought the concept was weird, especially because dating in a foreign country not only seemed futile but also because my heart was still closed and continuing to heal. However, I was craving a heavy dose of *normal*.

Elizabeth and I clicked, immediately. She was probably 5′2″ with long wavy blonde hair and a smile representative of the "Thai smile" that is the national treasure. I was immediately drawn to her quick wit and barbed sense of humor. The first night we met, we stayed up too late watching Seinfeld clips on YouTube, each of us taking turns quoting the next line in real time. " . . . and yada, I'm really tired today," she playfully joked the next morning.

"You know, I have a guest room that you can stay in. It's silly to spend money on a hotel," Elizabeth innocently offered over breakfast. I didn't disagree, and probably in a previous life, I would have thought it was silly to move in with a woman I barely knew, but that was the old me. I woke up three weeks later, and Thailand felt like home. It definitely was not what I would have planned, as if I had planned much of anything the previous months, but somewhere along the way, Elizabeth and I were dating, and it felt normal.

During the final, agonizing year prior to my separation from Emma, we lived as roommates but not roommates who liked each other. By the end, we were the roommates who wouldn't come out of our room to make dinner if the other person was in the kitchen. I felt like a neglected dog, shamed and yelled into a corner, feeling undesirable and worse, unworthy of affection. Elizabeth changed all that. She made me feel attractive and wanted again.

Elizabeth was a teacher at an environmentally-focused, Buddhist-based international school in Chiang Mai. During the day, I would do house-husband things like take the dog for a walk or wait for the electrician in between trips to the grocery store. After work, we would zoom our bicycles down the soi (smaller local alleyways) in search of the best authentic street food, something Elizabeth and her friends were very adept at finding. The food was prepared on portable food carts that showed up around 6 p.m. each evening. None of the menu was in English; the people didn't speak English, and only a few carts had pictures of food. I quickly learned that only tourists eat pad thai. My favorite was the woman who operated a juice cart who wore a t-shirt that read: "Sorry I'm So Rad," whose brilliant smile always ticked up a notch when she saw us approaching. I have no idea if she knew what it meant, but it didn't matter, because she was " . . . so rad." One day I drank so much fresh beet juice that it stained my teeth, and I peed crimson for a week, but it was totally worth it. After dinner, we would treat each other to $2 foot massages and $6 body massages downtown before pedaling home through the thick Thai air to watch more Seinfeld.

"You used all the cold water!" I shouted down the hall to Elizabeth the next morning as a spotted green gecko scurried up the tiled shower wall.

She laughed in a distant, sinister way. "Someone has to work to put food on the table," she mockingly joked back.

March and April are the hottest time of the year in Chiang Mai and many days it was over 90° *inside* Elizabeth's house, and sometimes surpassing 100°. The floors were hot. The walls were hot. The water that sits in the pipes in the ground—was hot. It was not uncommon to take three showers per day, simply to cool off, so that first fleeting burst of cold water was something to be cherished.

A few weeks later, the Swiss showed up. They had traveled through Myanmar for nearly a month with ZZ, our Czech friends from Kathmandu. They all looked shattered. It was mid-March, and I had not seen Ivo and Brigitte for a month and Zbenek and Zusanna since early December. They were understandably surprised yet happy to see me so comfortable and well-adjusted in Thailand—a far different picture from the nomadic wanderer they last saw. I proudly introduced them to Elizabeth over dinner one night at her house before playing tour guide and showing them where the best fruit juice carts and foot massages were. I laughed when I saw them lose their minds in the decadence of Chiang Mai. Now, I felt like a local and fondly remembered when I first arrived, a day that seemed so long ago. I had been the third and sometimes fifth wheel with my friends, but now, I felt like a part of the gang, and it felt normal. Elizabeth had met my friends, and I had met hers, and somehow without much notice or effort, we had become part of each other's worlds.

One afternoon, I motivated to get my bike fixed and stumbled into a local bike shop. I looked on the shelf and saw water bottles emblazoned with the Colorado state flag. "Why, or should I say, how do you have Colorado water bottles?" I asked.

"I lived in Boulder for twenty years," replied Stu, the owner. Of course. Elizabeth had ties to Boulder, and it had been nearly two weeks since I had another *random* encounter, so I suppose I was due.

Stu was a tall, lanky fella in his late 50s, and over the next week, he helped rebuild my bicycle to a pre-Himalayan tour status, including a new rear wheel and non-melted handlebar grips. And like that, 4,000 abusive miles were stripped away. After nearly a month, we (the collective again) were now ready for the next chapter. But I was far from motivated to leave this place that I was slowly calling home.

For nine months, I had been lured by curiosity and the exploration of travel, but now, I was lured by another type of curiosity—exploring what a life would look like with Elizabeth, in Thailand. We were getting closer, and really, I had no place to be. But as close as we were getting, and as special as she made me feel, deep down, I knew she wasn't my girl. I had learned throughout my travels that people come in and out of your life. Some only in passing, and some who will be part of your life forever. All serve a purpose. Elizabeth had slapped me awake and made me smile in a way that I hadn't since I first met Emma, nearly five years ago—reminding me that I'm not that dog that peed on the rug, and I am worthy of affection.

Over the course of several days, the voice in the back of my head, in between fresh fruit shakes, was getting louder, telling me that I was getting too comfortable here. Part of me wanted to stay in Chiang Mai and see what would happen, but I knew that if I didn't continue on with the journey, I'd never forgive myself, even though I had never set out with any semblance of a plan. Deep down, I think Elizabeth knew I was going to leave.

I thought I would be back in Boulder in December, but it seems that didn't happen. I tried again in February but missed that flight too. One day over lunch, Ivo said something that again altered my world. "We're going into Eastern Tibet for three months. Do you want to come?"

Mae Hong Son loop

Food suicide. Street sushi!

Reunited with the Swiss and ZZ

Beet juice? Elizabeth agrees

A night out in Chiang Mai—with Elizabeth

PART 7

China

April 3 – June 28, 2017

"If it's not Here, that means it's out There."

– Winnie the Pooh

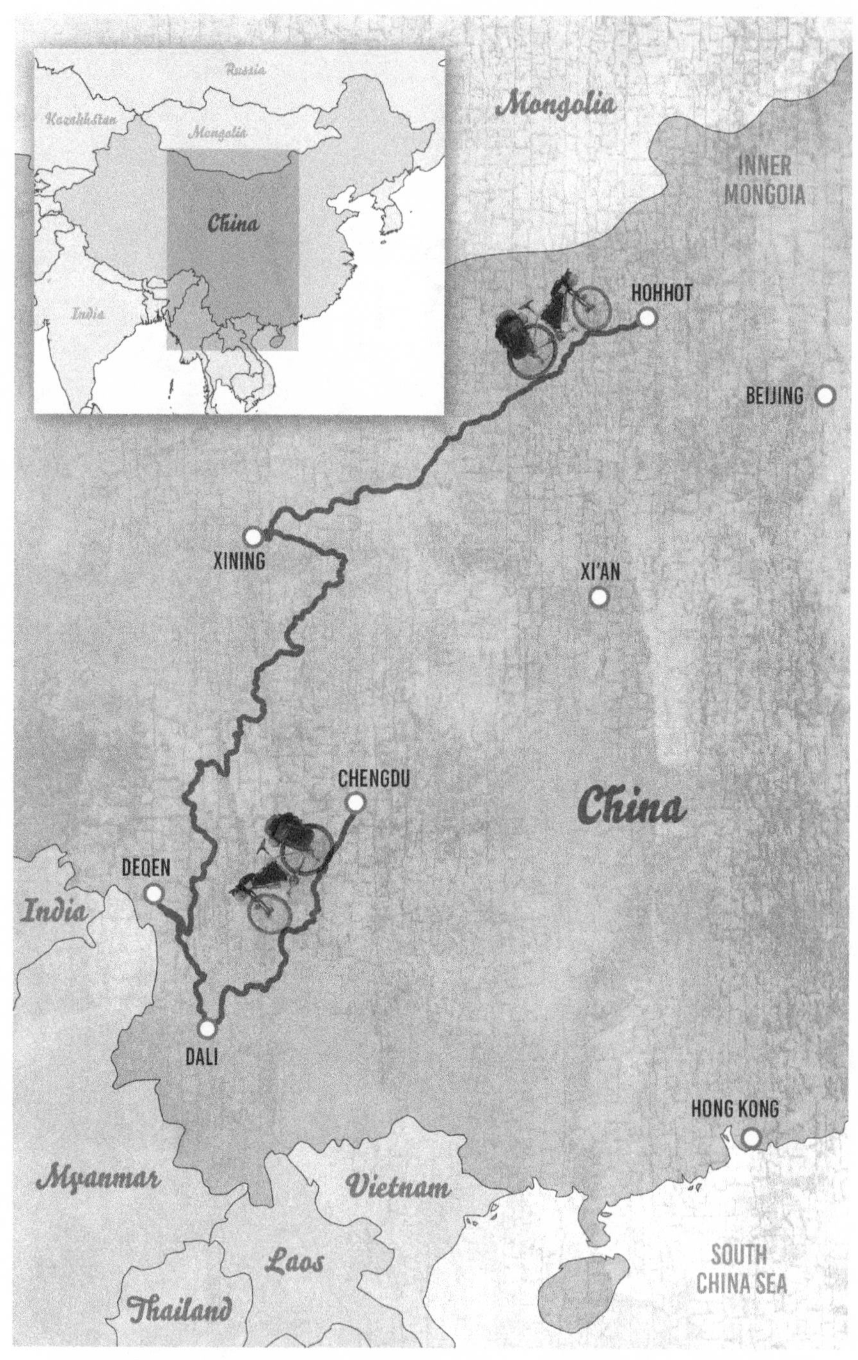
Russia
Kazakhstan
Mongolia
China
India
Mongolia
INNER
MONGOIA
HOHHOT
BEIJING
XINING
XI'AN
CHENGDU
China
DEQEN
India
DALI
HONG KONG
Myanmar
Vietnam
Laos
Thailand
SOUTH
CHINA SEA

CHAPTER 1

Same but Different

It was 2 a.m. I had been riding around in not one but two different taxis for nearly three hours since landing in Kunming, China. I just wanted to find my hotel. I missed Elizabeth, but that feeling had been overcome by my curiosity of a new adventure.

However, based on how it was beginning, I questioned my decision and wished I was back in Thailand.

I was smart, I thought. I had made an online hotel booking. All I needed to do was pick up my bike, which was neatly packed in a box, find a taxi, and tell the driver which hotel. I had done this numerous times before. It was easy. But this was China, and the language barrier here is legit. It was like nothing I had ever experienced. I told the taxi driver the name of the hotel and even showed him my phone. Nothing, because, of course, he couldn't read it. He handed me his phone and asked me to type in the address, which was equally as nonsensical, yet from the complete opposite perspective. We both stared at the other with a look of bemusement.

I found the phone number of the hotel and implored him to call. He did, but for some reason handed me the phone. Even if the person on the other end spoke *any* English, I still wouldn't have been able to communicate those directions to the driver—as if I even knew where

I was? He just simply couldn't fathom that I didn't speak Chinese, as was evident by the way he continued to carry on a complete conversation *at* me. I get it. China has 1.4 billion people, more than four times the population of the US and nearly 20 percent of the earth's population. Why would anyone in China think that there was anything else outside? But this was stupid, illogical thinking. It was my own myopic arrogance that was fueling my frustration that *he* didn't speak even a few words in *English*, which is also spoken by 20 percent of the world. But of course, why would he? I was in his country. Language had never been such an insurmountable problem as now. What would I have done in the US if someone from China showed up in the middle of the night and started talking *at* me, waving their arms with crazy gyrations and hand gestures?

We were lost. After an hour, the driver having felt he had invested enough time and gas in this scavenger hunt, put me out on the curb and sped off. Instead of being at the airport with a slew of taxis to choose from, I was on a street in the middle of the night somewhere in Kunming, a city of 6.6 million people.

Unfortunately, now, all of the taxis that zoomed by were much smaller, Volkswagen sedans, and my bike did not fit. I know because I tried several times. I pushed. I pulled. I twisted, but the doors simply would not close. "*Mei you*" all the drivers would say, waving their hands and shaking their heads when I tried to cram my bike into one of their taxis. I officially knew my first and only word in Chinese, and it meant "no." It was now 1:30 a.m. The convoy of drivers each looked at me as if to say: "What the hell are you doing here?" At that moment, I was wondering that as well. The comforts and familiarity of Chiang Mai seemed like a world away.

I took a deep breath and prepared to take my bike out of the box and build it. At least then I would have transportation since it clearly was not going to fit in the taxi anyway. As I was tearing into the box, an older, larger model Volkswagen from the late 1980s rolled up. It was dented, beat up, and had a loud, loose exhaust. The driver was an older fellow, and the few teeth that he did have were badly decayed but showed a kindness in his smile. With the windows in the back seat rolled all the way down, the corners of the box could stick out, allowing the doors (with a strong, full shoulder thrust) to close. I climbed in the passenger seat. The seat was torn, the dash was cracked, but we were once again on our way in search of my hotel.

At 2 a.m. the driver was excited, thinking that he had found this mystery hotel. I walked up to the front of the building and was stopped at the door by an intimidating man, dressed in a military uniform and holstering a gun.

"Lossen hotel?" I inquired politely, trying to fake a smile to hide my stressful fatigue. I put my hands together at the side of my head, giving the international signal for sleep.

"Mei you." Without so much of a hint of a smile, he shook his head and shooed me away.

My heart sunk and despair flooded over me. That was it. I had spent nearly three hours searching for a hotel and in thirty seconds was dismissed. It was 2:30 a.m. and I was emotionally bankrupt.

How could something as simple and benign as finding a hotel prove so challenging? I had ridden my bike over the highest motorable road in the world in a snowstorm in India, across the Annapurna Circuit in Nepal, through a wild game reserve in Zambia, but I was succumbing to Kunming, China, and I had been here less than four hours. It is a modern, developed city where everything is available. I just didn't know how to ask for it.

The driver, nearly as frustrated as me but seeing the dejection in my face, looked at me with sincerity as if to say, "What do you want from me?"

"Fuck, man. I don't know," I said audibly to him, assuming he didn't understand, yet he actually did. I again made the sleep sign with my hands and waved my hands around in a circle indicating, "Just find me a place to sleep, anywhere, I don't care."

Twenty minutes later we arrived at a hotel. I smiled with exhausted gratitude as the driver pulled away. I walked in the door, woke up the night clerk who was face down at the front desk, and checked in. By 3 a.m. I was asleep, in China.

The next morning I awoke refreshed after the nightmare of several hours prior. When I walked out the front door, the once dark alleyway was alive and gave way to the bustle of a modern city. Electric scooters (so quiet I began calling them "ninjas") stealthily zipped by me, a starkly different experience than the blue cloud-spewing motorbikes that sputtered down the narrow alleyways in Kathmandu.

I strolled across the street to an open-air restaurant. Inside was a glass case with dozens of fresh meats and vegetables, many of which I had never seen before. I looked around at the others who were eating, and they looked back at me with perplexing stares. A smiling woman handed me a basket. She pointed at the case and signaled for me to place whatever items I wanted into it, and she would prepare them into a soup—a soup that I soon discovered was essentially served in a bucket.

I was the only westerner around, and I fumbled comically with a combination of chopsticks and a giant ladle, while the spices triggered a waterfall of sweat that gushed down my forehead. The girl sitting next to me, who spoke at best seven words of English, said, "They like you," pointing to the staff, who were all standing around giggling at the spectacle I was putting on. I chuckled along, but this time, not from embarrassment, but from a feeling of connection.

When I was a kid, I was so embarrassed by my dad's unabashedly outgoing personality, and still am even a bit to this day. He himself is impossible to embarrass because what's the point of being embarrassed? We're all people, just trying to figure it out as we go. Big Jer would honk and wave out the window as we drove down the street, any street, in any town. "Hey, Tom!" "How you doin', Frank?" "Lookin' good, Charlie!" I was an awkward, insecure, and gangly boy and would cower in the front seat of his 1984 two-toned Chevy Caprice Classic, in complete and utter embarrassment. He was just making up names and being friendly (and truthfully, probably having fun embarrassing me, too), but almost always, the people would see my dad waving at them with a big, warm smile, and they would instinctively smile and wave back. He has this amazing gift of disarming people with his gregarious charisma, making them feel comfortable. He understood the human experience and the beauty of connection. I had been in China for less than twenty-four hours, and despite the incarcerating language barrier, which felt like solitary confinement, those lessons from my dad were paying back. Although it was a new country, with a new language, it was still a familiar storyline, one that revolves around connection. I get it, Dad.

—

"Where are you from? Where are you going?" I jokingly yelled across the common area of the quaint hotel where I found the Swiss a week later. They were seated at a small wooden table and, in familiar fashion, were nose down on their iPad, scouring maps, satellite images, and weather forecasts for the next week.

"Ah, the American!" replied Ivo as he excitedly leaped from his seat to give me a hug. Immediately, when I embraced my Swiss friends, any frustration or anxiety that had accumulated in me thus far in China was flushed from my system. I had traveled solo for the first five months, but I had no idea how much I had missed these two.

After slogging over three hundred miles through congested Chinese cities on my bike, I had once again joined my Swiss friends in the ancient city of Dali, a fabricated, cliché village with newly cobbled alleyways, tucked away in the mountainous Yunnan province in the southwest part of the country. There wasn't much *ancient* about it as most of the city has been rebuilt to satisfy the droves of Chinese tourists that blanket its streets, armed with selfie sticks. It did, however, provide a very comfortable resting and planning spot before heading north into the Kham region of Eastern Tibet.

Eastern Tibet is not to be confused with the Tibetan Autonomous Region (TAR). In 1950, the People's Liberation Army invaded and defeated the outmanned Tibetan army. Then, in 1951, the Tibetan representatives signed, under duress, an agreement with the Chinese Central People's Government affirming China's sovereignty over Tibet and thus the incorporation of Tibet. Under threat of death from Chinese forces, the Dalai Lama fled to India in 1959 and has been living in exile since. The Tibet Autonomous Region was established in 1965, thus making Tibet an administrative division that is essentially equivalent in status to a Chinese province. Many Tibetans fled to what historically has been called Eastern Tibet, where they enjoy a more relaxed and less regulated traditional Tibetan life. The TAR is marked by a strong Chinese influence, a heavy military presence, and a $200 per day tourist visa—all things we were happy to skip.

The Swiss had set out two weeks ahead of me and ridden overland through Thailand, Laos, and into China. They were either more concerned about *connecting the dots* or more tolerant to heat, but probably the former. Instead, I hung back in Chiang Mai with Elizabeth for a little while longer before hopping a plane and reuniting with them.

"Go fooding?" I inquired. "The soups here are big!"

"Sure, we know this. We have been here for two weeks already."

Why does he have to be so blunt and a know-it-all all the time? I mumbled under my breath. *Just once, I'm going to tell them something about a country that they didn't know.*

CHAPTER 2

3 Types of Fun

Loaded with five days of food, we crammed every nook in our bike bags and headed out, anxiously anticipating whatever we would find. Gradually, the tarmac road gave way to dirt before dwindling down to the familiar footpath then vaulting up into the sky and, with it, that old tingle came flooding back. Lungs expanded. Pulse slowed. Mind calm. Jubilant giggles seeped out of me like that young schoolboy just released from math class out to recess. I remember this feeling.

A few days later, that euphoria cratered, our psyches—hemorrhaging. Nobody said a word. Nobody complained, and nobody hung their head because surely, nobody was going to help us. This is what we signed up for. We occasionally looked at one another, if only for a check-in, but then solemnly just marched on. Complaining was a waste of time, and energy. Somewhere deep in the mountains of Eastern Tibet, we knew what to do and we knew what had to be done. There is some contention, however, on who got us into this situation, but at this point it was irrelevant. We were all in it. Deep in it. Together.

I had chatted with a local tour guide a month ago about traveling through the mountains in Eastern Tibet. He was the same guide that I had talked to more than a year prior when I was planning my trip to

Nepal, and when I told him I was from Colorado, he scoffed, "Colorado has hills." Yeah, that guy. After being in the Himalayas for four months, turns out he was right, and before leaving Thailand, he sent me a note, cautioning me about Eastern Tibet. "Many people go out into the mountains there, lose their way, and disappear. It is very remote, so be careful." As a result, I was now paying attention, though I thought of myself as far more seasoned and confident from my recent forays through India and Nepal. He didn't realize that his cautionary deterrent was actually a sales pitch. It's like when your father tells you to be careful with your new bike, and the first thing you do is dig a hole and build a jump over it. I did that, too.

It had been nearly two weeks since we left the comforts and cozy heated beds of Dali (it is very common in this region for hotels to have electric blankets since the buildings themselves have no heating) and disappeared into the mountains, arriving on the Tibetan Plateau. In India, even though we were in a remote area of the country, we were still following a relatively standard route of primitive roads across the country. In Eastern Tibet, that all changed, and seeing the Swiss poring over maps in Dali should have tipped me off.

We were back above 10,000 feet, arduously crisscrossing the rolling, velvety green passes between 13,000 and 16,000 feet. I had been at sea level in Chiang Mai for a month, drinking beet juice while both my bike and my body (and all my red blood cells) lazily dissolved in the Thai heat. Now, my muscles burned, my lungs wheezed, my head throbbed. I felt stupid, unable at times to construct coherent sentences, let alone thoughts, all distinct byproducts of the altitude. After traveling through the high mountains in India and Nepal with no effects, this was an unfamiliar and unwelcome feeling.

I had also been experiencing a phenomenon that I had only heard about: sleep apnea. I remember talking to travelers on the Annapurna Circuit about it, but it never affected me. It was terrifying at first, but actually, it was just terrifying. I woke up that first night on the Plateau because I wasn't breathing. I understood the burning legs and wheezing lungs, but I thought that breathing was just one of those things that I didn't have to think about? Instead, for over a week, I was jarred awake several times each night in a panic, sitting up and immediately gasping for air. After a few minutes, my heart rate slowed, but in order to fall back asleep, I had to consciously take deep breaths for fear that if I didn't, I just wouldn't breathe.

"I will push," said Brigitte as she got off her bike one day early on in our Tibetan adventure, the road continually climbing sharper as we inched our way into the sky. I smirked and continued to pedal on the narrow, rocky footpath, intent on proving Brigitte (and the laws of inertia) wrong while willing myself back into shape. Clearly, women are just smarter. I'm certain of it, and Brigitte had continually drilled this realization into my psyche over the three months I had known her, but my ego just blissfully droned on, "La, la, la, I can't hear you." That is the problem with the male hubris, I suppose; as she was pushing her bike faster than I was pedaling.

"Snickers break?" We had been climbing for four hours when Ivo called over to me.

"Sure, sounds good! What's our target today?" I inquired as I was looking for any excuse to preserve my honor and stop pedaling before I eventually tipped over. The track that we were following was relentless.

"Ah, Peanut Jerry is back!" Ivo chided as I dug into my frame bag and pulled out a bag of salted peanuts the size of my head, and weighing nearly as much.

"How're your Snickers?" I jabbed back. At any given time, the Swiss were always loaded with at least six Snickers each, which seemed odd since, as Swiss, they were so snobby about their chocolate.

"Good, man. You're missing out. Snickers are American. You should like them! I think we ride until probably six or seven, then find somewhere to camp." Ivo calmly replied with a specific, yet vague plan.

"You want to ride until 7 p.m.?" I questioned.

"Of course! If we only ride until 3 p.m., we will never get anywhere!" Brigitte chimed in with a smile, although I'm certain she wasn't joking. I didn't know where we were trying to *get,* but we had a 60-day visa, and China is big.

Through India, we typically rode into midafternoon, rarely the evening, until we found a village with a school, restaurant, or church to sleep at. I had gotten accustomed to having a target on the map, and in my mind. This was likely the last stronghold of my old, Type A, structured mentality that I was slowly letting go of, this goal-oriented, need-to-know mindset. But in Eastern Tibet, those villages were sometimes seven days apart, and I was softening to the idea of just riding without a plan. As remote as I felt in Arunachal or Nagaland, that experience could not prepare me for the vastness of the mountains in China. Though at times in India I felt like I was in another world, here, I was in another universe—not seeing a person or village for days.

With nicknames such as "the Roof of the World," "the Third Pole," and "the Asian Water Tower," the Tibetan Plateau stretches approximately six hundred miles north to south, sixteen hundred miles east to west, and is surrounded by the highest peaks in the Himalayas, Karakoram, and Pamir mountain ranges. It is the world's highest and largest plateau, sitting at an average altitude of over 14,000 feet, with an area of 970,000 square miles, and also where the headwaters of most of the streams in the surrounding regions originate. The Council on Foreign Relations stated in 2016: "Ten of Asia's major rivers flow from the Tibetan Plateau and fill river basins that provide water to more than 1.35 billion people, a fifth of the world's population."

The peaks were not daunting or sinister like the Himalayas in Nepal but were actually the opposite of dramatic. They were almost serene, like fluffy, velvety mounds, except, of course, those mounds were at 16,000 feet. Instead of feeling like being surrounded by the walls of a protected fortress, there was a vastness that made me feel alone and insignificant. We would ride for days and feel like we had gotten nowhere, with horizons that stretched like an ocean. A perfect simultaneous paradox of allness and nothingness.

But we carried food for a week, and clearly, water was abundant. With plenty of fuel to cook with, warm sleeping bags and tents, and driven by a deep-seated, passionate curiosity, there was nothing else that we needed. It was a new experience for me that took some time to adjust to, much the way the altitude shock did, but I quickly realized that there's something liberating about being that "lost" in the mountains.

"*Tah-shi de-leeeh*!" belted out a Tibetan man on his motorcycle, sloshing down the broken, muddy road, his wife and child clinging on precariously behind him. The family was completely enveloped in yak skin coats and hats with only eye holes cut in their face masks to see.

"Tah-shi de-leeeeeeeh!" I shouted back, even more emphatically as we began pedaling again after our Snickers and peanut break.

Sometime during that first week, we were cycling toward another colossal 16,000-foot saddle that was still easily an hour away.

It was clear that a storm was coming. Spring was slowly giving way to the summer monsoon season, bringing violent storms most afternoons, storms that were even ever angrier the higher into the mountains we went. They were all rated somewhere on the scale of "*pedal through it?*" to "*oh shit!*" For this storm, in particular, we rated it as *"pedal through it?"* and continued our ascent up the pass. At this altitude, weather happens fast, and we quickly changed our rating to *"oh shit!"*

From the ridge, I looked across the lush emerald plateau and saw the calculated clouds billowing, like a wild animal ready to attack, its chest expanding, lungs heaving, fangs piercing. We collectively decided we would pull over and make camp, for if nothing else than just to have shelter. Five minutes later, I could hear the roar. One minute more, I felt the first breath, and thirty seconds after that, it was raining sideways as we secured our gear and dove inside our tents. The fangs, a violent deluge of rain and sleet, tore at our tents for about twenty minutes, threatening to shred the fiber and snap their poles—and as quickly as it came, it was gone.

That was two weeks ago, and now, we found ourselves in something much deeper. This situation commanded a focus, the depths of which we had thus far yet to dip into. It was after 2 p.m. and the schizophrenic weather system had gotten us again. We were officially in monsoon season. Only moments ago it was sunny, but now, I looked over at Ivo, his chin tucked and head tilted from the shards of glass blowing in at an angle, careening off his two-week-old unshaven cheeks, thunder cracking all around. Brigitte, as always, was unshakable and barely blinked when I glanced over at her.

We had come over a 16,000-foot pass and dipped into a 15,000-foot valley that seemed high enough that we should have been able to simply reach up, turn the valve, and shut off the freezing rain that was thunking off our helmets like bb's. Earlier in the day, we had been on a dry road for several hours through the valley but had recently come around the mountain and found ourselves on the northerly aspect, void of any sun, with another storm charging in.

The chalky, dry track we had been following was now smeared with oozing, sticky gruel that clung to the edges of cascading ankle-deep rivers of melting slush, left behind from the long spring thaw and stretching even beyond the horizon. There was no way out. Pedaling was out of the question, and to turn back would have meant several days of detour without a promise of anything different. We pushed on.

The wrathful, charred sky continued to descend on us, swallowing up the peaks and the horizon everywhere we looked. We were following the remnants of a motorbike track that had carved a trough into the mud but was slowly freezing as the sun continued its escape into the blackened horizon. Three weeks ago, I had been melting in the 100° Thai heat. Now I was layered in Gore-Tex, my feet wrapped in plastic bags and jammed into my sandals, any effort to stay dry and retain heat.

"Man, this place would be great if there weren't so many people!" I joked aloud to the Swiss, trying to feign any semblance of fun.

There are three types of fun. Type 1: This is genuinely enjoyable in the moment. "Wow! This is awesome!"; Type 2: This is shitty, but when looked back upon two weeks or two months from now, having lived to tell about it, your recollection dulled, you think, "Yeah, that was amazing. I would totally do that again!"; and Type 3: This is shitty and will be shitty no matter how long I look back on it. There is no fond recollection regardless of the timeline. We started the day with Type 1, had slid subtly into Type 2, but were now teetering towards Type 3.

"Ha, ha, the American is so funny!" Ivo glared over at me, his sarcasm unmistakable, even for a Swiss. It didn't matter. I would take that over silence any day as I grasped desperately at the Type 2 fun that was slowly floating away down the stream of freezing slush.

"What's our stopping point? I think I see a dry place to camp over there," I said jokingly, pointing out into the white and grey abyss that was now creeping in from all sides. Spending the night here, cold, wet, and exposed to the elements, would have been dangerous and was simply not an option (think: Type 3 fun). We all knew we would keep pushing—for as long as it took—until we did find that dry spot to camp, which turned out to be ten miles and five hours later.

As miserable as it was, I was with two great friends. The memories of the pain I left behind in Colorado, while still lodged in my soul, were even further away than the beet juice in Chiang Mai. This is where I wanted to be, as grim and desolate as it may have seemed. Ultimately, I knew we would get through this valley, but this gift of time and freedom in my life would someday pass. *You'll miss this when it's gone*, I said to myself.

We eventually came around the mountain to a clearing just as the last light from the day was escaping. The muddy track that we had been following dried up and we began a gradual descent through a silky emerald meadow, mud and ice flinging off our wheels the faster we went. We stopped at the first dry spot we saw, just as the sun was beginning to peek out from the haze one last time before it went to sleep.

"Good thing we rode until 7 p.m. Otherwise we would never have gotten anywhere!" I joked, all of us collectively shivering, yet somehow laughing, and relieved to be putting on dry clothes, having survived another round of Type 2 fun in Eastern Tibet. After four months of traveling together, there were few things that I strove for more than getting a laugh out of the Swiss.

CHAPTER 3

The Chicken Soup of Buddhism

"*Here comes the sun . . .*" I began softly serenading outside the Swiss' tent as the first rays of light began to cascade over the furry green ridge, slowly melting off the overnight layer of frost from our tents.

"*It's all right . . .*" returned Ivo in a groggy voice, he and Brigitte still burrowed inside their tent.

This song had become our unofficial anthem in Eastern Tibet as we gradually came to anticipate the capricious, violent mood swings of the Plateau's weather. Each day that we started out with sun on our backs was a good day, but we were eventually sent scurrying for cover each afternoon right before the next storm scolded us for being here.

The previous night's storm had passed, and I woke to a hangover, the product of a potent cocktail of simply being above 14,000 feet, constantly looking over my shoulder for the next lashing, but also the *permafunk* of having put on dirty, wet clothes for two straight weeks.

By 9 a.m., my not quite frozen socks had thawed into a chilled, sopping heap of wool, and even though I was now accustomed to it (but you never really get *used to* it), putting on cold, wet, dirty clothes has got to be one of the worst ways to start your day. At least the Swiss had taught me to jam them into the bottom of my sleeping bag at night to keep them from freezing. We had been on the Plateau for over three weeks, every day growing more resilient, but cracks were starting to show. We needed a reset.

Following a slow, lethargic morning, the footpath from the day before joined a road, and a few hours later we found ourselves in a tiny Tibetan village just before the regularly scheduled midafternoon deluge. It was a simple village, not unlike any of the others that we had come through, with a handful of whitewashed structures dispersed along the seldom-used muddy road. Villages here were more a collection of buildings rather than any formal establishment.

Without surprise, there were no guesthouses, yet in our current state of debilitation, none of us were excited to camp. On schedule, raindrops began to splash on the already saturated, murky walkway as we exited a small shop, having restocked our frame bags of instant noodles, and reluctantly prepared to pedal out of town in search of a place to take shelter.

"Lama?" ironically joked a Buddhist monk pointing at my shaven head. He had kind eyes, a gentle, soft handshake, and was wrapped in the traditional, heavy burgundy robes, that despite the muddy conditions of the village, were otherwise pristine.

"Yes!" I laughed, rubbing my fuzzy head and playfully pointing back at his.

I pressed my hands together and rested them against my ear before waving my right hand around in a circular motion, asking if there was a place in the village to sleep for the night. He smiled and waved his arm, indicating for us to follow him up the sloppy hillside to his modest cinder block home. A line of welcoming, yet weathered, faded prayer flags were strung across the front, flapping turbulently in the wind as we approached.

There was a stream of smoke billowing from the chimney, and we were quickly ushered inside his cozy den. It was a single room of at most five hundred square feet that he shared with his 11-year-old sister and his ailing, bed-bound grandmother. Despite the humble, unassuming exterior, inside was an elaborate display of ornate tapestries on the floor and walls, accented by a small, framed picture of the Dali Lama that he pointed to with pride. Any picture or even mention of him is a crime in China, punishable by prison. In the middle of the room, there was just enough space for the three of us to roll out our air mattresses as our hosts looked on with perplexed astonishment at the inflatable beds.

They all had glowing, warm smiles that could not even be matched by the roaring fire in the stove, fueled by yak dung, in the center of his home—both of which were slowly thawing my persistent internal chill. Instead of us feeling like we were imposing in their very intimate and tiny space, they made us feel welcome and seemingly could not have been happier to share their home with us.

The three of us all stepped outside to clean up and put on some dry clothes only to return a few minutes later to heaping bowls of *tsampa*, the yak butter and barley soup I had not had since I left Leh nearly five months ago. It was a welcome refresher and reminder of the simple Buddhist culture. With another proud, almost mischievous smile, the lama reached into a box and pulled out a hunk of dried yak meat, which he used to make into fresh *momos* for us, something that struck me as odd, since weren't all Buddhist monks vegetarian?

While the Swiss practiced English and Tibetan with the lama, I attempted to work out my Plateau-inspired muscle kinks. Seeing some of my sprawled out yoga poses, the younger sister playfully joined in. *Note to self: never do backbends with an 11-year-old girl. They're like Play-Doh.*

Two days later we arrived in Yachen, a small pilgrim village for thousands of Buddhist monks and nuns. It is located in a valley at 13,000 feet and is one of the only places that allow both monks and nuns to worship in the same monastery. While they practice alongside one another, they live in separate dwellings bisected by the river that flows through the center of town. Their homes, one-room wooden shacks even smaller than the lama's, were clumped together in a sort of sprawling, burgundy shantytown. Additional white *boxes* (because that was essentially how large they were) speckled the surrounding hillside where monks and nuns would spend days and sometimes weeks in peaceful, solitary meditation, protected from the often less than tranquil weather.

To our relief, we found a simple guesthouse, the allure of its hopeful existence had propelled us all the way to Yachen after the lama's generosity. It had been nearly two weeks since our last reset, and, although there was no heat or running water, it was everything that we needed.

"*Cesuro?*" I asked of the man who showed us to our rooms, knowing thus far in Eastern Tibet that "toilet" was mostly a mixed bag.

More often than not it is outside, and nothing more than a hole through a couple of boards. Sometimes it is an elevated structure hanging over a river. Sometimes it is just—the river. On several occasions, it had been a concrete building, one side for ladies, one side for the gents. Inside these, there is usually a row of spaces, partitioned with a half wall, offering privacy if you choose, but low enough for social interaction otherwise. Sometimes there is no privacy, just all social.

"Mei you," he said, waving his hand and pointing out the window, downstairs, to the familiar wooden box perched atop a ladder, set over the river, likely with a hole in the floor.

"Okay," I said with a smile, having already expected that.

A month ago this would have been disturbing, but now, it just *was*. We were all happy to have shelter, especially when I unzipped my sleeping bag from inside my dry, yet unheated room the next morning to go pee. I shuffled across the drafty, weathered, wooden floors in a sleepy stupor, the feeling you only get when it's 4:30 a.m. It was still dark outside when I made my way to the window and scraped off the frost to see an old familiar friend outside: snow. While it was warmer than being in a tent during a snowstorm, the drawback of having to get dressed, walk downstairs, go outside, and scale the now perilously iced-over ladder leading up to the wooden box where I would begin my day, nearly offset my overnight accommodations. Especially when I had to wait in line.

"Go fooding?" I softly spoke through the door to the Swiss' room. It was nearly 11 a.m., which seemed reasonable based on "Swiss time."

"Sure. Give us thirty minutes," Ivo shot back, a distinct rasp in his voice indicating that he was still in bed.

"Bah. Shitty cold," griped Ivo as he and Brigitte emerged forty minutes later from their room wearing puffy coats. It's true, cold and wet was indeed *shitty*, and this had been the weather for the previous few weeks.

We wandered out into the *shitty cold*, down a snow-covered alley, where we found a restaurant. Inside were about fifteen men, all wrapped in the familiar Buddhist uniform of heavy burgundy robes, loudly slurping fresh *thukpa (*noodle soup).

"*Jee dan*?" I inquired of the man in the back of the kitchen as I tried to order an egg with my thukpa. A perplexed yet blank look glossed over his face. I probably could have asked where to get a leash for my pet goldfish, and likely would have gotten a similar look.

"*Jee daaan*?" I tried again, more slowly and pronounced.

Nothing. I flapped my wings and cackled as I reached behind my butt and feigned pulling out an imaginary egg, much to the laughter of the few people in the restaurant.

"Oh, *jee dan*!" he replied back.

Yeah, I just said that.

One of the monks at the table across from ours noticed this display and introduced himself. His name was Gu Lin, and he was 43, from Beijing, educated in London, and had been a reporter for the BBC in his prior life. He was the first person we had met in China that spoke *any* English, and as a result of his education, his was flawless, quite possibly better than the Swiss. I had so many curiosities about this region, and the religion, but was thus far prevented from asking any real questions due to the language barrier. Well, other than "Do you have eggs?" and "Do you have a toilet?" both of which I was only moderately adept at.

"Wow. So, how did you go from working as a reporter for the BBC in London to a monk in Yachen?"

"Well, it was pretty simple actually," Gu Lin explained in his soft voice and polished English. "I got tired of the rat race and pressures of society and just wanted to live more simply, so I pulled the plug."

"That's it?" I pushed back.

"Mostly," he responded with a smirk, indicating another layer that I didn't pry into.

"What do you know about Buddhism?" he asked me, quickly diverting the focus from him.

"Well, it's about simplifying your life and being content, questioning your emotions, being non-judgmental, and of course being present and living in the *now*," I replied.

"Well, that's kind of the *chicken soup* canned answer," he observed, chuckling. Touché.

Later in the day, Gu Lin invited us into the main monastery. Countless pairs of sandals were aligned neatly at the entrance before the heavy wooden doors swung closed behind us, effectively locking out the chill of the outside air. Initially, I was curious how anyone kept track of their own shoes, but that probably didn't matter.

Golden pillars at least thirty feet tall held up the brilliantly colored murals on the ceiling and walls. All around, there was a tangible hum that reverberated through my soul from the hundreds of monks and nuns, flowing in a sea of burgundy, who were seated and chanting in unison.

There was a part of me that just wanted to be a fly on the wall and take pictures, to document and observe this intimate experience. Ultimately, I felt that by doing so, I would be treating them like animals in a zoo, so instead, I resigned myself to drink in the potency of this tonic and enjoy my *chicken soup*. I found an open spot on the floor in the midst of the burgundy canvas of monks, closed my eyes, and slowed my breath. Before I knew it, ninety minutes had tranquilly melted away.

I had gotten several text messages from friends and family over the previous months—before leaving Nepal to go to India, before leaving India to go to Thailand, before leaving Thailand to go to China. They all asked the same thing: "When are you coming back?" When I replied simply, "I don't know," the perplexed reply was always, "Well, how much longer can you go on living like this?"

I had been gone from Boulder since September, a span of nearly nine months, two of them in Eastern Tibet. There are so many things that I used to take for granted, things that I once casually deemed *normal* or *basic*, things that I *needed*: like heat, or indoor toilets and a septic system (not a box over a river or simply *the river*), a hot shower, a faucet that when turned on the water came out, and maybe I could actually drink it. Now the things that I previously thought of as *normal,* were foreign.

I don't think there was a distinct line that I crossed from this being a "trip," but somewhere along the way, my perspective changed, and this simply became—*life*. I was relishing this rare gift of time that so many people are never given. Not only did I not know the answer to "When are you coming back?" but most days I didn't even know what day of the week it was. My focus instead shifted to wondering *what's over that next pass?*

This is Eastern Tibet, the land of snows, where birds soar, yak bells clang, and prayer wheels spin. In spite of the weather, I was not cold, nor was I miserable. There is a warmth and glow surrounding this place, and I was exactly where I wanted to be.

Many times there was no internet and thus no news, email, or text messaging. I was here. I was in it. In this vastness, I could disappear, and nobody would ever know. Yet instead of fear, I was calm. I was in my place, and each day I could feel my heart swell and my soul sing. We would ride and push our bikes all day and feel as if we had gotten nowhere, lost so far into a timeless and forgotten landscape, along nameless paths that stretch on for days.

Periodically, I would squint my eyes and for a moment think I might be tucked away in a canyon somewhere at home in Colorado, but really, I couldn't have been further away. Nine thousand miles, give or take. Nine thousand miles from everything familiar, even though I was completely at home, right now.

CHAPTER 4

Taking the Yak Track

"There is a 5,000-meter (nearly 17,000 feet) mountain pass that we could cross, but with the snow, we would need to buy a yak or some other animal to port our bikes. We have done it before. What do you think?"

This was the discussion over our *thukpa* breakfast in the restaurant of a tiny village that we had found ourselves in the night before. To a casual eavesdropper, it would have sounded nonsensical, as we collectively laid out the details of this caper. However, it was not the first time the Swiss had come up with what might seem even to an adventurous person as a ludicrous endeavor. But I had come to look forward to this Disney Pixar, anything is possible creativity, and now actually expected it.

But "*Buy a yak*?" This was a new one, and if I didn't know them, I would assume that they were joking. But I did know them. We had been together for three months in Nepal and India and now two months in Eastern Tibet. They're Swiss and didn't have an outlandish sense of humor, so like a judge listening to the defense attorney, I calmly sat back and allowed them to make their case, even though they had me at "buy a yak."

"Mei you," we heard too many times after showing people a

picture of a yak on our phones and then lifting our bikes up to demonstrate loading them on its back. Most of the time we got a look of bewilderment, followed by a subtle chuckle when they grasped what we were asking. Others just simply waved their hand and walked away.

After a few hours of haranguing passersby on the street in front of our hotel, orchestrating a myriad of charades and gyrations, ultimately, we could not locate a guy selling a yak or any other pack animal for that matter. I'm sure even without the language barrier this would have sounded absurd to the dozen or so people that we asked. Without a yak, we revised our route.

Hardly any of this vast region is mapped. Instead, it is a web of ancient dirt paths mixed in with newly-minted tarmac, but just because there is tarmac is no confirmation of a continual road. Many times they just end. But the Swiss are amazing route finders. They had learned to use several off-line mapping apps, Google Earth, and recently discovered Russian satellite maps of China from the 1980s, which were incredibly detailed. Who knew? Sure, there were plenty of roads on the map that we could have chosen that would go around the high pass, likely at a cost of a week's travel, but we agreed that the greater cost would have been to our inherent sense of adventure. We were collectively drawn by the insatiable lure of being "out there."

To complement all the mapping data, we ultimately found that the best solution had simply been to ask locals, which required a hodgepodge of thus far newly-acquired Tibetan charades, because aside from the language barrier, even charades took some adapting. Most of the time we heard the familiar "*Mei you,*" which simply meant that it was not possible as they showed us the sign for a dead-end road by cupping their hand in a "C" while ramming the other hand into the concave area.

Eventually, we met an old man who told us about a path that went over the ridge as he pointed off into the distance.

"With bikes?" Ivo inquired, knowing that the man didn't understand the words but got it when he pointed at our bikes and then over the ridge making a walking motion with his two fingers. The man nodded his head with a smile.

Through a series of hand gestures, followed by perturbed looks and chuckles, then cross-referenced against Ivo's downloaded Russian satellite maps, we figured out that the route started out briefly as tarmac, then turned to gravel, dissolved into a footpath, and then simply dissolved.

"About four miles from the summit the path stops. Locals take their motorbikes up to the end, leave them, then go forward on foot. The route would go over this pass, down about 900 meters (about 3,000 feet), continue up another 5,000-meter (16,400 feet) pass to a false summit and climb again up and over a near 5,500-meter (18,000 feet) pass on the other side, before dropping nearly 2,000 meters (6,500 feet) to a small town, where if all went well, we would find a guesthouse to rest for a few days. Or, we could ride seven days around the mountain on a busy Chinese highway," Ivo subtly persuaded, already knowing I would take the bait.

—

"Good sleep?" Ivo asked with a hint of Swiss sarcasm the morning after we had committed to this new route.

"Um . . . not really," I replied back with a grin, having mentally made my peace with the guy on the other side of the wall from me in the hotel last night.

Thus far our lodging had been a potpourri of camping, homestays, and places labeled as *guesthouses* but were more accurately just tiny, dirty rooms with a wooden frame and a piece of foam on top for a bed. Our guesthouse last night was just that, with porous walls constructed of weathered and rotted wooden planks that not only didn't keep the light out from the adjacent room, but worse, none of the noise.

"What the hell?" I said with a perplexed tone of disgust to Ivo as the guesthouse owner was showing us to our respective rooms the night before.

It appeared that she had a pet cat, which was for some reason tethered to a post by a three-foot piece of twine on the open-air patio just outside both of our rooms.

"Leave it alone," replied Ivo. "It's their way."

Three hours later, as we were all struggling to get to sleep, Ivo and Brigitte had heard enough of the cat's pathetic wallowing cries for freedom, and I had been patiently waiting for them to reach this breaking point.

"Ahhhhh! I can't take this! What should we do?" Ivo asked from outside my door just before midnight, already knowing what I was planning.

"Uh huh," I replied calmly, yet without any subtlety to mask my annoyance.

I went to my bag and took out my knife, looked around to see if anyone was looking—then cut the twine (you didn't really think I was going to kill a cat, did you?). The cat bolted down the stairs and into the night. I just hoped that the guesthouse owner wouldn't be pissed, or at least not know that it was me who set her *pet* free. But at this point, I didn't care.

I climbed back into the rickety wooden bed and within a few minutes was immediately unconscious, only to be rustled from my slumber by the tumultuous rumblings of my next-door neighbor's incessant snoring. It sounded like a 1978 Camaro with a rusted-out muffler, vibrating my bed through the walls. Even with earplugs and supplemented by utter cycling exhaustion, I spent the better part of the night pounding on the wall, momentarily jarring him awake, allowing me to fall asleep for about forty-five minutes, only to repeat the process for the next six hours.

I awoke the next morning with a headache but looking forward to waking him up with my passive-aggressive racket during our early departure, only to glance around the corner and see an open door and an empty bed. With childish revenge snatched from my eager grasp, I stumbled downstairs to find the Swiss loading their bikes, and the cat lounging in the lobby, basking in the morning sun.

We were all excited to get back into the mountains again. After a couple of hours of pedaling, we reached the end of the path and saw several motorbikes abandoned, with their owners somewhere further up the ridge.

We learned that many of the locals who come up here are in search of the *yarchagumba* or its proper name: *Cordyceps sinensis*. It is a caterpillar fungus that is the result of a parasitic relationship between the larva of the ghost moth and the fungus *Cordyceps sinensis*. The fungus germinates within the larva of the ghost moth, killing and mummifying the insect. Over time, the fungus will grow out of the insect's body and then into a small mushroom that can be used in many types of medicinal concoctions. This hand-foraged, intact fungus-caterpillar body has been used for at least 2,000 years for its reputed abilities to treat many diseases related to lungs, kidneys, and cancer. It is also used as an aphrodisiac and is reportedly sold for about $10 each in local markets. *Well, I was "single" . . . Never mind.*

Leaving the trail behind, we spent the next six hours dragging our bikes through the grassy, overgrown, yak meadow, straight up 2,000 vertical feet toward the saddle of the summit. Fortunately, it was a windless, blue-sky day with no imminent storms. In a simplistic yet sadistic way, it was an intoxicating struggle (Type 2 fun), bundled up in a blanket of peaceful *nothingness*, disconnected from any person, road, or path; the satisfaction of being "out there."

Two hours later, just before 4 p.m., the lumpy yak meadow abruptly transitioned into a shin-deep snowfield as we crested the summit, shrouded in weathered, fraying prayer flags flapping violently in the biting wind. Without a celebration, we quickly armored up and descended the backside of the pass.

Initially, there was no path, just an undulating, fuzzy carpet resembling a golf course putting green, an inviting sight after lugging our bikes up the ridge, and now begging to be ridden.

"Take care!" yelled Ivo. "There are no doctors out here," as I eagerly charged down the pass, overcome by the exuberant feeling like the first day that I learned how to ride a bike. There were no wrong directions and no rules. I could carve my own path and ride wherever I wanted. It all went down.

After about a half-hour, we were funneled onto a ribbon of seemingly manicured single track, with canyon walls towering over us from both sides, before crossing a river, joining a dirt road, and exiting into an expansive valley.

"Passport?" said a stocky man, likely in his 30s, with a peculiarly friendly smile as we approached a checkpoint. He stood up from his camp of white canvas tents where four other Chinese men, all dressed in grey t-shirts and red hats, were playing cards and having lunch.

A few days earlier, we had crossed over into the Amdo region from Kham, and it seemed that the further west into this region we went, the more *presence* there was. In many towns, and all cities, regardless of size, it was not uncommon to see cameras mounted on most street corners, monitoring everyone's movements. Throughout China, common apps like Google and Facebook are blocked and to get around that, I downloaded a VPN (Virtual Private Network) to my phone. It essentially tricks the government, or whomever else might be tracking you, into thinking that you're actually in Chicago, New York, or someplace other than a restricted area in China. However, this was our first physical checkpoint.

Instead of an interrogation, the officers were jovial and mostly curious about our travels and bikes, a distinct divergence from what I was expecting. However, it seemed like the only words that they spoke in English were "passport" and "beer," so I was not about to pass up the chance for a beer at a Chinese checkpoint when one was offered to me. We sat around for an awkward hour, all wishing we were able to interact more than we were, but it was only 2 p.m. and, after my beer and some friendly handshakes, we were allowed to pass without incident.

We pedaled along the narrow dirt road into the early evening, making sure not to stop before 7 p.m. Through an open meadow, we came upon a rushing river, gorged and hemorrhaging from the spring runoff, that had carved out this valley like a surgeon's scalpel. The crystal water was so clear that all I wanted to do was stick my entire head in it and drink myself full, but an icy river bath would have to do. Even after two months here, camping at 14,000 feet on a cloudless night on the Tibetan Plateau would never get old.

Tucked away in my tent, the temperature plummeted into the 20s overnight, making the stars glisten like a million pieces of ice; so close that I felt I could grab a handful to take inside to light my tent. But before I could do that, a few moments later the full moon exploded over the ridge and illuminated the valley, making it difficult to know when the sun had set and the moon had risen.

"*Here comes the sun . . .*" I once again serenaded the Swiss from my adjacent tent the next morning. The sun had begun to creep over the peaks, eroding away the frozen fringe from the river, and melting the ice crystals from the inside of my tent, waking me up with cold drops of water on my face. I peeked my head out to see several cranes swooping in to land on the frigid water.

Later that morning, we continued rolling through this carpeted, green steppe. The surrounding hills rippled and undulated like the comforter on an unmade bed. An hour later, we continued along the yak track before vaulting up again into a canyon as we clawed our way up a series of seventeen switchbacks (it was slow, so I had time to count). The fractured gravel road was bisected by a muddy river of flowing ice and slush that attempted to deter our progress, before entering a tunnel of fluttering prayer flags at the summit.

Clouds and an approaching storm seemed imminent again, yet only thirty minutes prior we were basked in a sky of pillowy clouds speckled against a sun-splashed sea of blue. For weeks I had been lulled into complacency by the rolling velvety hills of the plateau. But off in the distance, the 21,000-foot Chola mountain range exploded into the horizon, with snowcapped peaks intent on scaring off anyone who might be traveling in this direction.

The razor-like ridgeline seemed oddly misplaced in the familiar and welcoming green hills of the plateau, yet despite its inhospitable appearance, it beckoned to me like a bottle of whisky to an alcoholic. "Just one more?" they subtly prodded. The plateau had been magical thus far, but it was those sinister peaks that provided the intoxication that we had all been craving. Goosebumps covered my entire body as I took a deep breath to quell my emotions before descending the ridge to the town below, just as the Swiss (and Russians) had planned.

"We know it. We were here seven years ago. It is an ugly town with maybe not many guesthouses," warned Ivo an hour later over a Snickers break.

"Well, it's either that, or we make camp in the rain again," I pushed back not so passively before another soon to arrive drenching occurred.

We tucked our chins and fought ahead, the rain thickening, at first coming down in sheets, then finally in blankets, as it ultimately overwhelmed the limits of our Gore-Tex. On the map, it appeared that this small town we were about to descend upon was just that, but upon arrival, we discovered towering buildings and hotels that flanked the four-lane paved streets. The ugly, dusty village had grown into a city of more than 45,000.

It was not the first *pop-up* city that we had stumbled upon. In spite of all the new development, bringing with it an abundance of hotel choices, it was often difficult to find one without carpet. Smoking is a very real thing in China, with approximately 30 percent of the population who smoke (about 350 million people and roughly a third of the global smoking population). Culturally, it is custom to spit or put out cigarette butts on the carpet and as a result, we had walked out of countless hotels whose reeking floors and walls threatened to asphyxiate us from the second-hand smoke embedded in every fiber of the building.

For the next two hours, we battled physical but mostly mental fatigue as we wandered in and out of a dozen hotels, staggering through traffic as cars whizzed by, further saturating us with murky puddles of sludge from the afternoon storm.

"What's wrong with this one?" I asked, almost pleading with Ivo as we walked out and prepared to get back on our bikes. I was nearing my threshold of patience for his reluctance to simply choose a place and get out of the rain.

"If you don't like it, you can find your own guesthouse!" fired Ivo, "this is my trip too!"

Shocked, I looked over at Brigitte only to see her glancing away, her face red, either from the cold, but more likely, embarrassment.

This was the first time in nearly five months that any friction had surfaced between us. Up until this point, we had forged a bond so tight that we felt like brothers, but even brothers sometimes have a scrum.

When we were young, my brother Bobby and I would go at each other ferociously, most of the time without logic. We were kids, without the maturity to see past insignificant squabbles. At that time in our lives, we were probably fighting over a *Star Wars* toy or who got the next turn on Pac-Man. This particular day, Big Jer had had enough.

"All right. Down to the basement."

He pulled the string on the light bulb that was hanging from the rafters in our musty, unfinished concrete basement in Michigan as Bobby and I followed him down the creaky wooden stairs. Big Jer yanked back a sheet that was covering the entryway to a storage closet, pulled out two sets of boxing gloves, and suited us up.

"Okay, boys, you need to work this out," he said with an annoyance loosely masking his curiosity of what was about to happen.

I was probably eight, a full three years older than Bobby, probably eight inches taller, but nearly the same weight, so I wasn't sure what to do when he came charging at me with his psychotic windmill attack of circulating punches. After slugging each other into exhaustion, we eventually did work it out, just as Ivo and I did—however, without the windmill of punches. Apparently, Ivo and I possessed the maturity to see past inconsequential things. We were both just tired, and tired of being wet.

Through determined persistence, we found a newly constructed hotel with shimmering white tile floors, soft beds, modern bathrooms, and blazing fast internet with a modem in each room. The familiar stench of secondhand smoke had been supplanted by the permeating smell of newly drying plaster. We eagerly took it, before realizing only moments later that the *structure* had outpaced the *infrastructure*; there was no running water, only an empty twenty-gallon bucket in each room.

"Come," said Ivo very succinctly as he peered out the window from the hallway. He seemed to always have a plan.

By this time, the rain had begun to let up, and I followed him down the stairs to the back of the hotel, where a hose that was easily a hundred feet long lay strewn about on the newly poured concrete. Nearly as soon as Ivo picked it up, Brigitte had already lowered a thin rope from their bag out the window. Ivo promptly tied the rope to the end of the hose, and Brigitte hoisted it up two stories, through the hallway window and dragged it into their room. I retreated up the stairs to await my water delivery.

When our buckets were full, we went out to restock our food supply. Convenience stores in large cities, or tiny shops in the front of someone's home in a remote mountain town, always had instant noodles. For us, it was the cheapest and most easy food to buy, carry, and cook. Also available everywhere were the popular pickled chicken feet or pig snout, which in spite of my natural curiosity somehow evaded my desire. Usually on the same shelf, however, were vacuum-sealed tofu packages, and when doused in ketchup and cooked with a salty stock cube, were a great upgrade to make the three-times-per-day instant noodles seem a bit less like a poor college kid experience. Kinda like the first time I discovered that I could add hot dogs and salsa to mac & cheese and make an entirely new meal. But college was a long time ago, and after two months of subsisting on this diet, we eagerly looked forward to reset days in larger towns with restaurants.

"Boo yao rou," I leaned over the counter and said to the cook of the small restaurant that we walked into a few minutes later. He was busy stretching dough into homemade noodles, something that we had come to crave, in spite of the fact that we were thoroughly sick of instant noodles.

"You're a vegetarian? You're gonna starve," I was told by someone prior to entering China. "Even the Tibetan monks eat some nasty shit."

It's true, if you don't say "Boo yao rou" (I don't want meat) before you order any meal in this region of China, expect a healthy offering of either yak meat or various chicken and pig parts, mostly because up here on the plateau there aren't a lot of vegetables that grow. One thing that does grow here however is yak. Lots of them. Throughout India, Nepal, and Thailand, being a vegetarian was never an issue. Culturally, a vegetarian diet was common, and trying to find meat was the challenge. Many restaurants in India had signs on their front doors that read "Non Veg is not allowed," something I always found humor in.

"I'll figure it out or just order from a menu," I fired back in an overconfident '*I've traveled for years*' arrogance.

"Oh? Can you read Chinese?" I was rebutted even more arrogantly.

Over two months, we had a system, albeit a primitive one. When we did order something that by blind luck we liked, I took a picture of it and showed it when attempting to order at a new restaurant. We learned that each vegetable that you point at comes as a unique dish. If you point at a tomato in the glass case, they scramble up two eggs with it. We called it "tomato egg," which was not very original. I'm sure there is a proper name for it that I couldn't pronounce, but it worked for us. Eggplant was another staple that we ordered whenever it was available. It came presented on a bed of sautéed greens with ginger. Most of the time, however, fresh noodles were the only option.

"*Boo yao la*," Ivo said just after me to the cook behind the counter as he was dropping our noodles into the searing oily skillet.

I had been traveling with the Swiss for nearly six months and was convinced that they are biologically averse to "*la*." Each time we ordered food, I would say "boo yao rou" pointing back at me, then "boo yao la" pointing at the Swiss. Typically the cook would laugh, throw up his hands as if to say, "What the hell am I putting in there then?" It was a fair question. I could always pick out the yak bits, but picking out the *spice*? Not so easy. Ultimately, the pan that the food was prepared in had been seasoned with thousands of meals, so a bit of *la* inevitably seeped into our meals, and the result never got old to me.

We sat sorta patiently at the plastic table, draped in the familiar red and white vinyl tablecloth that we had seen throughout China. Spices were emanating from the kitchen as the searing sound of fried noodles made me salivate.

"Oh man! Soooo good!" I said through my first bite, a mouthful of noodles with oil dripping down my chin, the taste now so familiar and addictive.

I glanced across the table, and on cue, observed small beads of sweat beginning to form on Ivo's forehead. He reached for a napkin to dry it, trying to play it cool. Then, a subtle cough.

"Fuck. I can't eat this shete!" he choked out in his Swiss accent and stormed out of the restaurant, likely in search of yogurt to put out the fire.

Part of me felt bad for him as Brigitte and I (well, mostly I because she was struggling as well) laughed hysterically at Ivo's literal *meltdown* from the heat of the noodles.

Brigitte and I finished our noodles and Ivo his yogurt, but before going back to our rooms for the night, we struck gold. We (mostly the Swiss) were growing tired of bathing in the frigid rivers of the spring melt off or tepid bucket water in dingy guesthouses and had been actively looking for portable heating devices that could be dropped into a bucket to warm the water. We had seen them in some of the larger guesthouses that we stayed in and always fantasized about owning one. Yes, this was one of the luxury items that we felt we could not live without (that, and my hair clipper). They were small, about the size of your fist, weighed maybe two pounds, and fortunately, we found one in the shop next to where we bought our tofu. It was only about $20, and we knew it would have a limited lifespan as we had discovered with most cheap products in China. Still, we all chipped in, and before going to bed, we each enjoyed a long-overdue *warm* bucket bath, after about twenty minutes of heating, of course. With a steady water supply, our own heating device, and otherwise flawless new hotel rooms, we committed to a long-overdue four-day reset.

Throughout our nearly two months on the plateau, villages and landscapes had all passively and indiscernibly melded together like the running colors of a child's watercolor painting, and with them, my childlike curiosity had continued to flourish. Unlike in India, here, town names simply didn't matter. We were living in the moments of one another's growing bonds, clinging on to their finite grasp. What we did know is that we were making our way west to the desert city of Hohhot just before our visas expired in June, and where another decision awaited.

CHAPTER 5

You'll Miss it When It's Gone

Banma. We had traveled through countless inconsequential villages, none of them any more remarkable than the rest. But Banma, that name I would remember. We were decimated, physically and emotionally bankrupt, the cycle of relentless assault over another seemingly punitive mountain pass while dodging the now very predictable and inhospitable afternoon monsoon storm, having taken its toll.

We plunged down what could best be described as a mineshaft to the valley floor, heating up the brake rotors and skidding my back tire down the scree field of loose rocks. We once again fell upon the same lush green carpet that was this time snaking its way along a thunderous river in between two vertical granite walls. It was after 5 p.m., and our sights were set on a much-needed reset day, or three, in the small town of Banma. It was a town we would never see.

Slowly, the familiar path we were traveling along gave way to the expected tarmac road and, after making a left turn, an hour later, would theoretically deposit us in Banma. But there was a catch. The road was blocked. Soldiers shouldering automatic weapons patrolled the street and immediately demanded our passports. This time, nobody was offering me a beer. Since crossing into the Amdo region from Kham, the further west we went, the more patrolled the region was. The less welcome we felt. But then we entered Qinghai province, and things got serious. Entire towns or cities, we would learn, would close to foreigners without notice.

A soldier, slight of build and no more than 20, took our passports and returned ten minutes later informing us that we were in a restricted area, closed to foreigners.

"We go to Banma, just to sleep," Ivo explained, a slight prickly irritation creeping in through his accent.

"*Mei you*," the soldier replied back without any hospitable inflection in his tone, confirming that there would be no negotiation as he pointed off in the opposite direction of Banma.

"It's too far. It is soon dark, and we are tired," Ivo countered, knowing that the next town was about thirty miles away.

The officer again pointed off in the direction opposite of Banma, becoming more insistent and shorter in his tone, his eyes now stern and creased. Before long, the locals who were walking about, including other military personnel, began to take notice. This back and forth continued for about ten minutes, and like a mystery movie, Brigitte and I stood at a distance and watched the drama unfold. Finally, in defiant protest, Ivo sat down on the street, much to the soldier's disdain, and likely embarrassment.

Maybe I had read too many stories about Chinese protests, about people who would simply disappear in the middle of the night. Ivo's show of defiance scared me.

"They want us to pedal to the next town. It will take easily three hours. I will not do it. If they want us to leave, then they must move us," Ivo explained to Brigitte and me.

The soldier began yelling at Ivo, apparently trying to get him up and get back on his bike, but Ivo didn't budge.

"We are tired. If you want us to leave, you must provide transport," Ivo unflinchingly demanded through his poker face, as if he knew he was holding a full house.

"Ivo, are you sure about this?" I inquired nervously, less confident of the hand we were holding.

"Sure, we know this. We were here seven years ago, and same thing happened then. There are three of us. Nothing will happen," Ivo replied confidently.

"Send a jeep to transport us," Ivo calmly demanded of the soldier.

"*Mei you,*" replied the soldier again, even more sternly, before walking away and sending over his supervisor to hopefully quell this uprising.

An officer approached as Ivo remained sitting on the street. He had a sturdy build and carried an air of a person with the ability to make something happen, either to make us go away—or in my rabbit hole brain—*make us go away*.

"You must go," said the officer in more decipherable English.

Barely looking up at the officer, Ivo doubled down and instinctively responded with the same demand of a transport.

"No jeep. Not possible. Bus come soon. You take bus," the officer countered in an attempt to diffuse the escalating situation as attention continued to mount around us. My eyes bulged at what I was witnessing, but I silently stood by, unsure how this story would play out.

Thirty minutes later, a local bus did in fact arrive.

"Here. You go now," as the officer ushered us onto the bus.

"We don't have money. We are traveling by bike and cannot afford the bus. If you want us on the bus, you must pay," demanded Ivo, fully going *all in* without even a crack in his poker face.

Surely, we could afford the $2 bus ride as I was about to reach into my pocket for the money, but Ivo didn't back down. And all this time, I had thought I was the brash American. Class was in session, and I was taking notes.

With a look of disgust, the officer said something to the bus driver. We were told to load our bikes and shortly thereafter sped away.

Ironically, twenty minutes later, we arrived in Banma. From its initial appearance, it didn't appear to be a strategic military town or anything warranting a ban on foreigners. Nonetheless, we were not allowed to depart the bus, even as locals exited while others from Banma boarded. Clearly, the officer had made a call as soon as we got on the bus because, the moment we reached Banma, another soldier stepped onto the bus to ensure we were still on board—and that we did not get off.

Two hours later, after making a seemingly gratuitous loop through Banma, we arrived in Bayiu, the town to which the officer originally wanted us to pedal. Another soldier was waiting for us and took us directly to the only hotel in town that would accept foreigners. It looked like any other hotel that we had stayed at, with long echoing hallways and smoky rooms. We were allowed to stay, but in no uncertain terms were told that we could not leave the hotel and had to depart by 7 a.m. the next morning, which we happily did.

For the next two weeks, we pinballed our way through the region as I watched Ivo talk his way through countless checkpoints, all in an attempt to navigate this vast, unpredictable area while staying ahead of the increasingly volatile yet predictable summer storms on the Plateau. I had always been the most chatty and gregarious with locals through Nepal and India, but in this realm, I was happy to defer.

"There will be seven days of rain and shitty cold. We will stay here until the storm passes. There is no point in being out in this weather," Ivo told me after we checked into a hotel in another nameless, innocuous village. We were past due for a reset and fortuitously stumbled upon a new hotel owned by a local family, and most importantly, that allowed foreigners.

The tile floors shimmered as we dragged our weathered and filthy bikes inside the cavernous abode, the squeak of our grimy chains echoing throughout the main lobby. Upstairs, there were two master suites on the top floor, and knowing that our visas would be expiring in three weeks, we all agreed to splurge and spend the $11 per night. Behind the heavy wooden door was a spacious, almost decadent room, with a plush, queen-size bed, a sparkling tiled bathroom with running water, a flushing toilet, and a giant geyser, yet unsurprisingly, no heat. However, given this relative opulence, a reset week never felt so enticing.

Immediately after checking into my room, I noticed something. On the bed was a subtle, if not ominous sign: a pillow with an American flag embroidered on it, gently foreshadowing another looming decision. Down the hall in the Swiss' room, there was no pillow with an American flag. In fact, there was no pillow. The rooms were otherwise identical. By chance, I could have gotten their room, and they mine, but I didn't.

It was now the middle of June, just over one full year that I had been wandering the world on my bike, stepping through doors that opened, living life one pedal stroke at a time, and reminding myself to *always say yes*. The messages from home were again beginning to flood in, only this time, not just into my phone, but also seeping into my thoughts. This seemingly benign pillow, combined with an expiring visa, had unlocked the gate. Soon, another decision awaited.

"We will be going over three 5,000-meter (about 15,000 feet) passes, possibly in the same day," Ivo shared with me the next night while violent storms crashed against the windows in their room as we sat around their coffee table bundled up in puffy coats. He and Brigitte had spent most of the day poring over maps and weather reports, after they awoke at 11 a.m. and had taken two showers, of course.

"The final one, I cannot see a path over the pass on the satellite. It's likely that there isn't one. We only have one, maybe two days without storms, so we'll have to move fast, otherwise we will be camping in the rain and possibly snow at over 4,000 meters. We won't die, but it won't be fun," he said, with that familiar twinkle in his eyes, knowing I would take the bait. After nearly five months together with the Swiss, I would have been disappointed with anything less.

"Everyone needs a friend who will call you up and say . . ." Brigitte said to me with a smile.

"Get dressed fucker, we're going on an adventure," I said, finishing her statement. Everyone laughed.

One night back in India when we hardly knew one another, I had sent this quote to them on a text exchange during one of our reset days, the same one my friend back in Colorado had sent to me before I had left for Africa. It had become our unofficial anthem. A week later, we set off for one last adventure.

—

We had been here before. Not *here* specifically, but *here*, embarking on a similar crusade, in a place that was not in any guidebook or at the end of a bus route, traveling along a 12,000-foot plateau, over a perpetual swath of green velvet turf, in what is likely the loneliest place I had ever been. This faint track we were following was discernible the way a line appears when you run your finger the opposite way along velvet.

Everywhere, turquoise streams pervasively gushed from centuries-old glaciers and cascaded down the rocky ridges like fingers, as the path meandered its way through an endless valley. In sections where the river had formed a calm eddy, the morning sun glistened off the tranquil stillness like puddles of sky, framed against the lush, Crayola-green hillsides.

We crossed the first two passes on eroded footpaths, scars from a prior life, where maybe there was once a road, or perhaps there never was, just a seldom-used path etched into the hillside. Intermittent rays of summer sunshine pierced the hazy sky, briefly chasing the storms away.

By 4 p.m., we calculated that we had approximately another five miles to get through the valley, up a thousand feet and over the final pass. Two hours seemed like a reasonable estimate—until the path we were following (which was not on the satellite) abruptly ended, depositing us into the first of four, thigh-deep, swiftly moving rivers of summer snowmelt that not so politely offered to sweep us, and our bikes, away.

After forging the rivers, the sun began to hide behind the peaks, and the wind started to whip up, our jubilant optimism slowly dissipating into something just north of regret. Each switchback up the final pass brought either a gentle caress on the backside or a crisp slap across the face. There is definitely a point when there's no going back—when that pain far exceeds the pain of going forward, even if the destination is unknown. And we had reached that point.

"I just wish there were more people up here," I said sarcastically.

"Ha, ha. The American always talks," chided Ivo.

Two steps, drag the bike over a soggy clump of earth, through the slop, breathe. Step, step, breeaaathe . . . and repeat. Unlike when I was slowly making my way up Thorang La in Nepal more than six months ago, this approach had a significantly different feel. On the way up the final pass, I stopped frequently, not because I was winded, but rather because I wanted to drink in each moment, to take dozens of mental photographs to keep with me and pull out whenever I needed beauty. In the midst of my suffering, I knew this was it.

Slow down, I said audibly to myself, remembering back nearly three months ago to my first experience of slogging through the snow and slush when we had first arrived on the plateau. *You'll miss this when it's gone.* That moment of realization, so clear and obvious now when faced with the finality of this situation, seemed like a lifetime ago, both in time but mostly in my mentality. In spite of how tired, filthy, and hungry I was, I knew unequivocally that I *would* miss this when it was gone.

We had been in Eastern Tibet for about ten weeks. Despite daily challenges, it had flowed by, swiftly, like the spring runoff on the Plateau's snowcapped peaks, and faster than at any point of my journey over the past year. Vaguely, I recalled my frustrations with a culture and language with which now I had since grown so comfortable—to the point that I now embraced those very same things—and was heartbroken at the thought of leaving this magical place that I had called home for nearly three months.

Growing up, my friends would always race each other. It wasn't unique. It was just something we did, something I assumed all kids did—everyone wanting to prove who was the fastest. Initially, it was a running race, but when we all learned to ride bikes, it was always bikes. Always. "Do-over! I wasn't ready!" You would ultimately yell if your buddy beat you. This time, *time* had gotten the better of me. It had snuck up on me like a burglar in the night and stolen my time, and I wasn't ready. I wanted a do-over.

But time waits for no one, and when you're learning to live each moment, in the moment, the moments can have a way of passing you by if you're not paying attention. I remind myself: *reach out and grab them. Hold on tight as long as you can because there's no getting them back once they're gone.*

"I hope it's rideable on the other side," Ivo sighed, fatigue evident in his tone. We were all clinging to that same hope.

Just before 7 p.m., with the last rays of light gleaning through the now dense clouds, we crested the final 15,000-foot pass. On the other side, the real adventure began. The path that did not exist, did not resume. Instead, three miles of navigation across countless frozen and nearly frozen stream crossings, rock gardens, and sprawling brush fields patiently awaited our naive, yet ambitious fumbling. Perhaps the lesson is: if you can't see a path on the satellite, there likely isn't one. Relentlessly we dragged on. It was now nearing 8 p.m., and we dejectedly conceded that we would not make it out of the valley that night.

We eventually found a clearing next to the now only half-frozen river and set up our tents. There was a small Tibetan camp about a quarter mile down the river. Within a few minutes, we were surrounded by twenty Tibetan men, carrying clubs, picks, and one even was brandishing a bow and arrow, which seemed an odd tool to lug around. At first, I thought they were just coming to quell their curiosity as all others that we had encountered had done. However, upon seeing their weapons, it was clear that they had other intentions. They were up in this area in search of *yarchagumpa*, the medicinal mushroom, likely the main and only source of commerce for most of the people in this region. They were coming over to see who had crossed the pass into their territory. Once they realized that we weren't after their bounty, they lost interest and went home. And with that minor drama averted, we all drifted off to sleep.

"*Here comes the sun . . .*" I sang aloud through my tent as I woke up one last time on the Tibetan Plateau. Inside their tent, I could hear Ivo and Brigitte chuckling, then responding in unison, "*Sun, sun, sun, here it comes . . .*"

In spite of the lethargy from yesterday's battle, our spirits were high, realizing that this was it. Our last night of camping. Our last day on the Plateau. It was a day that had been benignly looming out there, just the way it had been in India. But now, here it was. By tonight, we would be in a Chinese city, sleeping in a hotel.

We packed up and continued our traverse of the gauntlet of dozens of stream crossings and countless fissures in the green, mossy earth. They appeared like crevasses in a glacier but were in fact just places where the ground had split, leaving gaping cracks filled with mud, large enough to swallow a Volkswagen with plenty of room left for three cyclists.

Within a couple of miles, we picked up a path, which eventually turned into a dirt road. Zooming down nearly 4,000 feet, I experienced a feeling so unreal—like I was pedaling off the end of the earth. As I looked back in the distance, I could somewhat make out the snowcapped peaks peering over the rolling green hills, euphoria still plastered on my face as we left the plateau behind.

In the blink of an eye, the Plateau was gone, and I was back in China. Almost at a line, trees appeared. Everything was green, and the flowers were in bloom. It was summer below the clouds and storms that had chased me down from the mountains that I love. This is how I would depart Eastern Tibet, abruptly, yet only slightly more smoothly than how I had entered, nearly three months earlier. It came too fast, and I wasn't ready. I *did* miss it when it was gone.

CHAPTER 6

It Was All a Dream

"Go to your room and lock the door. Don't open it until the morning," read the text message I received from Ivo, only moments after he had left my side in the hotel lobby and retreated to their room.

It was nearly 10 p.m., and we had been out getting supplies for the overnight train ride the next day to Hohhot. We had checked in four hours earlier without any grievance but returned back and were immediately headed off by the hotel owner as we tried to make our way to our rooms. The warm smile we had seen only a short while before was replaced with dizzying anxiety. She was frantic, waving her arms, a monsoon of words that we could not understand flooding out. Evidently, she was not authorized to offer rooms to foreigners, and when someone had found out, we had to leave.

"It's late! There are no other hotels, and we leave in the morning. No problem!" I said, trying to quell her anxiety.

It was futile. She wanted us out, or more likely, she needed us out. Somewhere during this ten-minute exchange, Ivo and Brigitte had stealthily gone to their room, leaving me to wage this war. When I read their text, I smiled and nodded, giving the impression that I would go upstairs and pack, but twenty minutes later, when I heard a pounding on my door and a stern male voice, I turned off the light, put in my earplugs, and went to sleep.

Early the next morning, as we were trying to sneak out of the hotel to avoid any conflict, we were greeted in the lobby by the hotel owner, this time a smile had replaced her previous look of distress. Based on our experiences in the region thus far, I had thoroughly expected to be greeted by police or, worse yet, escorted out the night before.

We boarded an overnight train out of Xining to Hohhot, a city with a predominantly Muslim population located near the desert in the Inner Mongolia province. If it wasn't *real* before, dismembering my bike and wrapping it in garbage bags and three rolls of clear packing tape sobered me up from the intoxicating elixir that had been the Tibetan Plateau.

"Okay, okay, I can see you're upset—but *what is it, man*?" my voice now slightly elevated, reflecting the agitation at being woken up for the fifth time by this guy. This time, with the flashlight from his mobile phone beaming me in the eye, jolting me out of a slumber at 2:30 a.m.

A Chinese man in his 40s, of slight build with a potbelly and sporting a soiled white tank top that was much too small, smoking a cigarette, was berating me as I lay on the top bunk for our twenty-two-hour overnight voyage.

"What?" I yelled the first time as I was awoken by him yanking at my blanket.

"Okay, fine. Take the blanket!" I conceded, throwing my blanket down to him just after 1 a.m.

"Is he *drunken*?" inquired Ivo from the bunk across from me, also awake from the commotion. Even in my agitated, exhausted state, Ivo's English still made me laugh.

Finally, three members of the train staff showed up to help resolve the situation just before I was about to smash the mobile phone that was still searing my eyes.

"Sir, can I see your ticket?" one of them asked me. "Sir, you are in the wrong bunk," she said, pointing to the vacant bunk just an arm's length away after she examined my ticket.

"Are you insane?" My patience was now noticeably tested. "It's the same bunk. Who cares? We're docking in four hours. I've been in this bunk for eighteen hours, and *now* he wants it? There are three other vacant beds. Just tell him to pick one, *any one*, and go to sleep! Have you checked his ticket?"

"Oh, sorry. Sorry. Sorry," she repeated profusely, obviously embarrassed after realizing that this "drunken" man was actually not even in the right train car.

We got off the train in Hohhot, a city of about 2.5 million people, and found a plush hotel (that accepted foreigners) in a quiet nook of the city. All the buildings were yellow. The men wore traditional white hats and the women, headdresses. Ten weeks of living simply in the Tibetan Himalayas was washed away in an instant with a hot shower and a bowl of fresh yogurt. Fancy cars lined up in all directions, waiting for the stoplights to change on the six-lane roads. I had not seen a stoplight in nearly two months. Culture shock was a gross understatement.

Transitions. Like spring to summer. The Tibetan Plateau to a Chinese city. Rain and snow to sun and heat. Living simply to plush hotels. Yaks and motorbikes to Audis and BMWs. Shared horses to bike share stations.

It was time, and this time, I actually booked a flight. In three days I would be back in Boulder, unaware of what I was going home to nor how I would fit in.

No doubt I would be asked repeatedly from day one to day *forever*, "How many miles did you ride?" The simple answer is, "I don't know." The better counter is, "Who cares? Why does it matter?" Instead, ask me how many smiles I inspired or how many times *I* was inspired? Ask me what I learned from this or how my life has changed. Yvon Chouinard, the founder of the outdoor outfitter Patagonia, once said, "So, it's kind of like the quest for the holy grail. Well, you know, who gives a shit what the holy grail is. It's the quest is what's important."

On June 25, I heard a knock on my hotel room door. It was 6 a.m. but I was already awake, dreading this moment. I opened the door to find the Swiss, bags packed, and already a few stray tears escaping down their cheeks. I gave them both a hug, the kind of hug reserved for the really important people in your life, making no attempt to choke back any of my tears this time. Never would I have guessed that a random encounter (is anything ever random?) back in Nepal in early December would have led me on this journey. What should have at most lasted six days with two complete strangers grew into more than six months, and even after that time, I still wanted to yell, "Do-over! I wasn't ready!"

—

After thirty hours of travel, I arrived back *home* to Colorado, into the engulfing, spine-adjusting embrace of an old friend who absolutely would not take "No" for an answer when she asked if I needed a ride from the airport.

"Well, I won't be the only person to ask you this, but at least I'll be the first. How does it feel to be home?" Sara inquired almost rhetorically, knowing what answer I would give her. Already, Eastern Tibet felt like a lifetime ago and India and Nepal, a dream that never was.

I had been gone for the better part of thirteen months, and the term "home" just didn't seem to register anymore. My home had been wherever I was pedaling at that moment, everything that I needed with me on my bike. I had been living simply, trying to blend in and experience life, not through the privileged gaze of an American tourist, but rather through the eyes of locals. By their uncompromising generosity, I had slept in their homes and shared their meals as we laughed at each other's stories through a jumbled potpourri of their local language and mine. Looking back, I often ponder, if the roles had been reversed, would I have been as open to welcoming a stranger into my house with the same offering or would my western societal norms and fears have prevented that? Perhaps another rhetorical question.

Before arriving home, I had wondered, would I fall back into old patterns and habits? Or would I continue to see the world through a new lens acquired over thousands of miles, countless mountain passes, and polished by never-ending smiles? How does it feel to be home? This question would occupy my mind continuously, the answers emerging unpredictably like that of a shaken Magic 8 ball.

I spent the first few days in my house processing the avalanche of emotions that were churning and tumbling down at me. I began to notice things, like my array of Banana Republic and Hugo Boss work clothes, remnants of my prior life, still pressed and hanging in dry cleaner's plastic from more than eighteen months ago, glaring at me from the open closet. It seemed strangely opulent to wear something other than the same shirt, shorts, shoes, and yes, underwear, that I had worn every day for over a year.

My house, a place I had spent the better part of five years remodeling with blood, sweat, tears, and of course thousands of dollars, felt like a cold and barren shell of a home—my voice echoing and bouncing off polished oak and heated tile floors. By American standards and those of people in Boulder, my house is average. By the standards of the world I had been traveling in, however, it is a palace.

For weeks, I restlessly paced the hallways, intermittently peeking into the room that Emma had occupied before she had left. The sheets were still tucked neatly beneath the draping comforter, but by now, not a smell or any sort of reminder lingered. It was just another empty bedroom. Although I had made my peace with our breakup along the way, seeing the sterile space provided the final resolution. "How does it feel to be *home?*" In this moment—lonely.

And then there was my mom. For over a year we had been estranged, and I was fretting over our first encounter, which I knew would happen at some point when I arrived home. Torn by my love for her and the need to have her in my life, yet passively annoyed by her lack of communication, I put off our meeting as long as I could, which turned out to be nearly a month.

While still in China, on Mother's Day, May 12, about a month earlier, I had sent her an email. It was like a confessional. Because it was an email and I was 9,000 miles away, in a different time zone, with spotty internet, I felt that I could cut loose and truly unload my heart on her. I just needed to get everything off my chest, knowing that even if she did reply, it would be at least a week before I would see it.

The motivation had arrived one week before in the form of a text message she had sent asking a ridiculous question about a repair for her Subaru. It was a problem so benign that, if it hadn't been a year since we'd spoken, it wouldn't have bothered me. But this was her way to break the ice, I suppose. Instead of being excited to finally hear from my mom, her veiled attempt at connection left me even more upset. I sat on my emotions for a week, and by the time I reached the next hotel in China with internet, I let her have it.

Hi Mom,

Happy Mother's Day. I received your text message regarding your ailing Subaru. I'm not quite sure how to respond. Part of me wants to tell you to simply go buy a BMW, the way Luther did, and fully bring this full circle. But that is just a hurtful reactive emotion and not what I want to convey. I know that you have had a lot of losses the past few years and so have I. We are both hurting, struggling to gain strength and direction.

After not really hearing much from you since I have been traveling for nearly one year, I am inside hoping that this is your way of reaching out to me, telling me that you're thinking of me, that you miss me, that you're proud of me, sentiments and emotions I feel that I have had to pull out of you.

I cannot and will not dwell in the past. I have learned so much about myself over the past year and I am getting ever closer to becoming my best self. I didn't get a choice in the hospice, but I do now. Life is short and I choose happiness and to move forward. I truly hope that we can at some point talk, really talk, and not be afraid of what the other person might feel and say. That is the only way that I think we can have a relationship again. It is something that I very much want, but I can only stretch so far.

I have been harboring this hurt for too many years and if we are ever going to be able to move forward, I need to get this out. I truly want us to restore, or at least create a relationship. I miss my mom . . .

I anticipated an equally long and emotional reply, something to justify her actions, to help me maybe understand a bit better. Instead, I received a very brief response stating that she looked forward to seeing me in person when I returned home. And that was the last I heard from her until I returned home. I didn't even reply.

Through this gift of time over the past year, I was afforded hundreds of hours on my bike, an opportunity to dive deeply into my emotions, confront and dissect my fears about confrontation and vulnerability. For the last three months in China, I had packed that away so when I returned home in August, I had built up the courage to see her—not knowing what she would say.

On a sunny day in early September, my mom's grey Subaru pulled into my driveway. I saw her drive up and peered anxiously out the window as she walked up to the front door.

"How does it feel to be home?" she asked after finally breaking from a long and overdue hug, her slight frame nearly dissolving into my embrace.

"Funny, you're the first person to ask me that," I replied back with a chuckle as we both wiped away some inevitable tears.

"Right. I'm sure." She still knew my humor.

We waded slowly and cautiously into the tepid stream of more serious conversation, lightly tiptoeing around the elephant that was prominently lounging in the room, perhaps both of us too afraid to simply dive headfirst into the emotional questions I needed answers to. After only about thirty minutes, her phone rang.

"I have to go. Luther needs me for something. I'm so happy you're home. Can we do this again soon?" my mom asked as she stood up and made her way to the door.

"Of course. I'm glad you came over," I chimed back, not even trying to mask my disappointment at her abrupt departure.

We hugged in a way that we hadn't in far too many years, neither one of us wanting to let go. I watched her walk down the driveway, climb into her Suby, and drive away.

While it wasn't the emotional exchange that I had hoped for, it was something. An opening. It took years to dissolve our relationship, so perhaps it wasn't realistic to fix it in one sitting. Rome wasn't built in a day.

I had been home for six weeks, and almost immediately, people, friends, family, and even strangers felt free to fling the same mix of questions at me, like a battalion laying siege to a formidable castle.

There was "*How does it feel to be home?*" And, "*What did you learn?*" My personal favorite, loathsome question was, "*How many miles did you ride?*" Really? While I struggled to form a cohesive response to that barrage, the one thing I was sure about pertained to work. The hospice had been my identity for ten years. Without it, who was I? What now? Everyone asked this. But this one I felt I had on lockdown. This question I had the answer to.

While in China, I had been actively interviewing for a position in the mountains of Steamboat Springs, a place I had grown fond of over the years. It is a small ski resort town about three hours to the north. Traveling through the Himalayas, the possibility of a move from Boulder to the grandeur of living in the mountains seemed exciting. The job was an executive position, running a healthcare company, something well within my wheelhouse. This is what I thought I was "supposed to do" after traveling and being absent from the working world that long. To immediately pick up where I left off and assimilate back into the normal routine. The job was familiar, but I had changed.

In an odd paradox, the closer I got to the job, the less I wanted it, the more I knew that part of me was slowly dying. It seemed my desire for another high-profile position was created and fed by my insecure ego. I wanted to feel *important* again, not just like the drifter that I now saw myself as, or worse, how I felt others saw me. I was already rehearsing my speech declining their offer, and was relieved when it went to an internal candidate instead. It turns out, sometimes not getting what you want is the gift. Maybe I didn't know what I wanted, but it was becoming more evident what I didn't.

After traveling nearly thirteen months on a bike, through some of the most remote corners and over the highest mountain ranges in the world, I returned home, ideally bringing with me all the direction and answers I had been seeking. But it was an illusion. It seems to me that if you go off consciously looking for something, rarely will you find it.

The one answer that I knew—to the question that was never asked—was that my soul yearns to wander. An unquenchable thirst for discovery and unbound curiosity drives me and was once again making me restless. The dull smolder of my desire to hit the road and travel by bike was not yet extinguished—and perhaps it never would be. I was different now, and there was no going back.

A few months mindlessly, effortlessly drifted by, the way time does when you're asleep. It was happening to me, even though I vowed that it wouldn't. I was sliding back into my normal routine. Had I not learned anything?

One day in February, as the snow was falling outside my window, a warm glow came over me and I began to laugh. I thought about the brief, not so random, yet awkward encounter I had with an Israeli man back in Pokhara in November, over a year earlier. I had met countless people on my trip, many framed by awkward moments, but this one stuck with me.

"Is that your bike?" I recalled hearing a male voice with a strong accent behind me. I was immediately defensive, having felt that this person broke a code by approaching me at a cash machine, as if I might actually be robbed in broad daylight? In Nepal?

"Yes," I replied curtly as I spun around to see a man about my age with olive-colored skin and wavy brown hair, standing too close.

"I want to talk to you about it. Come sit and have a tea with me," Yuval said, almost politely demanding, yet with an inviting smile.

I had just gotten back to Pokhara and was taking out cash before returning to rest in my hotel room. As social of a person as I am, at the time, I just wasn't in the mood to answer the same barrage of questions I had mindlessly checked off over the past six weeks.

Maybe it was my fatigue or his persistent interrogative Israeli personality, but I agreed to have tea. Yuval was from Israel and worked for an Israeli NGO helping with disaster relief efforts after the earthquake in Nepal. He was also an avid biker in Israel and had noticed my bright green bike leaning against the wall by the ATM. For two hours I recounted tales from the prior six months as Yuval looked on with intrigue; moments and adventures that now seemed insurmountable, even though at the time they felt very ordinary.

Yuval said politely, yet almost demanding again as we parted ways, "On your journey, if you ever find yourself in Israel, come and stay with my family,"

I took a sip of tea as I watched the snow fall from my couch in Boulder, over a year later. Even though I had not talked to him since, I thought, why not drop him a text?

"Hey, Yuval! Remember me? We met briefly over chai in Pokhara back in November 2016."

"Hey, dude! Yes, of course!" he responded an hour later. "Great to hear from you. Where are you now?"

"I'm home, whatever that means."

"Are you coming to Israel? Come! You can stay with me and my family."

"What about the *temperature?* I've been watching the news and it seems like things are heating up over there," I asked with trepidation.

"Fake news! Things here are fine. Your news media doesn't know what's really happening. There is always something in Gaza. I heard there was a shooting in Chicago. Does that mean I shouldn't come to Colorado?" Yuval joked back.

"Yeah, okay. That makes sense," I replied, my concerns assuaged, and my spirit once again excited.

Two months later, in April, I packed a bag, grabbed my bike (which had yet to be unpacked) and boarded a plane to Israel.

The Tibetan Plateau...before the storm (Ivo Jost @bikepackground)

...and then, the storm

Crossing another 15,000 foot pass (Ivo Jost @bikepackground)

And down... (Ivo Jost @bikepackground)

Lama? (Ivo Jost @bikepackground)

Camping below 14,000 feet (Ivo Jost @bikepackground)

Taking the yak track (Ivo Jost @bikepackground)

Military check point. (Ivo Jost @bikepackground)

Yarchen Gar

Gazing off at the Chola mountains (Ivo Jost @bikepackground)

Crossing peaks and lakes (Ivo Jost @bikepackground)

Last group photo in China

PART 8

Israel

April 5 – 30, 2017

"You can't stay in your corner of the Forest waiting for others to come to you. You have to go to them sometimes."

– Winnie the Pooh

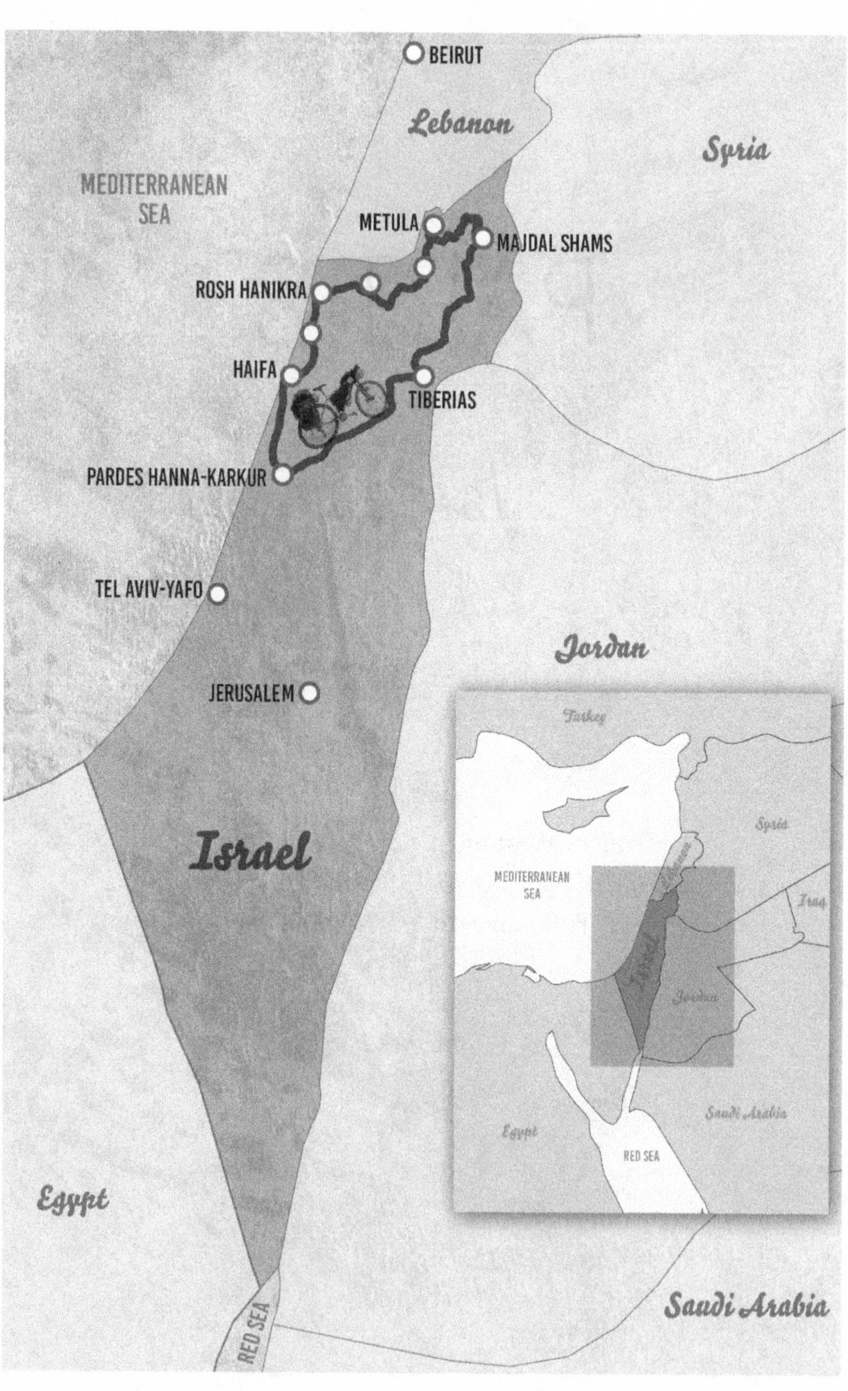

BEIRUT
Lebanon
Syria
MEDITERRANEAN
SEA
METULA
MAJDAL SHAMS
ROSH HANIKRA
HAIFA
TIBERIAS
PARDES HANNA-KARKUR
TEL AVIV-YAFO
Jordan
JERUSALEM
Turkey
Syria
MEDITERRANEAN
SEA
Iraq
Jordan
Israel
Saudi Arabia
Egypt
RED SEA
Egypt
Saudi Arabia
RED SEA

CHAPTER 1

Don't Go to Israel!

"Don't let them stamp your passport," I was told matter-of-factly by countless people. "Israel doesn't have many friends in the Middle East, and there are plenty of countries that will not let you in if they find an Israel stamp in your passport."

This flashed through my mind as I went through a second, more intense airport security check just for passengers bound for Tel Aviv. All of our carry-on bags were rechecked, our bodies rescanned. Hours earlier, the camp stove and fuel bottle that I needed for the trip were seized by security agents prior to checking my bags in Denver. I had flown with them before without issue. Maybe it got missed by security on prior trips, or maybe security was tighter now, going to Israel.

To be honest, I didn't know much about the Middle East. I had grown numb to the stories that proliferated the headlines, much the way the white noise of a fan drones on in the periphery. There seems to be a continual newsfeed about Israel dating back as far I can remember involving tense border relations with Syria, Palestine, Gaza, Lebanon, and the West Bank. For me, and most people living in the West, the words "bombing" and "terrorism" were synonymous with the Middle East. However, I never thought much about them because it was always "over there." But now, I was going.

Israel, and the greater Middle East is the Holy Land. The history dates back thousands of years, and one could spend months reading up on it and a lifetime trying to understand it. As a boy, I remember all the Bible stories about Jerusalem, the Red Sea, Moses, and Jesus. As an adult, I was enthralled by the confluence of the entire Christian, Muslim, and Jewish religions in this region.

Outside of the biblical history of the region, the actual history of the country is much younger. After World War II, Britain found itself in intense conflict with the Jewish community over Jewish immigration limits in Europe. Its people had been displaced. Hundreds of thousands of Jewish Holocaust survivors and refugees sought a new life far from their destroyed communities in Europe.

On 14 May 1948, David Ben-Gurion, the head of the Jewish Agency, declared the establishment of a Jewish state to be known as the State of Israel. The following day, the armies of four Arab countries—Egypt, Syria, Transjordan, and Iraq—entered what had been British Mandatory Palestine, launching the 1948 Arab-Israeli War. Contingents from Yemen, Morocco, Saudi Arabia and Sudan joined in. The apparent purpose of the invasion was to prevent the establishment of the Jewish state at inception, and some Arab leaders talked about "driving the Jews into the sea." The Jewish people turned back all their invading enemies and built a country out of the ashes and memories of their heritage. Almost immediately, an influx of Holocaust survivors and Jews from Arab and Muslim countries flowed into Israel. During the first three years, the Jewish population increased from 700,000 to 1.4 million. By 1958, the population of Israel rose to 2 million. An official Jewish state was born. But there seemingly would never be peace.

A breaking headline came across my phone as I was waiting to board the plane out of Denver. The US was threatening military action on Syrian President Bashar al Assad over United Nations reports that his regime had used chemical weapons on thousands of its own people. Things were again heating up. Syria and Israel share a border in the north, and the former's capital, Damascus, is less than fifteen miles (as the crow flies) from the Golan Heights in Israel—the place I would be starting my trip.

What is it about fear that can be so paralyzing? Is it just fear of the unknown? We only know what we're told, and most of us never question it. I had seen too many videos of terrorism, bombings, and rocket launches. "Don't go to Israel," I heard on a loop in my brain, only moments before I reread Yuval's message: "Fake news. Things here are fine!" Who was right? My friends, my family, the news media? Maybe this was a bad idea? "Don't go to Israel," I could hear my dad saying as I took a deep breath and boarded the plane.

I had met Yuval only once for about two hours over tea in Nepal, back in November of 2016. What should have felt like seeing a complete stranger in another world, didn't.

"Dude! It's great to see you!" he said as I stumbled bleary-eyed off the plane after forty-three hours. I'm certain my bloodshot eyes looked like those red and white hard peppermint candies my grandma always had on her coffee table.

Yuval wrapped me in a warm hug and gave me a kiss on the cheek, his own eyes twinkling in the midday Israeli heat. Like two brothers reunited, in an instant, all my preconceived fears melted away.

"After meeting you in Nepal, I've been getting into bikepacking. I thought maybe I would join you on your trip for a few days. What do you think?" Yuval asked during the drive out of Tel Aviv to his small town of Pardes Hannah.

"Hell yes!" I blurted out, casually wiping off the drool that was seeping out of the corner of my mouth as I tried to fight off my jetlag delirium.

"Good, so we leave in two days. It is Passover, a holiday for us, so I will have some time off."

While I wasn't expecting a tour guide, I was happy to have one, though still somewhat nervous about what I was walking into.

On Monday afternoon, just after lunch, Yuval and I pedaled through a pissing rain along a harrowing four-lane highway for about thirty minutes to a bus stop.

It never rains in the Middle East, I grumbled quietly, becoming increasingly more salty with every car that doused me with sheets of water from oil-streaked puddles—yet another thing about this country that I had already gotten wrong.

The plan was to take a bus three hours north to the Golan Heights, where we would pick up the Israeli National Trail that snakes its way through the country from north to south, ending in the Negev desert at the Jordan border. With only three days, Yuval would peel off, leaving me to meander the rest of the way on my own, something I was quite looking forward to.

Holy shit! No way that just happened! No way!

These were the thoughts painfully scorching my brain, paralyzing me with a panic, the emotion so visceral that initially, I could scarcely utter anything audibly to Yuval.

"Yuval, where's my bag?" I finally summoned some words, my voice quivering, knowing inherently that something was horribly wrong.

"I don't know. Don't you have it?"

It was over before it started. My heart was pounding, audibly in my ear. A deafening thumping. How did this happen? I had taken a dozen busses in a dozen countries. I had never lost anything, not even a set of earplugs. What had gotten in my head, breaking my track record of flawless travel flow? Was it the rain that we pedaled through to reach the bus stop on the highway, cars whizzing by at 70 mph in a place where it isn't supposed to rain? I swore I saw him grab my bag, but clearly, he hadn't. Everything happened so fast, but it didn't matter. There was no blame, nor time for answers or rationalization. The clock was ticking.

"We have to stop the bus. I have to go back for my bag!" My voice now slightly more elevated and panic-stricken.

Everything I had with me was in that bag: my wallet, credit cards, passport, laptop, and clothes. Everything—left at the bus stop on the bench, in a foreign country I had been in for only three days. Yuval politely pleaded with the bus driver to pull over, but the next stop was still ten miles away, and he could not stop before that.

"I think it will be okay," Yuval calmly stated in his Hebrew-accented English. "Many times in Israel when a bag is left, people call 911 because they think it is a bomb."

I laughed at that comment partially because it is a mentality foreign to most of the western world, but mostly *because* of this mentality, I might actually get my bag back. Because they think it's a bomb, nobody will steal it.

"I have a friend in the CSI (Crime Scene Investigation) who works in the area. I will call him. I think it will be there."

Two hours later (but actually only about ten minutes), the bus driver arrived at the next stop on the highway, and we got off. I was breathing now, sorta.

"Relax, dude. I think it will be fine. But if the bomb squad does show up, they will blow it up. But I think it will be fine."

I had already thought about what was in the bag and how I would replace everything. I sat on the bench, motionless, going through the steps, yet hoping for a miracle in this religious country. Minutes dragged on agonizingly.

Yuval's phone rang, and he smiled. Five minutes later, his friend arrived in his covert, black police vehicle with a very familiar backpack. Strangely enough, nobody had called the bomb squad, and I had my life back. We boarded the next bus and resumed our voyage north.

The Golan Heights is a mountainous region in the northernmost part of Israel. It is bordered by Syria and Lebanon, two countries that, unfortunately, Israel is not friendly with. This region is claimed by both Israel and Syria, and although it was annexed by Israel in 1981, the annexation is unrecognized by other nations. Due to this contested nature, much of the area is a military zone and littered with minefields left over from previous wars. In the Golan Heights, it is advised that travelers should never deviate from marked trails due to the danger of stumbling into minefields or firing areas. Once again, I could feel fear creeping in.

The landscape was not as I expected. As we neared the Syrian border, no bombs were audibly or visibly detonating. Where were the endless peanut butter-colored expanses of the Middle East? Just like the baseless fear that was propagated on TV, instead of endless beige, bright red poppies appeared like polka dots scattered across a lush, yet rugged, green blanket. It was spring, and Israel was exploding with life. To the north, several mountains framed long-distance views into Syria. In the fringe, ruins (including many disused army bases) gave a sense of this region's contentious history.

Yuval and I got off the bus in Majdal Shams at 5 p.m. to a now drizzling rain. It is a small military town near the border of Syria. I expected to look for a hotel and start fresh in the morning, but Yuval had other ideas.

"Ready to go down?" he inquired.

"Um, it's 5 p.m. and raining, in a place that you said never rains, so I guess I figured we would start tomorrow? How far do you think we can really get tonight?" I inquired, in jest but mostly annoyed.

But as soon as I threw a leg over my shiny green bike, I was back. Traveling, wandering, exploring the world and even though it was a new country, it felt like home. The months of pacing through the doldrums in my mind, wondering what I *should be* doing, were gone in a single pedal stroke, and everything made sense.

But a few minutes later, across a field, gunshots cracked. To my left, through the cool, foggy mist, I saw soldiers running, crawling, and yelling, some diving behind rocks. *What the fuck? What am I doing up here?*

Yuval looked back at me and saw the concern (not quite panic) in my eyes, and smiling, he said, "Military training. This brings back memories. All men and women serve two years in the military when they graduate high school."

Right, I knew that.

We continued downhill, the weather gradually improving. Remnants of a prior Syrian civilization dot the landscape, a crumbled wall, an abandoned mosque. This was contested land, but make no mistake, we were in Israel, and the Israelis had no intention of giving it up. Along the fence line, yellow signs clearly displayed the words: "DANGER. MINES!" and, together with army posts perched atop strategic peaks, notified me of the wounds of the past and places we should not be. There was something eerie and chilling cycling through this war-torn place, knowing its history of sacrifice.

For these three days, I resigned myself to being a tourist and letting Yuval play tour guide. This was, of course, his country, and I had only a faint idea of how much it meant to him to be able to share it with me. We meandered our way through dense forests, rocky green meadows, down from the Golan Heights to the shores of the Sea of Galilee, where we camped on our last night together.

As we rolled through a bustling town the following day, April 10, at 10 a.m., sirens began to wail. It was a disaster siren, the kind you would hear if there were an earthquake, a storm—or war. Yuval put out his hand, indicating for me to stop pedaling.

"Holocaust Day," he whispered solemnly.

Immediately, my body shuttered. Goosebumps crawled along every inch of me while a chill ran down my spine. The entire town, and all of Israel, literally, stopped. Busy six-lane highways became parking lots as people got out of their cars and off of buses, and stood still for two full, uninterrupted minutes. The rest of the world was still spinning, but not in Israel. This was a time for the entire country to remember the six million Jewish lives lost in the Holocaust, and to vow never again, and to never forget. For those two minutes, I tried to imagine the terror that Jews faced, just for being Jewish. This is why I came to Israel.

After a long embrace, Yuval continued to head west, and I made my way back to Majdal Shams where I discovered that there is actually a ski resort named Mt. Hermon, which I cycled up to. It is the highest point in Israel at just over 5,000 feet, a comical claim when compared to the dizzying Himalayas. The top of the mountain is over 7,000 feet, but that road is closed for military use only, because, at the top of the mountain, off the backside, is Syria.

There was no place to camp, mostly because I didn't feel comfortable camping in a place where tanks roamed freely throughout the countryside, so I found a local bike shop to inquire about lodging. "I have idea," offered the slender, bald man, likely in his 30s with bicycle grease smeared across his cheek. "You need place to sleep? Hold on. I will call a friend."

Five minutes later, a man in his late 20s showed up. "I have the most reviews on Airbnb in Majdal Shams," he proudly boasted.

I followed him around the corner and up a short flight of stairs. He opened the door to his six hundred-square-foot studio apartment, and for 100 shekels (about $30), I had a place to sleep. While I hadn't had any experience with Airbnb in Israel, I was pretty sure, based on the state of his apartment, that he was just a guy who got a call to rent his space. There were dishes in the sink, empty beer bottles on the counter, and the bed wasn't made. But I looked out the window and saw the border fence separating Syria from Israel and realized that in this contentious region, a complete stranger had given me his home for the night.

The following morning, I woke up to a barrage of text messages and emails from friends and family in the US. "Are you okay?" was the common thread. "Where are you?"

The US had launched a targeted missile strike in the early morning hours on Damascus, at most fifteen miles from where I slept. Yet throughout the night, I never stirred.

Rolling through town later that morning, life seemed the same as the day before. The sun was cascading down on the distant green mountainside as I gazed off into Syria without seeing a hint of any billowing smoke. People were embarking on their day, drinking coffee, going to the market, or scurrying off to work. Living in the United States, it's unfathomable to think of war going on around us in Canada or Mexico. It's so ingrained in the lives of people here that they don't even notice. For us, it would be like a traffic jam on the way to work. It's just life.

I continued out of town, now paralleling the border of Lebanon. A ten-foot metal fence, wrapped with razor wire, was just to my right and most of the time within arm's reach. I was heading toward the village of Metula along a lightly traveled two-lane paved road that stitched back and forth along the chunky hillside. I periodically gazed through the metal fence, foolishly expecting to see men in camouflage lobbing grenades into Israel. But just like looking into Syria, the hillside into Lebanon was peaceful and serene, with no suggestion of any inherent conflict.

I stopped at the village of Gjarha, which sits precariously on the border of Lebanon and Israel. I was naively eager to enter and catch a glimpse of Lebanese culture. The four soldiers dressed in full battle fatigues and brandishing automatic weapons at the gate, thought otherwise.

"This is a split village. Half Arab. Half Jewish. Foreigners not allowed. You must go back the way you came," I was told without a hint of compromise.

Not wanting to backtrack, I glanced at my map and prodded, "There is a secondary road heading west. Can I take this?"

In the back of my mind, I could hear Big Jer quoting Cool Hand Luke again. "What we have here is . . . failure . . . to communicate."

Shut up, Dad, I said under my breath, trying to suppress my anxiety.

"This is a military road that goes along the border. It would probably be okay but also could be snipers, but is probably okay."

What the fuck was I thinking? In what world does, " . . . probably be okay but also could be snipers" sound like a good idea? I looked on the map and saw that just to the south of this military road was the Israel National Trail, and a nature preserve, so somehow that justified its safety.

Two miles down the dusty, bombed-out road, a fully-armored Humvee came racing up the road towards me, a cloud of dust in its wake. My heart stopped. *Was I someplace I wasn't supposed to be? I didn't cross a border by mistake? Shit! What am I doing here?* "Don't go to Israel" was once again going through my head on a loop. I went through a dozen excuses and reasons to justify my existence here. The chalky beige vehicle barely slowed down, the helmeted driver and passengers barely waving as it thundered by me. This was all normal, whatever normal is, I rationalized again. Just like a traffic jam. "Fake news. Things are fine!" I could hear Yuval.

Four hours later, I arrived in the small mountain village of Metula and found a café to refill my water. Dried sweat formed a salty paste on my face. Despite its proximity to Lebanon in an otherwise unstable region, Metula is a wealthy village of only several thousand people. It is picturesque, with cush hotels, European-style cafes, and set against a tapestry of rolling green hillsides. The streets are lined with freshly blooming flowers, and on every corner, crisp white and blue Israeli flags flap in the warm breeze.

"Are you Jerry?" I heard from the man behind the counter as I walked in the door. Before I could pick my jaw up from the floor, he continued, "I read about you on Facebook on 'Bikepacking Israel.' You posted that you were traveling through Israel by bike and looking for homestays. Someone responded to you. I will call him."

A man answered, and the man behind the counter handed me his phone.

"Are you Jerry?" the stranger on the other end asked.

Chuckling, I replied, "Yes?" wondering what sort of ruse was happening.

"You need a place to sleep?"

"Yes! Is there a place where I can camp? I have a tent," I replied enthusiastically.

"Give me your phone number. I will drop a pin on your phone. Follow it to my house. It is very near. My neighbor will be waiting outside to let you in. I'm away for the holiday but will be back next week. Stay as long as you need. If you are there when I return, then great. Otherwise, safe travels."

Ten minutes later, I was staying in the home of someone I had never met, and likely would never meet, along a war-torn border, just another example of the human experience.

After a much-needed shower, I ventured out. At the edge of town is a park where children play, and families have picnics. There is laughter in the air. Across the road is a wall. It separates Israel from Lebanon. Humvees pass by so routinely, intermittently drowning out the children's laughter, that nobody even notices. Soldiers walk around with machine guns like businesspeople carry briefcases. The sounds of circling helicopters are constant. It's no big deal. No one even looks at them but rather at me, curiously, as I photograph the military presence, and they wonder what I'm looking at. Yet still, everywhere I go here, I am greeted with beaming smiles and "*Shalom! Manish ma*?" (Hello! How are you?).

My plan for Israel seemed reasonable. Ride the length of the country from north to south, a thousand miles over four weeks, cross into Jordan, and then back north to Tel Aviv. I would be home in a month, with an authentic Middle East perspective, an itch scratched, and maybe then with a few more answers—or so I thought. Instead, I rode for one week and maybe two hundred miles before that plan blew up (I probably should have chosen a better descriptive, given the environment).

The further south I traveled into the middle of the country, the more the mercury rose, and like a line, the rolling green hills gave way to dusty cow fields lining busy highways. It was like riding through Michigan in the summer. There were no historic, unique villages that predated the *now*. Instead, I found myself in a modern industrial country. Still, my mind was set on the Negev desert, the final slice of truly unique landscape in Israel. The *real* Middle East, I thought. The three hundred-mile, newly built Israel Bike Trail carves through the region and zigzags down to the Red Sea at the southern tip of Israel on the border of Jordan. However, a quick check of the forecast showed temperatures there in excess of 95°, with minimal trees or water.

"It is too hot by now. Come back in October," I was told by nearly everyone I asked.

I was barely two weeks in, and it seemed my cycling time in Israel had ended. I resigned myself to pulling the plug and going home early, satisfied with my time spent here. I had plenty of things I could do in Colorado, I reasoned.

CHAPTER 2

What Are You Entrepreneuring In?

"Dude, what are you doing here? I figured you would be in the Negev by now?" Yuval asked as he arrived home from work to see me slumped on his couch.

"It's too hot," I replied with a failed attempt to mask my frustration.

"You have to start early. Maybe 5 a.m. Then ride until noon and take a break until 6 p.m. Then ride again," his advice bounced off me as if I were traveling in an armored Humvee. My mind was already made up.

"I was thinking of changing my flight and heading home this weekend. I have some things I need to get done back in Colorado."

I didn't, but I didn't know what else to say, and really, I didn't know what else to do.

"Well, I'm back at work next week, but you should take a bus to Jerusalem. It's a special place. You will love it," Yuval said encouragingly, clearly seeing through my thin sheet of disappointment.

"Yeah, maybe," I replied unconvincingly.

To this day, I don't know why I did it. After dinner with Yuval, his wife, Na'ama, and their three kids, I retired to my room, which was really just a tiny space used as an office with a narrow foam mattress laid out on the tile floor. Small enough that I was essentially sleeping *under* the desk. I opened my laptop and found a flight to Denver leaving in three days, but before pulling the trigger (maybe another poor Middle East expression), I logged onto the dating app I had used in Thailand. Yuval was busy with life, and I just wanted to see more of the country, without a bike, if even for a couple of days before going home.

I indiscriminately swiped through too many names, faces, and profiles the way one would pass people in a busy airport. But then I saw Sharon, and to my luck, on the other end of her phone, she saw me. She is a sociology professor in Haifa, a city just north of where I was. Born in Norway, educated at Penn and Cambridge, and living in Israel. Jewish, but not Israeli. She had straight, shoulder-length brown hair, freckles, and eyes that pierced through me from her profile picture.

"What are you entrepreneuring in?" She asked in a message to me a few minutes later.

On my profile, I had listed my job as an "entrepreneur," I guess because I had founded a company, but even now, over the past two years, I felt like I was kinda just doing my own thing. So, an entrepreneur, I guess.

We traded text messages for about an hour before I finally wrote: "Do you wanna just call me?"

"Right, forgot about that option," she replied, just before my phone rang.

Her accent was a mashup of English, Norwegian, and Hebrew, a combination that she was embarrassed by. We talked late into the evening, and I was immediately captivated by her wit, her brain, but mostly because we made each other laugh. I didn't think it was possible that someone who was living on the other side of the world with a completely different upbringing could "get me" the way she did—immediately that first night. A little after midnight, I closed my laptop and temporarily put off purchasing my flight.

"Who were you talking to last night?" Na'ama asked over breakfast the next morning. I was embarrassed to admit that I had met a woman on a dating app, but I could tell she was on to me.

"Oh, sorry. Did I keep you awake? I was talking to a friend back home." I'm a terrible liar, and Na'ama knew it, but she didn't push it.

"Dude, there is a fun trail that I'm riding with some friends tomorrow. It's maybe a one-hour drive. You will like it. Do you want to come?" *Dude* was clearly Yuval's favorite English slang word as he chimed in over breakfast.

"Hell yes!" I replied. Yuval and I hadn't spent much time together, and mountain biking in Israel seemed like just the authentic experience that I was craving.

The next day as Yuval and I were driving home from the ride, childhood exuberance once again restored, I got a message from Sharon, sending my teenage insecurities into a frenzy.

"Hi! What are you up to? I have to pick up kids from school at 12, but was somehow hoping to have time to hang with you . . ."

"Yes! I'm in Tiberias now with three other friends riding mountain bikes. I will be back around 12," I replied, not even trying to hide my excitement in my text.

"I got no plans until family dinner this evening, but got my kids with me so if you want to join me it will have to be kids friendly."

"I'm pretty good with kids."

"Can you be dropped off in Haifa? I won't leave you stranded in Haifa after. I promise."

"We already passed the turn. Heading south through Afula."

"There is a bus to Haifa from there leaving at 13:00. Bus 301."

"Also, I'm filthy."

"I figured you would be filthy."

I put down my phone and turned to Yuval. "Hey, man, this is weird, but a friend wants me to get dropped off at the bus station at Afula. Are you okay with that?"

"A friend?" Yuval inquired curiously.

"Yeah, a friend. I met her through the *Bikepacking Israel* Facebook page, just like that guy I told you about who let me sleep in his house up in the Golan." It was clearly a lie, but like Na'ama, Yuval didn't push it.

"Also, do you have any money? I didn't plan on meeting my friend today and don't have money for the bus."

"You know it's Shabbat? The buses stop soon, and there are no buses tomorrow," Yuval said.

"Right. Yeah. I thought about that. I'll figure it out," I said confidently just before we pulled into the bus station, and Yuval handed me 50 shekels (about $16).

I was being dropped off at a bus station, without a bike, with just enough money for the bus, but not enough for a taxi later or even to buy food, to meet a person I had exchanged a few text messages with followed by an hour-long phone call. I was having Shabbat dinner with her, her kids, and her parents. Out of all the things I had done over the past two years, this might have been the craziest. I always had money and my bike, and thus was always in control. But I had neither now. However, in my mind, whatever could happen, a worse choice would have been to stay in the car with Yuval.

An hour later, on a muggy late afternoon in April, I stepped off the bus in Haifa. This person whom I had never set eyes on before stepped out of her white Volkswagen Golf, leaving the door open behind her. She was wearing white jeans and a long-sleeve button-up denim shirt, her hair flowing in the warm Israeli breeze.

"Shit," I said calmly to myself, my heart immediately sent racing.

Our eyes locked like a magnet. Shyly, yet confidently she strode toward me, her stare never diverting from my own, as she put her arms around me in a warm hug as if we had known each other for years.

"Hi. I'm Sharon (pronounced Shah-RONE)," she said with a giggle. The smell of her hair was salty after a day at the beach.

"Hi," was all that I could muster. It was the first time I remember ever being speechless.

We zoomed up the hill through winding streets, impatient Israeli drivers blaring their horns and swerving around us. Even with her twin six-year-old boys in the back seat clamoring on in alternating Hebrew and Norwegian, everything was white noise. All I could hear was her.

A couple of hours later, we walked down the street from Sharon's flat to her parent's.

"This is Jerry, my friend from America. He's in town on business."

I have no idea if they believed that, but regardless, welcomed me to their home, her mother handing me a glass of wine even before I could take my shoes off. The smell of fresh challah was wafting through their flat.

"Oh, so nice to meet you. How long are you in town for?" her father asked me.

"A few more days and then back to America, but maybe I will extend my trip until the end of the month," I said, peering over at Sharon with a curious smile. At this point, I hadn't changed my flight yet, and it was feeling like I wouldn't.

Fortunately, I had a clean shirt and pants with me in the car, so I didn't show up in dirty bike gear to meet her parents.

We sat around the table and held hands while her dad led us in a traditional Jewish prayer. Sharon glanced over at me throughout dinner with her own curious smile, if nothing more than to check in and make sure I was handling the situation. I later assured her that I had been at far more awkward dinners over the past two years because, if nothing else, everyone in this room spoke English.

"Okay, we're going out for a drink. I'll pick the kids up tomorrow," Sharon said a few hours later as we exited her parent's flat.

"Where should we go? It's early," she asked me.

"How am I getting home?" I countered playfully. "You said you wouldn't leave me stranded in Haifa."

"Are you worried?" she shot back, matching my joke.

"No, I think if you turned out to be crazy, I could take you," I volleyed.

"I'm not worried. Something about you. I had a good feeling as soon as we talked," Sharon said reassuringly. "I have wine at my place. Let's just go there. I want to talk to you more."

Sharon had great taste in American music, so when she was pouring the wine, I found a Norah Jones CD and pushed play. She handed me a glass of wine as I sat at the opposite end of the couch, too nervous to move. We talked about travel, politics, books, and even our favorite NPR podcasts. But it was blaringly obvious that there was more between us, a connection so unabashedly profound that it was impossible to mask. Unfortunately, I was paralyzed like an eighth-grader, afraid of his first kiss.

After nearly two hours of talking and listening to Norah Jones on repeat, Sharon slid down the black leather couch, looked at me, into my heart, tilted her head, and gave me a kiss. It was something I would never have had the guts to do. In my mind, she was way out of my league. But when I kissed her back, I felt a tear roll down her cheek and across mine.

"I'm sorry," she said, embarrassed. "I'm not sad. That's not why I'm crying."

I cowered behind my defensive wall as she slowly tore it down, one brick at a time, exposing a long period of fear, heartbreak, and insecurity. With that one kiss, I was defenseless. She knew me, in the span of a single night, in a way it would have taken anyone else years.

Maybe I let her in because I had nothing to lose. I was getting on a plane in less than two weeks so I gave her everything, but in that moment, I had no idea how much I was giving her. But I wasn't scared, nor was I nervous anymore. After that first kiss, I had known her for years. We talked until 2 a.m., laughing until tears streamed down our cheeks and our stomachs hurt, but it was the piercing stare of her brown eyes that delivered the decisive blow. I didn't know it yet, but I was in love.

Although I had met Elizabeth in a similar way in Thailand, this was different. Elizabeth and I felt like old college buddies in some regards, but with Sharon, it was deeper, immediately. Maybe I was in a different place in my life, further distanced from old heartache, more open to new emotions, but likely, it was just Sharon.

The next day, she walked back to her parents, and I drove her car back to Yuval's, with the mission of picking up a change of clothes.

"I can have a friend drive me to yours, or you can drive back to mine. Feel free to tell me whatever you prefer, and we can arrange it," was Sharon's message to me after I arrived in Pardes Hannah.

"Prefer to see you?" I replied.

"Why the question mark? I prefer that you prefer to see me."

"Okay. Just checking if you are into it too."

"Very . . . maybe too much," she unabashedly replied in her text.

Two hours later, Sharon arrived at Yuval's house to pick up her car, and me. I packed all my things, knowing that even with nearly two weeks before my flight, I wouldn't be coming back

"Ah, this is your *friend*," Yuval said with a glare in his eye, glancing at Sharon before smiling at Na'ama. "So she will take you to the airport on Tuesday?"

"Well, I decided not to change my flight after all," I replied. "Maybe we go to Jerusalem tomorrow."

—

"Fuck, I hate Jerusalem," Sharon griped the next day while we were making the two-hour pilgrimage from Haifa.

"What? Why are we going?" I asked in astonishment.

"You said you wanted to go. I hate all the tourists and religious *fuckery*."

"We don't have to go," I insisted, trying not to laugh at this new word I just learned, no doubt the product of the conglomeration of her three languages.

"No, it will be fine. We can stay overnight in my friend's flat."

Before arriving in Jerusalem, we stopped at a store to get some groceries. There was a guard out front of the underground parking garage. He had a machine gun slung over his shoulder. At this point, to me, this was no big deal. I had sat next to a soldier on the bus the day before who had a similar gun.

"What are you doing?" I curiously asked as Sharon popped the hatch on her car.

"He has to make sure there isn't a bomb in my car," she replied nonchalantly.

"Sure, of course," I said, unfazed. "No big deal," as I was trying to act cool, like a local.

"You know that each home has a bomb shelter, right?"

"Um, no, but I guess that makes sense."

"Mine is my bedroom. There is a heavy iron door over my window that I can close. If we hear the sirens, I have ninety seconds to get the kids inside and close the window because that is how long it takes a missile to arrive from Lebanon."

"Wow!" I said, this time now very much *fazed*, unsure of what else to say in the moment.

"Yup. But it's no big deal," Sharon replied, mocking my prior comment.

Inside the Old City of Jerusalem is the only place in the world where the three religions converge. Jewish, Christian, and Muslim followers all lay claim to this sacred space. The Western Wall is perhaps the holiest Jewish site dating back to 19 BC, while the Dome of the Rock, an Islamic temple completed in 691 AD, looks on just behind. Although it seemed completely unreasonable to come to Israel and not go to one of the holiest cities in the world, I had to prepare myself for the one thing I truly dread and try to avoid: tourist places. I simply couldn't get excited to battle thousands of western religious pilgrims, anxious to walk in the footsteps of Jesus.

"He's yours," joked Sharon, of the retired man, likely in his 70s wearing a Detroit Tigers baseball cap, white sneakers, and baggy blue jeans wrapped with a fanny pack.

We played a game where we tried to identify either the Americans or Europeans. Sometimes the lines were a bit blurred, but that hat made it too easy. He was clearly one of *mine*. Ugh. I had flown 43 hours to stand in line behind a guy from Michigan, the place I spent my youth. That was enough for me. We made a quick pass through the Old City, took a couple of snaps of the Western Wall and Dome of the Rock, and stealthily escaped—before anyone identified me as *one of theirs*.

Just outside of the Old City lies Mea Shearim, one of the oldest neighborhoods in Jerusalem. It is populated by Haredi and Hasidic Jews, and although only a few streets over from the Old City, it could not be further away from anything found in a tourist guidebook. No busses transporting eager religious pilgrims roll down these passages. Instead, the streets retain the feel of the small Eastern European towns (*shtetls)* that existed before the Holocaust. Men in their long black suit coats and pants, white shirts, black hats with *pais* (the long, curly sideburns) walk these narrow streets likely on their way to *shul*, the synagogue. Their eyes are perpetually scanning a book from behind their wire-rim glasses, occasionally stopping to read news or propaganda plastered on building walls

Young boys, also dressed in the traditional black garments, zip by on bicycles. Wives push strollers carrying their children, all dressed in the same clothing pattern, perhaps to identify their family. The women cover their hair or wear wigs to show that they are married. Apparently, a woman's hair drives men crazy, and they cannot be held accountable if the hair is not covered, so I'm told. The buildings are simple. Traffic is minimal. Two blocks over is a religious tourist mecca, but here, I was the only tourist. Yet nobody even glanced in my direction or picked their head up from their book, and for sure, nobody identified me as *one of theirs*.

"See. I told you. I'm easy. Nothing really gets to me," I said as we walked back to Sharon's car and prepared to drive back to Haifa. "That wasn't the *fuckery* that you suggested."

"I disagree. I saw the way you felt trapped in Jerusalem. It was as if you couldn't breathe. You say you're a simple guy and never get stressed, but I think the opposite of the minimum makes you the opposite of happy."

"Huh?"

"Sure. If things aren't simple, if they are in any way complicated, like the tourist *fuckery* that is Jerusalem, you get overwhelmed and can't handle it. It's okay, babe. You're just not a city person."

Maybe it was the way that she already knew me so well, or that she had started calling me "babe," but at that moment, my life changed.

For the next two weeks, Sharon and I were living together, as a couple, perfectly enmeshed in each other's lives and growing closer by the hour. When she came home from work, we would cook dinner together and afterwards go for walks with her kids or out for drinks with her friends. We stayed up late every night after the boys went to sleep with never a minute of boredom, the only silence coming after we finally agreed to stop talking and go to sleep.

I knew her and she knew me, intimately, and in an impossibly short spell, all of my protective walls were torn down. Unlike in Thailand, however, I wasn't anxious to go see what was over the next mountain. My bike got packed up after I left Yuval's, and I never looked at it again. But each day, as we grew closer, so too did my looming flight back to Colorado.

A couple of days prior to my departure, we watched the movie *Before Sunset* with Ethan Hawke and Julie Delpy. It's the second film in the trilogy. In the first film, *Before Sunrise*, Ethan Hawke meets Delpy on a train and convinces her to get off in Vienna, where they spend a day and a half just walking the city and getting to know each other, unexpectedly building a much deeper connection. The entire film is dialogue. The next morning at the train station, they make a promise to meet the following year in Paris, and that's how the movie ends.

In *Before Sunset*, we flash forward ten years, both characters having moved on with their separate lives, never meeting the following year as planned. Now, finally, their paths cross, in Paris. They spend their single day together discussing regrets and missteps in their lives, hinting at a decade of unfulfilled love, decisions they wish they'd made, and things they could not change.

It's clear that there is still a spark, as if they had been together every day since. In the final scene, before Hawke's character is set to depart for the airport, Delpy invites him to her flat. While he is sitting on the couch, she smiles across the room at him, Nina Simone (not Norah Jones) is playing on the stereo. With a cagey smile, she says, "Baby . . . you are gonna miss that flight." "I know . . ." was all that he could reply with that timeless twinkle still in his eyes.

This was us, but after only two weeks, and I was left wondering why I hadn't met Sharon sooner.

"It's getting near," Sharon said while we were laying on the couch, her eyes beginning to swell.

"You know, I'm not even supposed to be here now? I had a flight nearly booked the night you messaged me. So, yeah! It's your fault!" I said playfully, trying to change the subject and lighten the emotions sitting so forcefully in both of our hearts.

"Yeah, that would most probably have been better if you did," she replied.

"You're the one who called me!" I jabbed again.

"You're the one who said you're an *entrepreneur!*"

Maybe it would've been better if we hadn't met, I thought. Then I wouldn't have been dreading these last few days. Fuck. This wasn't supposed to happen. I would have already been home, but instead, in only two weeks, she knew me deeper than any person ever had. Whatever happened next, I would never be the same.

I had done my best to not think about it. This was just another experience, something that would shape my life and open my heart to new possibilities, I tried to tell myself. To once again remind me to always say yes. But this hurt.

She would later say that she knew before me, but I don't know. Maybe. Or maybe I was just too stubborn to admit that I had fallen in love with a woman the first time I saw her. At least I finally knew the answer to that age-old question: *How do you know?*

Throughout my years of traveling, I had met countless people and each one had played a role in where I was, right now. Just like in the movie, how would my life have been different based on decisions and circumstances? What if Emma and I hadn't broken up. If my mom had never sold Family Hospice. Then I would not have gone to see Ben in Zambia. I would not have met Ian, who told me to go to Madagascar, and I would not have met the professor at the airport in Madagascar who told me to go to India and Nepal, and then I would not have met Yuval at the ATM in Pokhara, and thus not be in Israel with Sharon. Or what if I had not met the Swiss and traveled with them? Would I have gone back to my old life as planned after only being away for two months instead of twelve? Or even if all those things *had* happened, what if I *had* gotten the job in Steamboat Springs—then for sure, I would not be in Israel, right now, with Sharon. Fuck. It seemed like all roads had led me to this moment, which, as best I could see, was clearly not *so random.*

On April 28, we boarded a train to the airport. I was going home. To what—I hadn't a clue. We watched the stops on the overhead display, and in my mind, I kept waiting for her to say, "Baby . . . you are gonna miss that flight." What would have been my response? Did Sharon want me to stay? To change (or cancel) my flight? Why hadn't we talked about this?

I had fallen in love with a woman on the opposite side of the planet. I wasn't looking for this, but once again, when you go looking for something, rarely do you find it. Everything had happened too fast, and I didn't know how to process it. Although we had not said *those words*, we both felt it. But now, I was boarding a plane for home. After several minutes of a sobbing embrace, neither of us wanting to be the first to let go for fear that we may never be here again, I finally turned and walked away. I hated that we had unfinished dreams. After only two weeks, there was so much we still hadn't done together, and I wondered if I would ever see her again.

Pay attention to these signs

The border wall looking into Syria

No big deal

Pedaling through Haifa with Sharon

Touristing around Jerusalem

Hummus with Yuval and Sharon

EPILOGUE

One More

April 5 – 30, 2017

"How lucky am I to have something that makes saying goodbye so hard."

– Winnie the Pooh

EPILOGUE

Sure, I could have concluded the story after China. It was neatly wrapped. Tied with a bow. A forty-something white guy comes home after traveling the world, all of life's greatest questions answered, or his life questions, at least. But that wouldn't have been authentic because, after all, that isn't how it happened. It's cliché to say, "I went in search of answers but was left with just more questions." Life is messy, and it's impossible to believe that any of us will *ever* have all the answers.

Unlike so many other travelers, I never had grand ambitions of riding around the world or connecting a bunch of dots on a map. The goal was never to do *epic shit* or take *sick* videos of me doing it to gain social media fame. There is no GoPro of life.

I had a loose plan when I started out. I would see an old friend in Africa for a few weeks in June 2016, then return home and figure out the next steps, a needed break from life. Instead, that plan morphed and gradually evolved into a nearly two-year exploration of the world, and myself. Along the way, I learned that plans are great, but you cannot control the outcome, so forego these insecure and lofty ambitions. Loosen your grip and resign yourself to what *might be.* Always say yes when opportunities arise and step through the doors when they open.

This was a difficult lesson as a 42-year-old man with a rigid, Type A obsession for control. What I discovered was that life is unscripted, and even though you may have a map, the true adventure happens at the intersections of fear and control.

Although I chose a bike, this was never a bike adventure, but rather an exploration of a deeper curiosity. On the surface, and at least initially, my journey was fed by the unfathomable physical and emotional highs of traveling through Africa and the Himalayas, but tempered by paralyzing lows as well.

Every day I was inspired and humbled by the human experience, and it started almost immediately by being offered a place to sleep and given food to eat by a family in Madagascar who took a chance on a tired, broken traveler. Then a *high five* from some children who ran out of their hut to greet me as I rolled through their village, and countless other high fives along the way. These opportunities to connect with others are never found in any guidebook, but are the true gems of the journey.

As a result of these experiences, quite simply, I've learned that traveling makes you less of an asshole. I'm sure of it. Like any place that you go, no matter how *weird* it is, people really are just people, with their own challenges, trying to get by. ("It's not weird, Culture Boy, it's just different than you're used to." Heidi's words are always with me.) Going to faraway places where I don't speak the language and trusting that the people I meet will do me no harm, was a powerful lesson. Each person showed me the world through a new lens, and it was immediately clear that despite our perceived differences, we're really not that different.

So then, what's the point of all this chest-thumping, self-aggrandizing suffering on a bike? Quite simply, it reminds me that I'm alive, and my greed for these experiences, these connections, is insatiable. Was I miserable on a shitty hike-a-bike for six hours? Sure, but it was still an experience, and as much as I may have hated it in the moment, those moments were gifts. I remind myself: *slow down. You'll miss it when it's gone.*

—

In the fall of 2019, I took a trip to see some of my favorite people. Yuval invited me to cycle through the Negev desert with him for his 50th birthday, something that I regretted having not done in 2018. And, of course, I got to see Sharon again. Just like in *Before Sunset*, the time apart seemed a mere illusion, as if we had never been apart at all.

A few weeks later, the Swiss invited me to come see what "real mountains" are because, as they said far too many times to me over the years, "Colorado has hills." So, Sharon and I went to Switzerland, and, dammit, they were right. The Alps seemingly are snatched from the pages of a comic book.

When I was completing this book in 2020, the world, both mine and the greater world, changed. COVID-19 shut down the world, but life kept going. The world kept spinning by. Ivo and Brigitte welcomed twins into their family, and their world will never be the same.

Although we had followed our hearts and chased each other all over the world for the better part of two years, sadly, one year apart from Sharon stretched us too far. Maybe it just wasn't our time, and just like the movie, it will come again. Maybe it never will be. But I know that whatever happens, I'm a better person for having opened my heart and spent time with her. We still talk, but her note to me the last time we saw each other pretty much sums it up.

> *"Babe, I love you. I miss you. I had such a good time. I want you in my life forever. FUCK YOU. I love you. I'm so happy that I met you. No regrets. Just love."*

In the fall of 2020, my mom was diagnosed with Stage IV Pancreatic Cancer. It was a shock to her and a devastating blow to everyone who was fortunate enough to share time with her. But I believe that something good comes from everything. She became my first editor and read every word of this book, and even provided some pretty harsh critiques.

"Don't read this as my mom," I initially demanded when she wanted to read it.

"It's quite the opposite," she would say. "I have to remind myself that you're my son because of the things you've done!"

Over the years, this gift of time has allowed us to mend all of our old wounds. I still see her often and talk to her regularly, and I know that her spirit and zest for life will live on through everyone she has touched.

One more is a sentiment that I have been embracing since I began this journey, a lesson no doubt learned from running a hospice. It has to do with the premise that time is finite. Opportunities are limited. It's easy when you know something is your *last*, so you should savor it because—it's your *last*. It's only when things happen that are unexpected do you say, "If only I had *one more* . . ." *One more* has a more optimistic feel than *last one*, giving us the feeling that perhaps we have some semblance of control. Like most, especially those of us in our now 40s or beyond, I have experienced losses that I have had to look back on with the curious despondence of *if I only had one more* . . .

If I knew that I could have *one more* talk with my mom, *one more* swim with my dad, climb *one more* mountain pass with the Swiss, or *one more anything* with Sharon—how would I change the way I experience that moment? Would I go slower? Would I be more patient? Would I smile more, laugh more, without fear or reservation? If I accept this truth—that every experience is a gift and opportunities are limited, thus striving to live in the *now* of each moment, maybe I can live more deeply. Instead, not relying on the mental scarcity of *one more*, but rather embed this into my daily life.

I read a quote recently that resonated with me. It drives me every day, and I shared it with about 150 seventh- and eighth-grade students to whom I gave a presentation in Colorado recently.

> *"Each day, you are given 86,400 seconds from the time bank. Everyone is given the same. There are no exceptions. The time bank won't tell you how to spend it. Time poorly spent will not be replaced with more time. Time doesn't do refunds. Time is your biggest gift. It is more valuable than money. You can always make more money, but you cannot make more time. Your time is limited. One day you will go to the time bank, and it won't have any more time. And it will be at that exact moment that you know the answer to this question: 'Did I use my time well?'"*

I began this story with a gift of time, and the question I posed: *What would you do if time was not a factor?* I named my book *The World Spins By* because time waits for no one. In the chapter, "You'll Miss It When It's Gone," I wrote, *When you're learning to live each moment, in the moment, the moments can have a way of passing you by if you're not paying attention. Reach out and grab them. Hold on tight as long as you can, because there's no getting them back once they're gone.*

So after nearly two years of travel, I didn't come back with *all* the answers, but really, maybe there is only one: do not waste time. You get one crack at this thing, so live your best life, without apologies, fear, or regret. Choose relationships and experiences over *stuff,* because at the end of the day, when things don't go your way, everyone needs a friend who will call you up and say, "Get dressed fucker, we're going on an adventure."

Home in Boulder for Dad's birthday

Sushi with Sara and Dad

Bobby's birthday with Mom

First Lake Michigan trip with Dad and Bobby since 2004

Giving a talk to a group of 12 year olds in Israel

Checking out "real" mountains with the Swiss. Dammit...they were right

Backpacking in Switzerland—with Sharon and the Swiss

Hiking in Switzerland—with Sharon

Mom taking me to the airport for my next adventure...

ABOUT THE AUTHOR

JERRY KOPACK is a wanderer, question asker, and recovering cubicle dweller. With a degree in finance from the University of Colorado at Boulder, he did his time in corporate America before founding a hospice and learning how precious time really is. His debut book, *The World Spins By,* is a travel memoir chronicling his rural Michigan upbringing, professional career, and his two-year exploration on a bicycle. To date, Jerry has pedaled through eighteen countries (and counting) and has been calling Colorado (and the world) home since 1995.

You can find more about what Jerry is up to at

www.jerrykopack.com

or on Instagram

@jerrykopack

ABOUT ATMOSPHERE PRESS

Atmosphere Press is an independent, full-service publisher for excellent books in all genres and for all audiences. Learn more about what we do at atmospherepress.com.

We encourage you to check out some of Atmosphere's latest releases, which are available at Amazon.com and via order from your local bookstore:

The Great Unfixables, by Neil Taylor

Soused at the Manor House, by Brian Crawford

Portal or Hole: Meditations on Art, Religion, Race And The Pandemic, by Pamela M. Connell

A Walk Through the Wilderness, by Dan Conger

The House at 104: Memoir of a Childhood, by Anne Hegnauer

A Short History of Newton Hall, Chester, by Chris Fozzard

Serial Love: When Happily Ever After... Isn't, by Kathy Kay

Sit-Ins, Drive-Ins and Uncle Sam, by Bill Slawter

Black Water and Tulips, by Sara Mansfield Taber

Ghosted: Dating & Other Paramoural Experiences, by Jana Eisenstein

Walking with Fay: My Mother's Uncharted Path into Dementia, by Carolyn Testa

FLAWED HOUSES of FOUR SEASONS, by James Morris

Word for New Weddings, by David Glusker and Thom Blackstone

It's Really All about Collaboration and Creativity! A Textbook and Self-Study Guide for the Instrumental Music Ensemble Conductor, by John F. Colson

A Life of Obstructions, by Rob Penfield

Troubled Skies Over Quaker Hill: A Search for the Truth, by Lessie Auletti

My Northeast Passage – Hope, Hassles and Danes, by Frances Terry Fischer

Love and Asperger's: Jim and Mary's Excellent Adventure, by Mary A. Johnson, PH.D.

Down, Looking Up, by Connie Rubsamen

CPSIA information can be obtained
at www.ICGtesting.com
Printed in the USA
BVHW040414171222
654331BV00010B/659